Steel Wheels

Steel Wheels

The Evolution of the Railways and how
they stimulated and excited Engineers,
Architects, Artists, Writers,
Musicians and Travellers

A F Garnett

CANNWOOD PRESS

Cannwood Press
Waldenbury, Chailey, East Sussex BN8 4DR
Tel: 01825 723398, Fax: 01825 724188
Email: sales@vinehouseuk.co.uk
www.steelwheels-cannwood.com

Published by Cannwood Press 2005

1

A catalogue record for this book is available from
the British Library

ISBN 0-9550257-0-2

Printed and bound in Great Britain by
The Cromwell Press Limited
Trowbridge, Wiltshire

Contents

		page
	Acknowledgements	vii
	Foreword	ix
1	Wheels and Steam	1
2	North-East England: the first Steam Locomotives	16
3	The Engineer Heroes	33
4	British Apogee and Decline	52
5	Across the Channel	73
6	North America	103
7	Astonishing Bridges and Buildings	138
8	Rails in and under Cities	167
9	Passengers	191
10	Pictures of Rails and Trains	218
11	Words and Songs	234
12	Change	258

Acknowledgements

I recognise my debt to the books and magazines that have been published about railways and about the arts from the middle of the 19th century to the present day. I apologise if any of the quotations or other matter are an infringement of any copyright. I also apologise for any mistakes or misinformation that appear in these pages.

Thanks and Gratitude

I owe thanks to everyone who has encouraged and advised me, or found new sources of information. I owe particular gratitude to Dr Heinz Fischer, Steve Fitzgerald, Diana Fuller, Francesco Gneechi-Ruscone, Richard Graham, Andy and Dee Hoare, Hildegard Kalt, Pierre Loustric, George Melly, Richard Needham, Fabio Semenza and Dr Robert Woof.

Seona Chapman, Denise Elliott, Sarah Flint, Joan Grohmann, and Daf Moray merit my warm thanks for their patience and understanding for turning shaky handwriting into typescript.

I am very grateful to Sheila Murphy for her enthusiasm for *Steel Wheels* and her determination to see it in print. I also want to thank Dick Knowles for masterminding the layout and appearance of the book.

I give the greatest thanks to my wife, Polly, for editing *Steel Wheels* and take this opportunity of expressing my love and devotion to her and to our three daughters for humouring and putting up with a Railway Enthusiast in the family. However, we have two small grandsons and I live in the hope that they will increase the number of enthusiasts from one to three.

Picture credits

'Most people think rail buffs are nuts. I don't know why. If I rode around in a Buick all weekend, no one would say a word.'

EM Frimbo, *The New Yorker*

Foreword

It began because of a girl; I suppose we were both about 13 years old. I forget how I met her, but I just couldn't get over her blondey beauty. We lived in the country and I used to bike 14 or 15 miles to lurk in the shrubbery outside her parents' house in the hope of a distant sighting.

Those watches, those missions were an important part of my school holidays. But even I had to admit there was a certain tedium to maintaining vigil hour after hour. However, beside the family's farm was a railway line, one of the two direct routes between London and Scotland and the artery for rail traffic between the great cities of Birmingham, Manchester, Liverpool and Glasgow with London. And – especially important in the early 1940s – it was the direct route to the English south coast from the River Clyde, where troops and ordnance were arriving from across the Atlantic to prepare for the invasion of France.

From my hiding place, I first heard the trains going past, and after a while began to watch them. Soon I started to look at them. Finally, I deserted my vigil and waited for them. It was a new and lasting love; I would take up a position as close to the permanent way as possible to get the full feeling of 700 tons of steam locomotive and train travelling at 70 miles per hour, 100 feet every second. I knew the gods had moved house; they had deserted the clouds, forests and waves to live with the steam locomotive.

I think it was the sensation of physical energy and power that summoned me to the side of the railway line. Many of us have stood on a station platform and been shaken and stunned by the sight and by the waves of energy of an express train hurtling through only a few feet away.

The station buildings, the station canopy and the waiting passengers remain shaken after the slipstream of the disappearing train has subsided into quiet. Raymond Loewy, the great industrial designer who helped design the Pennsylvania Railroad type S-1 locomotives gives a memorable description of locomotive power,

> I remember a day in Fort Wayne, Indiana at the station on a straight stretch of track without any curves for miles; I waited for the S-1 to pass through at full speed. I stood on the platform and saw it coming from the distance at 120 miles per hour. It flashed by like a steel thunderbolt, the ground shaking under me, in a blast of air that almost sucked me into its whirlwind. Approximately a million pounds of locomotive were crashing through near me. I felt shaken and overwhelmed by an unforgettable feeling of power and by a sense of pride of what I had helped create.

Of course the S-1 weighing nearly 400 tons and hauling 1,000 tons of passenger carriages on its way from Chicago to New York City was much more dramatic than the 140-ton Royal Scot class engine built in 1927 tearing along at the head of a troop train. But the feeling of awe and pleasure was much the same.

One of the great pleasures of watching a steam locomotive is the visual fascination of seeing the workings of the side rods of the valve gear translating the reciprocating motion of the piston into the rotary motion of the driving wheels. Henry Dreyfuss, who helped design the locomotives that hauled the *Twentieth Century Limited* train of the New York Central System, installed special lighting under the streamline cowling to show off and glorify the movement of the piston rod, eccentric cranks, connecting rods and the other rods driving the three 7-ft diameter wheels.

The steam locomotive is the only machine where this glorious and disciplined jumble of rhythmic and geometric movement is fully visible. The heavy side rods, hanging over the void outside the rails, work together to drive the locomotive's wheels in a seeming confusion of steam and noise. I suppose this ballet of steel and movement has something of the qualities of a dinosaur but a marvellous dinosaur when compared to the car with its sparks, con rods and crankshaft all hidden away in the engine block and blowing out a stream of invisible toxic gas, too often with a thoughtless and selfish driver at its wheel. There are millions of these cars and all too few steam locomotives.

From my earliest train-watching days, I have had a romantic idea about the 'iron men' on the footplate whose skill, vigilance and sometimes sacrifice made it all possible. Like many before me, I revelled in the marriage of man and machine, a marriage consummated with water and fire.

I have always understood the wide gulf between the railway enthusiast and the railway professional. The professional, whether manager, engineer, engineman, technician or workman belongs to an elite on whom the 24-hours a day smooth running of the railway depends, as do the lives of colleagues and passengers. The railway professional cannot relax his standards or vigilance; working on the railway demands the highest standards of professional conscience from all its workers all the time.

❖

I travelled by train during the years of World War II. The natural drama of the railway at night was heightened by the blackout and the sparks shooting out of the engine chimney glowed all the better. One of the most enduring memories of my childhood is half-sleeping in a train stopped under the great York station train shed and hearing the distinctive noise of the wheel tapper becoming louder and louder as he tapped each wheel with a hammer to test for flaws or cracks, and then the sound getting fainter.

My first train journey in Continental Europe after the war was in 1946 to an Alpine ski resort at the eastern end of the Swiss Valais. When I disembarked from the cross-channel ferry at Calais I saw three trains waiting, each with its blue carriages and each carriage with an elaborate and grandiose bronze coat of arms and the insignia *Compagnie Internationale des Wagons-Lits et des Grands Express Européens*. They were bigger than any trains in England and, because there was no platform, they seemed even more huge and grand. At the end of each carriage was a white destination board. The one on my train read *Calais Paris Lausanne Venise Trieste Zagreb Beograd*. The boards for the next train read *Calais Strasbourg Munich Salzburg Vienne Budapest* and the third train was the

Rome Express. The activity was confusing and madly French with porters pushing luggage up the side of the carriage and through the windows and then arguing over their tip with anxious English tourists on their first trip abroad. The train lurched and lumbered across Northern France and Picardy and finally ground its way into the Gare du Nord terminus in Paris. There the Paris section was detached and my section for Switzerland and beyond was shunted round the Petite Ceinture, that joined the main Paris rail termini. The train went through a narrow cutting under the bridges of the Paris streets and through Belleville and Ménilmontant Tunnels to the Gare de Lyon where it was coupled to the carriages originating in Paris. Once we left Paris I fell asleep in my couchette and woke when the train stopped in the middle of the night, to hear a deep voiced station loudspeaker repeat Dijon, Dijon, Dijon across the darkness.

The first time I found myself on the footplate of a working steam locomotive was in north-eastern Brazil in the early 1960s when I made my way to the Madeira-Mamoré Railway. The railway was built under the terms of a treaty following a war when Brazil annexed an eastern province of Bolivia. The rubber boom was at its height and the railway was built to bypass the river cataracts and give Bolivia access to an Atlantic port on the Rio Madeira, a huge tributary of the Amazon river. The South American rubber boom was over by the time the railway was completed in 1912, so it no longer had any purpose and just went from nowhere to nowhere, but had to be kept running to conform to the terms of the peace treaty. It was notorious because it was said that in its construction every 100 sleepers or crossties cost a life. Certainly there were the vestiges of mounds and crosses at each passenger halt. The projected line was jinxed from the start. Conditions in the jungle were appalling and the construction workers died from malaria, yellow fever and other hazards including poisonous snakes, alligators and piranha. The jinx followed the third contractor to tackle the project; his supply steamer sank in a storm with a loss of eighty lives, which resulted in near starvation of the workers on site. Finally the line was built by the Bahamians who had constructed the Panama Canal. I spent ten days trying to be helpful in the railway workshops in the eastern terminus, Porto Velho, the capital of Rondonia. Next to the train shed was the corrugated iron Baptist chapel and there I met Macaulay Nathaniel

Augustine, a retired engineman and the son of one of the men who built the railway. Almost completely blind, this dignified old man spoke or read no English apart from his daily Bible readings. I remember him saying, 'The vacuum brakes have gone asunder'. As indeed they had.

It was a pleasure to see that the descendants of the original Bahamians were now an elite running the system: the enginemen, workshop supervisors and train despatchers. I travelled on the footplate for almost all the 140 miles from Porto Velho to Guajará Mirim. The train crew consisted of the engineman and two firemen on the footplate and each of the three passenger cars had a conductor with various assistants, a brakeman and two militiamen. There were also half a dozen flat cars loaded with mining machinery. For the most part the line was level, running parallel to the river, but there was an occasional grade where the brakemen had to work their big iron hand-wheels furiously to prevent the heavy carriages shoving the train to disaster. The journey from Porto Velho took the best part of two whole days. We left just after dawn on the first day, and arrived at Abuna the same evening to sling our hammocks for the night in a communal room next to the track. The following morning we got up early to begin an eventful second leg of the journey. We finally rolled onto the overgrown tracks of the western terminus beside the Rio Madeira in the late afternoon. There were twelve stops along the route to take on water. Each water tower had a manual pump drawing water from the nearby river and everyone, apart from the militiamen, took turns to crank the pumps. I asked about the suitability of river water for a locomotive boiler and learnt that the problem was not alkalinity but the amount of mud in the water which choked the boiler tubes. On that journey we had one disaster after another. A series of hot boxes: in one, flames shot out of an axle journal and started licking the side of the passenger carriage. There were four or five derailments but the engine crew had heavy jacks and we levered the cars back on the rails. Most dramatic was our runaway train. We were going up a modest grade at a smart 15mph clip when the engine lurched over a section where one of the rails dipped. The lurch twisted the coupling between the tender and the first passenger car so that it disconnected. We knew instantly what happened because the engine jumped forward. The engineman braked and cranked into reverse. He hung right out of the cab as we reversed to overtake the train sliding back down the grade. There was little panic; clearly not the first time it had happened. I was lost in admiration for the engineman as he barely nudged the locomotive to the leading car of the train and the automatic coupling snapped closed and he was back in command. I was sad to leave the railway and take the ferry across the Rio Madeira to Guayaramerin on the Bolivian bank to wait for a bus to Riberalta.

Rain jungle, rails and steam are a good cocktail. In the early 1960s I travelled in India. I remember holding a cup and saucer of steaming tea on the swaying *Deccan Express*, with a steward always filling my slopping cup to the brim with boiling inky tea to the amusement of the posh Bombay commuters returning to their families in the Poona hills. I also remember travelling in the hills in a crowded narrow gauge boxcar with a hole in one corner to relieve an upset India tummy, and an authoritative moustachioed military person with a cane who whacked fellow passengers when they stared at my discomfort.

A highlight for any railway enthusiast who visits India is the Railway Museum in New Delhi. There are sidings with an enormous assortment of different steam, diesel and electric locomotives, a showcase with a pair of tusks from an elephant that walked in the path of an express train, and best of all, a 1909 steam monorail locomotive which once ran on a single rail beside a road in Patiala State. I once made a 24-hour stop in Rangoon. I spent the morning discussing the possibilities of developing business in Burma and the afternoon walking round the railway yard enjoying the sight of elephants unloading heavy timber from flatcars shunted round the yard by an elderly tank locomotive built in Glasgow 70 years previously.

❖

My most memorable day on the footplate was on one of the most famous of all steam locomotives, the *Flying Scotsman* on the East Lancashire preserved railway. There were two of us and we walked from the darkness of the stabling shed to see this gleaming, glorious great locomotive shimmering in a mixture of steam and sunshine. She was painted in her original colours: apple green lined in black, green wheels and a scarlet buffer bar. Built in 1923 for the 394-mile run between London and Edinburgh, she was an icon for every schoolboy, even for me though I tried to be sniffy because I was a West Coast, London to Glasgow enthusiast. I particularly admired the taper boiler design of Sir William Stanier as against the parallel boiler design of Sir Nigel Gresley's A3 Pacific *Flying Scotsman*. Ah! Happy days when monarchs bestowed knighthoods on distinguished railway locomotive designers.

As I climbed up and into the cab of this glowing machine ready to move off I felt the greatest excitement and pleasure. After I had unwound the brake and just touched the regulator, the locomotive and its carriages lumbered across the switches out of the yard, along the track, across the fields, over the streams and through the only tunnel on its route. After epic hours on the footplate we came back to reality and returned to our everyday lives. My companion drove off for a nearby meeting and I walked a few yards to the tram terminus to go to Manchester Piccadilly Station to catch the express train to London. At that time Manchester had just finished a complete revamp of its tram system. Riding at high speed on previously disused suburban rail tracks, the trams enter the city centre and join the road traffic as conventional street trams. The tramcars are swish, modern and streamlined. An empty one was waiting at the Bury terminus. I climbed in and sat in the front so that I could look ahead through the glass screen separating the driver from the passengers. I settled down and was lost in thought of the excitements of the day when I realised the driver had climbed in and was sitting in front of me: a slender girl with long golden hair falling well below the collar on her smart navy blue tunic. Her seat was raised so that her shoulders were on a level with my eyes and this height gave her authority over her machine and passengers. She never looked round and I never got to see if she had the face as well as the bearing of a Nordic goddess. Sitting behind her in the tramcar as she fairly whizzed along. and seeing her mastery over the controls with no apparent movement other than very slight nudges of her hands and elbows, made me believe she was a golden creature from a different planet. When we arrived at Piccadilly Station I raced round to catch sight of her face but the traffic lights turned green and the tram, trailer and goddess got away.

❖

When I was working in France and living in Paris, I had to make frequent visits to a works in Grenoble or to the construction site of the Pierrelatte uranium enrichment plant in the Rhône Valley. I went there and back in a couchette at least once a week and sometimes twice. I started very bashful, changing under a blanket so that there was not even the remotest risk of self-conscious immodesty for my four or five travelling companions to notice. After the first three months I used to change into my pyjamas while people were still embracing, boarding the train or saying goodbyes. Once, I climbed on the train, couldn't sleep, took too many sleeping pills and was dead to the world when we arrived at the platform at Pierrelatte where the overnight Paris-Marseille express stopped. I was woken by the conductor and had to tumble onto the platform still in pyjamas. In those days, the early 1960s, the return express train to Paris made a stop late at night to pick up Pierrelatte engineers and passengers. I remember arriving a little early on the platform one summer evening and seeing a succession of fast trains roar by, one after the other, each with 40 or 50 box cars full of melons on their way to the markets of Paris and Northern Europe. Each train left a pungent trail of the distinctive and heavy aroma of Cavaillon melons, which hung long and heavy in the warm night air. I imagined this aroma stretching right up across all France and bisecting the nation.

One memorable journey started with a delicious dinner in *Le Train Bleu*, the sumptuous starred *haute époque* restaurant in the Gare de Lyon, before boarding the train to Milan in a first class Wagon-Lits with a hot happy blonde. The erotic and the railway train make a pretty fancy combination; before the last world war there was a celebrated brothel close to the Parc Monceau that used decor and noise to conjure up a luxurious Wagon-Lits railway atmosphere in some of its rooms. A welcome change from the *ambience Tiffany*, which I believe was more the norm. Freud linked the traditional small boy's longing to be an engineman on the footplate to the 'exquisite sexual symbolism' of the railway together with the 'pleasureable character of the sensations of movement'.

In the late 1970s I worked in a small advanced-tech engineering business situated next to the railway from Bristol to Devon and Cornwall.

The company designed and made specialised equipment and it became apparent that we would have to establish sales and engineering bases overseas if the business was to expand. I had noticed how many American and Japanese businesses in Britain had chosen to establish their headquarters close to well-known golf courses. In something of the same spirit my firm established its overseas offices next to railway lines. First came France where we set up beside the once busy Paris–Dieppe line, by then becoming underused and rather haunted. In Germany we opened an engineering office in Emmerich on the Dutch–German border on the mainline between Amsterdam and cities of the Ruhr. Our top floor looked out over the train station and railway yards. When a train came in from Amsterdam, the Dutch locomotive was unhitched and its place taken by a Deutsche Bundesbahn machine to haul the train on to Oberhausen and beyond.

In the United States we hung up our shingle in New Jersey next to Ridgewood Station on the tracks of the Erie and Lackawanna Railway. The emergency exit door of our building opened straight onto the permanent way and the top of my office window was almost level with the engineman's cab window. Rail traffic consisted of identical clattering electric commuter trains slowing down or accelerating out of Ridgewood Station. Much more interesting was a daily freight train headed by two EMD diesels taking a seemingly endless procession of boxcars into Metro New York. The train moved at about 15 miles per hour, the heavy locomotives creaking over the rail joints. If it was a sunny day the engineman would sit on the sill of the cab window, his knees almost jammed to his chin. At first we waved to each other; then we started to shout greetings. If I was talking on the telephone and heard the roar of the approaching locomotives, I would say 'Just a minute, someone at the door' and then go out to exchange a salute and greeting.

Now, in the 21st century, I have a close association with a children's charitable company housed on the top floor of a disused railway station on the commuter line between Bristol's Temple Meads station and Avonmouth.

Once in the early 1990s, I found myself in New York waiting to meet a colleague who was driving north to Manhattan when he was surprised to hear the sound of a locomotive warning horn in Brooklyn's Sunset Park neighbourhood. It seemed an unlikely place to hear a train. When he caught up with the big Alco diesel hauling three boxcars it was halted, along with cars, bikes and trucks, at a road intersection. They all set off as soon as the lights turned green. Later I learned it was taking the boxcars for loading on a barge to make the two-mile journey across Upper New York Bay to the New Jersey Oak Island rail yard. I also learned that unless they cross the bay, railcars have to travel 120 miles north from the Jersey yards to cross the Hudson and then the same distance south to reach the New York City boroughs.

Later, we waited for a New York uptown local in 23rd Street subway station, when simultaneously, a downtown local stopped opposite while a crowded uptown express and a downtown express went roaring and crashing through the station in opposite directions, their fearsome sound amplified by the steel columns and beams supporting the concrete roof. We were on our way to lunch together and after the subway journey we walked through the most glamorous and glorious of all railway stations, Manhattan's Grand Central Terminal, to eat in the Oyster Bar. As I looked around at the huge magnificence of the station I felt sad at the present impoverishment of its rail system. The longest train journeys from the station's tracks are to New Haven, the outer northern dormitory towns, or up the Hudson to Poughkeepsie.

❖

I've sat in trains looking out of the window, I've waited for them, looked down at them from bridges, looked up at them from the bottom of embankments, read about them, been thrilled by them and admired them. I have even enjoyed watching the noise and sight of the wheels of the bogie of a 70-ton mineral hopper wagon crossing an uneven switch or rail joint with the springs reacting to the sideways lurch of the heavy load; and when there is hopper after hopper of a long slow train, the rhythm and monotony has much of the philosophic pleasure of watching an English three-day cricket match or a Japanese Noh theatre performance.

I write in a room with paintings and photographs of locomotives and trains on three of the four walls: a large oil-painting of a New York Central express heading north on the tracks beside the Hudson, a coloured print of an 1860s engine and tender decorated with fantastical coloured patterns for a visit by the Khedive of Egypt, and a large 1840 coloured drawing from a design office, probably Scottish, of a locomotive named *Edward Findlay* with its wood frame, brass dome and safety valve. There's an LNER poster of a blue streamlined engine heading an express train across the Forth bridge, a Winston Link photograph of a Norfolk & Western articulated giant on the Roanoke turntable, a Dubout exhibition poster of an overwhelmingly large dark locomotive with the beams of its front lights catching an elderly couple walking along the track in a loving embrace. Finally, and in front of my table, is a framed four-page spread from *Trains* magazine of a 552-ton Union Pacific *Big Boy* locomotive, the biggest[1] of them all, fairly batting along up a Wyoming hill. I'm drawn to it, to the world of the railway; it always has and always will captivate my interest.

This account of the evolution of some of the world's railway systems is seen through English eyes that believe that the best examples of steam locomotive design are among the most handsome and aesthetically pleasing objects ever made. The scope of *Steel Wheels* is what I have seen or read, noticed and enjoyed about the evolution of the railway and the excitement it gave to engineers, architects, writers, artists and travellers. I hope these pages convey my perceptions and pleasures.

1. Some argue that the Chesapeake & Ohio's Allegheny engines were bigger.

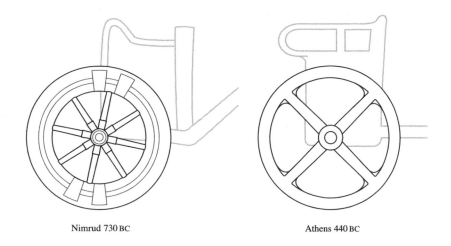

Nimrud 730 BC   Athens 440 BC

1 Wheels and Steam

The transportation of people, goods and freight over land was a problem until nearly 200 years ago. Towns and cities were therefore usually sited on or close to navigable rivers or estuaries. The great Gothic cathedrals and monasteries were either situated beside a quarry or a waterway and sophisticated systems of winches, levers and pulleys were used for handling heavy stones and for hauling them along slipways over short distances. The silver-coloured stone that built Canterbury and Winchester cathedrals in the south of England and the keep of William the Conqueror's Tower of London was shipped across the channel from quarries on the coast near Caen in Normandy. Paris is seldom thought of as a maritime city but its coat of arms incorporates a boat motif with the motto *Fluctuat nec mergitur*[1].

Despite the difficulties of overland transportation, a number of famous generals managed to organise the movement of great armies on a huge scale across inhospitable landmasses. In the fourth century BC, Alexander the Great of Macedon and his army made the epic march with horses, supplies and sometimes even carrying water for themselves and their animals across what is now Turkey, the nations of the eastern Mediterranean and 500 miles into western Egypt; he then doubled back

---

1. *Buffeted by waves but does not sink.*

1

and went east through Iran and Pakistan to Bokhara and the Oxus valley. Napoleon assembled an enormous army for the invasion of Russia and in June 1812 420,000 men and their equipment crossed the River Niemen from Poland into Russia – an astonishing feat of organisation, logistics and effort, never mind the fighting.

Trade routes have crossed continents since antiquity but the goods that were carried were generally high value and low volume, such as the silks that came through Asia from China to Europe and the salt trade that criss-crossed the Sahara and Arabian deserts with the caravans travelling at night and navigating by the stars[2] to avoid the scorching daytime sun.

The ancients did not need to transport coal or minerals overland but they needed to move massive stone statues from the quarries to centres of religious or imperial importance. The blue stones that form part of the henge at Stonehenge are known to have been quarried in the Precelly Hills nearly 150 miles away and each of these three-ton stones was hauled overland for a substantial part of the distance; there is no record of how the overland journey was accomplished. At Hetep, El-Bersheh in the Nile Valley there is a wall painting which shows four lines of hundreds of slaves or workers hauling a 25-ft stone colossus. The statue is fastened to a sledge that slid on wooden skids laid in the sand. A supervisor or slave driver stands on the knees of the colossus shouting out the rhythm for the heaves. More interesting is the man standing on the front of the sledge pouring oil onto the skids. This is supposedly the first known depiction of a tribologist or lubrication engineer at work, reducing the sliding friction of a moving load.

The next advance in moving heavy objects was the placing of logs or rollers under a load to convert sliding motion into rolling motion with its greatly reduced co-efficient of friction. An Egyptian bas-relief from about 700 BC shows rows of men hauling a large stone human-headed bull monolith on a sledge with some of them laying logs or rollers in front of the sledge, pulling the sledge over the rollers and then retrieving them from behind to place them back in front. A refinement in the use of rollers was devised 25 centuries later when Catherine II of Russia commissioned the equestrian statue of Peter the Great, immortalised by Pushkin, for the

2. The Qur'an (6:97): 'It is He Who maketh the stars for you, that you may guide yourselves with their help, through the dark spaces of land and sea'.

city of St Petersburg. The sculptor, Falconet, decided to mount it on a single monumental granite slab nearly 100ft long, 26ft high and 20ft wide. This huge lump of rock needed to be moved a considerable distance. Two parallel heavy wood beams, each with a V-section cut in the top and lined with metal, were laid along the path of the stone. Large metal spheres were placed in the Vs; the slab was winched onto the spheres and the load was rolled forward. The sculptor even designed a turntable using the same system so that the giant stone could be precisely positioned. An onlooker described the progress as being like 'a mountain on top of an egg'.

Possibly the earliest wheels still extant are a set of four wheels with very fine rims and six fine spokes found in a room of funerary litters in the tomb of King Tut'ankhamun in Thebes beside the River Nile. The tomb dates back to the middle of the second millennium BC and the presence of the wheels in the king's tomb is an indication of their rarity and their presumed usefulness in the afterworld.

The sections of the famous Parthenon frieze from Athens that are on display in the British Museum are a portrayal of the Panathenaic procession and were carved about 440 BC. They show crowds of musicians, water carriers and horsemen moving in procession toward the seated gods. Every detail of drapery and facial expression is carved with great beauty and precision. Therefore it is surprising that the wheels of the very few chariots in the procession are delineated as being heavy and crudely made; each wheel has four very coarse thick spokes, each with its hub fixed to the axle.

In a nearby gallery are two earlier panels dated about 730 BC, from the Central Palace in Nimrud, the Assyrian capital. The panels include carved images of three chariots. The wheels of each chariot are identical: they have eight slender decoratively shaped spokes attached to the heavy rim and it's clear from the detailing of the hub that the wheel revolves on the axle, allowing the chariot to turn tight corners or to be rotated round 360°. It seems curious that such a significant advance in wheel design was either lost or neglected over the years.

The Isthmus of Corinth between mainland Greece to the north and the Peloponnese to the south separates the Aegean sea from the Gulf of Corinth and the Adriatic. The isthmus is just over 3½ miles wide and the

Diolkos trackway, dating from the fifth century BC, runs across it either on a direct route next to the 1893 canal or on a slightly longer route to the south taking advantage of a more level profile. There are about 900 yards of track on the western end of the Diolkos that might possibly be grooves cut into the stone for wheels – inverted rails.

During the Peloponnesian War[3] warships were transported across the isthmus to avoid sailing round the Peloponnese with its unfavourable Aeolian winds. Thucydides wrote that the Spartans shipped a trireme or war-galley along the Diolkos. It obviously had to be fitted onto a cradle and hauled up a slip from the sea with a capstan. Some archaeologists choose to believe that the cradle rested on wheels which ran in the grooves in the trackway, that is to say that it was an early railway, but it seems very much more probable that the cradle and vessel, weighing some 30 tons, was hauled on rollers along the limestone track. The grooved 'rails' may have been made by the many successive journeys of commercial goods being transhipped in wagons across the isthmus.

The wheel is clearly man's most important contribution to solving the problems of overland transportation. The advance from placing logs rolling under a load to devising the wheel with its fixed position under the wagon or chariot seems obvious but, in fact, it is a very sophisticated advance and some civilisations never made the transition from roller to wheel. In the 16th century, the Spanish conquistadors were astonished to find that the Incas who had mastered astronomy, advanced mathematics and built large cities had not mastered the roller to wheel transition.

The introduction of the wheel brought its own technical problems. Although it solved the problem of maintaining its correct position below the wagon or chariot, the efficient rolling friction of a roller was exchanged for the sliding friction of the axle in its journal or the shaft in the hub. Tallow was the main lubricant but it has the unfortunate quality of melting when it becomes hot, losing much of its effectiveness. The Romans devised a forerunner of the ball bearing and there is a second- or third-century light cart[4] with bronze wheel hubs with axial grooves that probably held small rollers to reduce sliding friction. Leonardo da Vinci examined the problems

---

3. The war began in 431 BC.

4. In the National Museum in Copenhagen.

caused by friction and one of his notebooks contains sketches of various types of ball bearing and, most interestingly, shows a cage inside the bearing to prevent the balls touching, as otherwise their surfaces, moving in opposing directions, would rub against each other.

The Romans were renowned for their great roads radiating across the empire throughout most of Europe, Asia Minor and even North Africa. They knew that a straight line was the shortest route between two points and they built their roads straight unless there was an unavoidable obstacle. Roads over the hills and valleys were suitable for foot and mounted soldiers but could only be used by very lightly loaded wagons or chariots. Heavy equipment was probably transported on pack animals.

Early landscape paintings often include peasants with a horse between shafts, the shafts and load on their end dragging along the ground; no luxury of a wheel. Seventeenth-century European paintings and prints show heavy loads of wool and other bulky merchandise being moved on pack animals rather than in wagons. The combination of the problems of the wheel bearing, bad road surfaces and the lack of suitable springs meant that wheels were mainly used for lightweight carriages. Eventually the technology of roads and carriages improved and in the early 19th century horse-drawn stagecoach services travelling on well-maintained turnpikes could carry four passengers inside and eight or even more outside.

Finally, technical advances in the second half of the 19th century, such as Timken's tapered roller bearing in the United States and the double row self-aligning ball bearing developed by Wingquist in Sweden, largely solved the friction problems of the wheel. Interestingly, the introduction of the bicycle at the end of the 19th century contributed a number of important technical advances to the development of modern, reliable and low cost bearings. Today, wheel-bearing failure on trains or heavy road trucks or even on the millions of cars on the road is almost unknown.

❖

There are records of waggonways as early as the 16th century: crude wood rails making it possible to move heavily loaded wagons. They must have been a necessity in the dark in coal and mineral drift mines where loaded wagons needed to be pushed or dragged without hitting the sides of the tunnel. In some mines the wheel had a flat circumferential edge and ran along a waggonway – a series of flat wood rails with an L-shaped raised flange to guide the wheels along the flat section. In others the guiding flange was on the edge of the wheel rather than the rail. Each type had its advantages and disadvantages. The wide wheel for the L-shaped waggonway could be used on any flat surface, but it had the disadvantage that pebbles and dirt compacting in the L of the rails caused obstruction. However wagons with narrow flanged wheels could only be used on rails.

In time the rails inside the mines were extended to the nearby navigable waterways where the coal or mineral could be loaded into barges. By 1660 there were nine waggonways on Tyneside and a number of others in the Midlands. Generally, oak rails were fastened to sleepers or crossties laid in deep ballast. The rails needed replacing each year and so iron straps began to be fastened to the top of the rails to extend their life; this was probably only a marginal improvement because of the wear and damage caused by the heavily loaded wagons with their unsprung cast-iron wheels. By the end of the 18th century cast-iron rails, about three or four feet long mounted on stone blocks, began to replace wood rails. Much longer wrought-iron rails, especially John Birkinshaw's patent fish-belly rail with its thick section between the supporting chairs, replaced cast iron and by the mid 19th century this became the standard for railways or waggonways which carried a heavy volume of traffic.

In England, particularly in the collieries in Northumberland and Durham, a gauge of 5ft between the vertical outside plates of waggonways was adopted. It was a width and size suited to the horses which hauled the wagons and on a well-maintained level waggonway a horse could pull a 2¼-ton load as compared to less than a ton on a made-up roadway. On downhill grades the driver climbed up on the wagon to operate the brake and the horse was tethered to the back. The last stretch was downhill to the river staithes, and failure to operate the brake in time meant that load, wagon, dobbin and driver found themselves in the river.

The 5ft distance between the outside raised flanges of the waggonway meant that the distance between the inside of the two horizontal sections of the waggonway that supported the wheels was three or four inches smaller, and rails for flanged wheels started to be laid 4ft 8½ inch or 1,435mm apart. The first recorded instance of this dimension as the gauge between the rails was for the Willington Colliery three-mile railway running to the river Tyne. In time, and with only a few exceptions, this became the standard gauge for railways around the world.

There were many variations to horse-drawn wagons on rails. One of the best known was Ralph Allen's waggonway in Bath Spa which underwent a building boom in the early and mid 18th century when it became fashionable to take the waters. Allen owned a quarry on one of the high ridges surrounding Bath and he designed his waggonway with a series of ropes so that the loaded wagons descending the gradient to the city pulled the unloaded wagons up the hill back to the quarry. Gravity railways or waggonways became common, usually with loaded wagons running down the gradient and horses hauling the empty wagons back up the hill. One of the best-known gravity railways ran from Mt. Tamalpais to the Muir Woods redwood forest, a few miles north of San Francisco's Golden Gate. A steam locomotive hauled trippers to the summit half a mile above the surface of the bay and a series of open cars coupled together brought them down on a sightseeing ride through the California redwoods. At the start of the journey downhill the lead brakeman would tell passengers, 'This is not a thrill ride. Our speed will not exceed 12mph ...' and then 'OK, men! Turn on the gravity.'

The most splendid and elaborate gravity railway or roller-coaster ever must have been the *Roulette* of King Louis XIV built in the gardens of Marly close to Paris. Designed to simulate the fun of sliding down a snow-covered hill on a *Schlitte vosgien,* it was a highly ornamented and decorated carriage on wooden rails. A contemporary print shows the king with seven or eight gorgeously dressed ladies and courtiers on board with three valets pushing the carriage to the edge of the incline for the ride down the hill. The print also shows a classical-style building where the passengers boarded the fantastical vehicle, the *cabinet de la roulette,* possibly the first-ever railway station.

❖

The elasticity or expansive force of steam must have been evident to early man as soon as he began to use a pot for cooking. The earliest recorded use of steam energy comes from a text of AD 60, *Spiritalia seu Pneumatica* by Hero of Alexandria; a translation was published in 1851, the year of the London Great Exhibition. It includes a description of an aeolipyle or hollow sphere rotating on a horizontal hollow shaft. This shaft or axis was connected to a closed cauldron filled with water and heated by a fire. The steam from the cauldron filled the sphere and was discharged through a number of pipes which all pointed backwards; the sphere probably whizzed round once it filled with steam. It shared many of the characteristics of the steam turbine developed by Charles Parsons more than 1,800 years later; Hero's steam jets reacted against atmosphere and Parson's steam jets forced reaction into the blades of a turbine rotor.

One of the first recorded uses of steam was by Dennis Papin, a French scientist who studied under Huyghens, the Dutch physicist. He fled Paris in 1681, the year of the Revocation of the Edict of Nantes, and was welcomed to London by Robert Boyle who appointed him curator of the Royal Society. Papin made the discovery that boiling water rises to a much higher temperature than its free boiling point if the water and steam are contained in a pressure vessel. Papin also designed the weight-loaded safety valve to prevent a pressure vessel from bursting and the principle of this design became a standard for the next 250 years. Papin's best-known apparatus was the Digester and its purpose was to use the increased heat from pressurised steam to extract nutritious matter from animal bones. In his famous diary, John Evelyn gives an amusing account of a philosophical evening with the supper cooked in the Digester and served to the Fellows of the Royal Society. Six years after his arrival in London, Papin left to become the Professor of Mathematics at Marburg University, where he worked on the theory of using the elastic qualities of steam to raise a piston in a cylinder and then cooling the cylinder to create a vacuum so that the piston returned downwards, driven by the force of atmospheric pressure. Papin was the first, or one of the very first, to recognise that the piston in a cylinder was an effective way of harnessing the power of steam's expansive qualities. Today, a piston in a cylinder is not only used in steam engines but it harnesses the explosive qualities of petroleum or oil vapour to power millions of cars, buses, trucks, ships and machines around the world. Sadly, there is no record of Papin building a steam engine; he was a professor and not a mechanic.

Captain Thomas Savery, a military engineer born in Devon in 1650, was probably the first to design and build a working steam engine. Several of his engines were built to work pumps for draining Cornish mines. The engine's two boilers alternately heated and cooled so that atmospheric pressure in the cooled boiler sucked the water up past a non-return valve. Steam pressure from the heated boiler then forced the water up past another non-return valve. Considerable steam pressure was needed to force the water up the pipe and one boiler exploded and 'tore the engine to pieces' when it was at work in a Staffordshire coal mine. One of Savery's claims to fame was his comparison of the power of his engines relative to the quantity of work a horse could perform and the term horsepower[5] was in world-wide use until the introduction of the metric system. Savery finished his professional life as Surveyor of the Waterworks at Hampton Court Palace.

The beginnings of the industrial revolution brought an increasing requirement for steam engines in England. They were needed to raise water, to pump out mines, to lift water for distribution in the growing towns and to conserve water by lifting it from the tail-race back to the millpond of a waterwheel powering machines in textile factories.

Probably the first practical steam engines, or fire engines as they were known at the time, were built by Thomas Newcomen from Devon, an iron master or mechanic, with his assistant John Calley, a plumber and glazier. Newcomen built a number of model engines before attempting to build a full-size working engine. He used Papin's cylinder with a tight fitting piston connected by a chain to a rocker beam 12 or 15 feet long whose opposite end was attached to the pump rods. The cylinder was vertical with an open top; steam from the boiler was admitted to the bottom of the cylinder, which pushed up the piston. Cold water sprayed on the outside of the cylinder condensed the steam and created a partial vacuum forcing the piston to the bottom of the cylinder ready for another injection of steam; it

5. 1hp = 745.7 Watts in metric-speak.

was the atmospheric pressure forcing the downward stroke that raised the water. Humphrey Potter, a bright youth employed to open and close the steam and water valves, saw they could be operated by joining rods to the movement of the rocker beam and so made a substantial contribution to the early development of steam engines.

Fortunately there was an advance in the technology of smelting iron as Newcomen was preparing to build his first working engines. In 1709 'Dud' Dudley succeeded in smelting iron with coal instead of charcoal and produced a more consistent and dependable material. This advance was exploited by Abraham Darby, famous for the 1787 iron bridge over the river Severn in Shropshire, who had cast 22 cylinders for Newcomen by 1733. Henry Cort's 1789 puddling process to produce malleable or wrought iron with its qualities of predictability and greater strength in tension was another advance, giving engine builders a more versatile and dependable material. Even with the growing availability of new materials, engine manufacturers continued to construct their machines without the slide lathes, planing machines and boring tools that became available early in the 19th century. There were no suppliers with catalogues of available parts; there was not even a unified system of threads and measures. Each engine builder had to be a master mechanic, making each component part in addition to designing the engine.

Despite initial problems, Newcomen improved and developed his engines to become much more efficient; the initial six strokes a minute was speeded up to 15 strokes a minute and cylinders grew in size from 23 inches to 72 inches. The design worked well and was reliable as it used very low-pressure steam, probably not very much greater than atmospheric pressure, but the engine had severe limitations as it made use of only a very small proportion of the latent heat in the coal. The high cost of coal in Cornwall meant that the engines were often more expensive to run than using horses so they did not have many applications in the local mines. However, a large number of Newcomen engines were used for raising water in coalmines where fuel was cheap.

It has been estimated that 60 engines were built up to 1733 when Newcomen's patents ran out. More than 300 Newcomen-type engines were constructed by various builders between then and 1780 and sent to the United States, Germany, Hungary, Spain and Sweden; one engine was used to provide a 75-ft water lift to drive the fountains for Prince von Schwarzenberg's palace in Vienna. A Newcomen-type engine using the same atmospheric principle was in use in Oakthorpe Colliery from 1791 until 1918 and is now in the London Science Museum.

Newcomen was regarded as the first man who 'obtained mechanical power other than from wind, water or muscle'. His lasting memorial lies in the name of the organisation that researches the history of mechanical invention and technology: the Newcomen Society.

Everyone knows that James Watt watched a kettle boil and then invented the steam engine. In fact his great contributions were a number of important conceptual and design advances that made the steam engine commercially viable. They helped make steam a universal provider of power in every factory in the world and paved the way to harnessing it for the movement of people and goods along a railway. Watt did use a kitchen kettle in one of his experiments but perhaps the source of the kettle story comes from Samuel Smiles's life of Boulton and Watt published in 1878 in his *Lives of the Engineers* series:

> On one occasion he was reproved by Mrs Muirhead, his aunt, for his indolence at the tea-table. "James Watt," said the worthy lady, "I never saw such an idle boy as you are: take a book or employ yourself usefully; for the last hour you have not spoken one word, but taken off the lid of that kettle and put it on again, holding now a cup and now a silver spoon over the steam, watching how it rises from the spout."

James Watt was born in 1736 at Greenock on the river Clyde. His father was a general merchant, builder and shipwright and James spent most of his time in his father's workshops. He was a frail boy who suffered violent headaches and a tendency to self-pity and melancholy. At school he was unable to learn parrot fashion and only brightened up in maths class. After the equivalent of an apprenticeship in Glasgow and London, Watt set up as a mathematical instrument maker in Glasgow.

In 1763 he was asked to repair a model of a Newcomen engine. The model had a boiler smaller than a kettle and a 2-inch diameter cylinder with a 6-inch stroke. Watt recognised the principles of the engine and saw ways of improving them. Two years later he made the great advance of recognising that evacuating steam from the cylinder into a separate condenser meant that the cylinder was kept at the temperature of the steam and not subject to the inefficient cycle of heating and cooling with its consequent high fuel costs and low performance. He quickly made a model and proved the theory of the separate condenser. A subsequent model incorporated a jacket to maintain a high temperature in the cylinder and incorporated another great advance: injecting steam above the piston on its downward stroke as well as below it on the upward stroke, an improvement that almost doubled the power of the steam engine.

During this period of invention and innovation Watt's instrument business began to prosper. He found a partner and they moved their 16 employees to a shop and works at 'the Trongate where he sells all sorts of mathematical and musical instruments with a variety of toys and other goods' (advertisement in the *Glasgow Journal*, December 1763). Watt even made a barrel organ. However, most of his attention, energy and resources were devoted to developing his ideas for improving the steam engine. When his business partner died the instrument business folded and Watt was left trying to earn a living making surveys for canal builders, selling charts and even designing a bridge over the river Clyde.

The costs of building model steam engines submerged him in debt and so he approached Dr Roebuck, founder of the famous Carron Ironworks, to cover the debt and fund future development of the steam engine. They came to an arrangement for a partnership whereby Roebuck would own two-thirds of the benefits from the patent of an engine with a separate condenser that had been lodged in 1769. Shortly after the agreement Watt built his first full-size engine behind Roebuck's Kinneil house overlooking the Clyde. He had endless problems caused by the difficulty of making a tight fit between the piston and cylinder and by the lack of skilled mechanics and pipe fitters, and the engine never worked satisfactorily. Shortly after, Roebuck became over-extended and eventually went bankrupt, but in the meantime he had told Matthew Boulton about Watt's steam engine.

Matthew Boulton had founded the Soho Manufactory a few miles north of Birmingham. It became the leading manufacturer of metal buttons, buckles, watch chains, candlesticks and every kind of fancy or decorative metal hardware; the factory was regarded as the biggest and most advanced in the world. Boulton was not only an industrialist but he was also a substantial man of the world and a close friend of such eminent men as Erasmus Darwin, Joseph Priestley, Josiah Wedgwood and Benjamin Franklin. He was a leading member of the Lunar Society of Birmingham, which met each Monday evening closest to the full moon[5] to discuss their discoveries, their curiosities and the scientific advances to which they contributed so much.

When the power requirements of the Soho factory exceeded the power that could be supplied by the available water, Boulton looked for a solution and became enthusiastic about the idea of Watt's engine; he had enough technical background and aptitude to appreciate the improvements of Watt's design. Boulton's need for an effective engine to lift sufficient water to maintain the drive for the machines in his Soho works was complemented by the skills to manufacture it and the resources to purchase Dr Roebuck's two-thirds share in Watt's patent rights. After Watt's first visit to Soho, Boulton wrote to him, 'I was excited by two motives to offer you my assistance which were love of you and love of a money-getting ingenious project'. Finally Watt moved his family to near Birmingham and he and Boulton became partners in the business of building steam engines. The Kinneil engine was sent to Soho where the cylinder and other parts were reworked and the engine was installed and worked satisfactorily lifting water from the tail-race up to the mill pond.

So far, Watt's engine and work had cost money and had not provided any return. Both he and Boulton considered that an extended period of patent protection was necessary to complete development of the engine and derive some benefit. In 1775 Boulton used his contacts to persuade a Parliamentary Committee to extend the validity of the patent for a further 25 years. This extension was hotly disputed by mine owners who feared a situation of having only one supplier of engines that incorporated Watt's improvements. Other engine makers, including Joseph Bramah, famous for his hydraulic press and his design of the screw propeller, whom Watt

5. So that they had enough light to find the way home.

referred to as the 'eminent Water Closet Maker who called himself an Engineer', argued that Watt's patent rights not only covered what he had invented but also what he might invent in the future.

While supervising the erection of engines in Cornwall, Watt wrote deeply pessimistic letters to Boulton, who tried to reassure him and lift his spirits. Even when depressed, Watt had a good turn of phrase, referring to one customer with doubtful credit, '... he is like a shaved pig with a soapy tail', and on another occasion he wrote to Boulton '... a hundred hours of melancholy will not pay one farthing of debt'. He determined to retire from the partnership and wrote 'I wish to retire and eat my cake in peace but will not go without cake'. A twitchy and unattractive man, he whined almost daily to Boulton in a stream of long letters, convinced that customers were cheating him, friends betraying him, his workmen letting him down with poor quality and his rivals determined to steal his ideas and his rights. He built an elaborate barricade of patents to protect his interests and thus probably slowed down the development of using the expansive qualities of high pressure steam as well as other technical advances.

James Watt continued to make improvements in engine design. The introduction of steam into the cylinder had been regulated by manual operation of a valve or steam throttle at the entry to the cylinder; his design of an automatic governor provided consistent control; this was the one invention that he never tried to patent. Watt continued to innovate and introduce new designs, an important one being a parallel motion device to relate the vertical motion of the piston rod to the angular motion of the rocker beam. Even more important was the design to convert the reciprocating motion of the piston into the rotary motion of a shaft. He had just completed the drawings of the design, which was based on a crank similar to the foot treadle to work a potter's wheel, when what we would now call an industrial spy, James Pickard, a local button maker, listened to conversations between Watt's pattern maker and other Soho workmen. He was reputed to have posted to London and obtained a patent to cover the use of a crank for transmitting the drive of a steam engine. Watt was obliged to find a different solution and he and his principal assistant, William Murdoch, designed a device they called *The Sun and Planet Motion*, comprising a fixed toothed wheel attached to a rocker beam, driving another toothed wheel by rotating round it.

The combination of the patented designs, the experience, the increasing reputation of the engines that had been installed and their increasingly skilled and experienced workmanship made Boulton & Watt by far the most important builder of steam engines in the world. Boulton & Watt engines powered the *Charlotte Dundas*, the world's first steam-powered boat, and Robert Fulton's famous *Clermont* steamship that ploughed up and down the Hudson between New York and Albany. Orders flooded in for engines to drive sugar mills in the West Indies, cotton mills in America, flour mills in Europe and many other applications and the works were enlarged over and over again. Boulton wrote 'The people ... are *steammill mad*'. Watt wrote 'The velocity, violence, magnitude and horrible noise of the engine give universal satisfaction to all beholders.' Over the years Boulton & Watt licensed other engine builders and by the early years of the 19th century there were many hundreds of their steam engines in use around the world.

With increasing age and prosperity James Watt shook off his melancholy and most of his illness and died aged 83, outliving the energetic Boulton who had buoyed up and supported him through his illnesses and periods of depression. There is a statue of Watt in Westminster Abbey complete with a eulogy carved on the plinth and another statue in Handsworth church where he is buried. But the most lasting memorial is the Watt or W, the universal unit for expressing power. A great and innovative thinker and engineer, Watt made important technical advances and worried away at their detail until they made a positive contribution to the engines that powered the machines of the world. Finally, a word from Boulton: 'I sell here, sir, what all the world desires to have ... Power'.

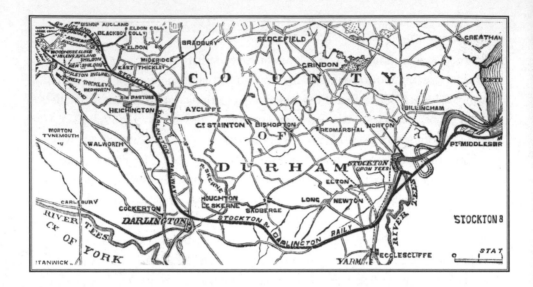

2 North-East England: the first Steam Locomotives

The first-ever steam locomotive or *fardier* – a bearer of burden – was built in 1769 as an artillery tractor by Nicholas Cugnot, a French military engineer. There is no record of it ever working or what became of it. A few years later Cugnot constructed a second and larger engine[1]. It had three wheels and two cylinders with the pistons connected to the single front driving wheel with ratchets; each piston stroke gave a quarter turn to the driving wheel. The *fardier*'s main design shortcoming was that there was no way of feeding water to its boiler so it could only maintain steam for a maximum of 15 minutes. It reached a top speed of $2\frac{1}{4}$ miles per hour and was supposed to have run in a Paris street, hit a wall and overturned, and then been declared a public danger by the city authorities. Certainly there is no evidence of Cugnot continuing with the development of the *fardier*; more likely, the Duc de Choiseul, the Minister of War who had been his patron, left office and there was no one of influence to help Cugnot.

James Watt took out a patent for a steam carriage but did nothing to develop it. William Murdoch, one of his principal engineers who was stationed in Cornwall to supervise the installation and start-up of Boulton & Watt pumping engines, made a model steam carriage, about the size of

1. The historic machine is preserved and together with a lighthearted audio-visual display can be seen in the museum of the Paris Conservatoire des Arts et Métiers.

a large tricycle; it had a two-inch piston and a spirit lamp to heat the boiler. Murdoch managed to make it work on a road late one evening; it outran him and legend has it that it terrorised a Redruth pastor who took it for the devil in person. However, Richard Trevithick was reported to have said that it 'wobbled like a lame duck'. Shortly after, Murdoch was on his way to London to take out a patent on his locomotive when he met Matthew Boulton on his way to Cornwall. Boulton was deeply shocked at the very idea of Murdoch's making any kind of invention and persuaded him to return immediately to Cornwall. He later wrote to James Watt 'I think it fortunate I met him, as I am persuaded I can cure him of his disorder and turn evil to good'. There were no more Murdoch locomotives.

Towards the end of the 18th century a number of patents were taken out for steam road locomotives: by William Symington in Scotland, Fourness and Ashworth in England with three-wheel steam carriages, Nathan Read in America with a four-wheel machine, and Oliver Evans, who built the *Oruktor Amphibolis*, a machine with road wheels and a paddle wheel for driving into the Delaware river and then supposedly dredging in the shallows. None of these pioneers made any contribution to the mainstream design or development of the steam locomotive.

❖

Richard Trevithick was the father of the steam locomotive and the railway, a system that was to serve almost every town in the civilised world. All his ideas were right, he built steam locomotives and made them work but almost everything he did or made ended in failure. One biographer wrote 'his hopeful character enabled him to enjoy life in the midst of neglect and poverty'. In addition to his other achievements, he founded a locomotive family dynasty; his son became locomotive superintendent at the London and North Western's Crewe works and two grandsons became locomotive superintendents in Japan.

Trevithick was a Cornishman born in 1771, the son of a mine manager. He was a big, vigorous man brought up in the world of mines and their steam pumping engines. He had no academic training, and according to the son of a one-time partner 'he would often run wild from want of calculation'. He helped lead a faction of Cornish mine owners in their disputes with Boulton & Watt and was not on speaking terms with James Watt. However, he had a natural aptitude for the workings of steam engines and a gift for recognising the potential of harnessing them for traction. In 1800 he made a model steam locomotive and a year later he built a steam road carriage. It broke down on its trials and everyone 'adjourned to the hotel and comforted their hearts with roast goose and proper drinks when forgetful of the engine, its water boiled away, the iron became red hot and nothing that was combustible remained'.

Trevithick and his partners took out a patent for a steam engine to drive a road carriage and in 1803 he built a steam locomotive for the Pen-y-Darren iron works in Wales. The design incorporated a number of important innovations that included using high-pressure steam, which reduced the size and weight of the engine and increased its efficiency. But the most significant advance was putting the locomotive on rails – so obvious with the benefit of hindsight, but it was the first time and it was a breakthrough in the world of land transportation. Both the wheels and the rails were smooth but there was sufficient adhesion for the locomotive to haul loaded wagons weighing nine tons at a speed of five miles an hour. The engine was too heavy for the track of iron plates; it was considered unsatisfactory and converted into a stationary engine. The following year, Trevithick visited the coal-mining region of northeast England to sell the rights to use the patents of his steam locomotive.

In 1808 Trevithick built the locomotive *Catch me who can* for demonstration to the public on a circular track in London; there is a Rowlandson print of the engine on its track with disappointingly few spectators. The demonstration was a commercial failure and Trevithick disappeared from the world of developing steam locomotion to become an engineer in the gold and silver mines of Peru. His reputation for building steam engines for draining mines was so great that he had an almost royal reception with a guard of honour when he arrived in Lima, and there was talk of putting up a solid silver statue of Don Ricardo, the eminent Professor of Mechanics. He even had an audience with the viceroy to propose building a railway line to service the mines in the high Andes. After a few years he returned to England penniless. There is a Spanish proverb: 'a silver mine brings misery, a gold mine ruin'.

Trevithick went on to use his considerable gifts to design an improved gun carriage, a new method for manufacturing ice and a system for superheating steam; he proposed plans for draining the low-lying parts of Holland and he made a design for a 1,000-ft monument to commemorate the passing of the 1832 Reform Bill. The qualities of mechanic and visionary are seldom combined in one man, but with such untethered energy it was probably inevitable that he would leave no concrete achievement – other than as inventor and pioneer of the steam railway.

❖

The valleys of the rivers Tyne, Tees and Wear in north-east England had rich seams of coal and they were situated close to navigable rivers providing access to the important markets of London and Continental Europe. By the beginning of the 19th century, the mines closest to the rivers had been exhausted and most of the working mines were several miles from navigable water. There was a maze of railway lines or waggonways, each with its horses and carts, taking the coal from the collieries to the river staithes where it was loaded into keels to go down river, to be loaded into sea-going vessels. The rapid growth in population and the large number of steam engines required for pumping mines dry and for raising water to provide power for factories were increasing the demand for coal; the consequent rise in production brought about the need for a quicker and more efficient method of transporting coal from the pit to the river. In addition, the scarcity of horses and the steep rise in the price of fodder caused by the Napoleonic wars compounded the difficulties of the colliery owners trying to meet the growing demand.

There was an obvious need for steam locomotives, and Trevithick had demonstrated that steam could be used for locomotion as well as for driving stationary engines. His visit to the Newcastle area in 1804 was well timed; he had a ready audience of colliery owners and engineers. The visit was such a success that the colliery railways in north-east England became the leading centre for experimentation, development and proving the steam locomotive as a technical and commercial reality.

In addition to the problems of designing a reliable engine with existing technology and materials, the early engineers faced a number of serious problems. The weight of the locomotive was a critical factor. The existing railways had been built for horse-drawn wagons and had not been designed to support machines weighing four or five tons. Satisfactory springs did not exist, and this lack of cushioning the heavy motion of the locomotive on the uneven rails exacerbated the problem of wear of both the rails and the locomotive. Many early locomotives had vertical cylinders housed in the top of the boiler to keep them hot, and the uneven downward thrust of the connecting rods increased the wear on the rails.

The solution of increasing the number of wheels to spread the load and reduce the weight on each axle was seldom acceptable because a locomotive with a long wheelbase could not then ride round curves. Curves were already hazardous, even for a short-framed engine with only two pairs of wheels, as cast-iron rails could not be bent; a curve was a succession of changes of direction between each rail. In 1812 William Chapman of Newcastle applied for a patent for a bogie: two wheels on a small chassis pivoting underneath the front of the frame of the locomotive to help guide it round curves. Chapman thought bogie wheels needed to be driven and he connected them to the driving wheels with a chain and sprocket. He built a locomotive that went to work at Heaton Colliery but the drive chain kept breaking and the trial was not a success. In 1815 Chapman had a second locomotive built in Newcastle and put to work at a Lambton colliery. As reported by the *Tyne Mercury* '… the engine is mounted on eight wheels according to a patent granted to Messrs William and Edward Chapman by means of which the weight is so far reduced upon each wheel as to avoid the expense of relaying the ways with stronger rails …'. The problems caused by the heavy weight of locomotives were only solved when wrought-iron rails replaced cast-iron rails. Wrought-iron also had the great advantage that it could be bent to the radius of a curve.

Another problem was the question of adhesion of the locomotive wheels to the rails. It appeared to defy common sense to think that a locomotive with smooth wheels on smooth rails could haul more than its own weight; surely the wheels would start to slip if the load was too heavy. This was despite the examples of Trevithick's engines with smooth wheels at Pen-y-Darren and the *Catch me who can* in London. John Blenkinsopp, agent of the Middleton Colliery, took out a patent for propelling a locomotive with a toothed wheel engaging in a continuous rack laid close to one of the rails. The asymmetric transmission of power from the locomotive put additional strain and wear on the wheels and moving parts, resulting in poor reliability. But the locomotive hauled 16 loaded coal wagons weighing about 70 tons at nearly four miles per hour for its maiden journey in front of a 'vast concourse of spectators'.

Other colliery engineers devised ingenious solutions for overcoming the supposed problem of adhesion of the wheel to the rail. The Chapmans drove one of their locomotives with a sprocket engaging in the teeth of a chain resting in a V-shaped trough between the rails. William Brunton of the Butterley Iron Company designed 'a horse to go by steam'. The engine was supported on two pairs of wheels but traction was by a series of legs sticking out the back like a gigantic grasshopper. The legs were worked by a series of links connected to the piston rod and walked the locomotive along. The engine was put to work but it did not have enough power, so it was decided to fit a bigger boiler. There is a contemporary account of the first journey of the rebuilt locomotive: '13th July 1815. The locomotive engine called the *Steam Horse* at Nesham's Colliery was destroyed by the bursting of the boiler. By this accident 57 people were killed or maimed'. Possibly the first steam railway train accident to cost lives.

Christopher Blackett, owner of the Wylam Collieries, had purchased a locomotive from John Whinfield of Newcastle but had refused to accept delivery because of problems with the machine. Following this disappointment Blackett relaid the wooden Wylam railway with cast-iron rails; the upgraded line was a great improvement and enabled a horse to pull two wagons in the place of a single one. In 1812 Blackett revived his enthusiasm for a steam locomotive to haul his coal wagons over the 4½ miles from the pits to the river. He asked his supervisor William Hedley, assisted by Timothy Hackworth, the foreman blacksmith, to arrange for the supply of a steam locomotive. Hedley had seen or heard of the various methods of propelling steam locomotives and he was determined to make a measured enquiry into the capability of a locomotive with smooth wheels to haul loads in excess of its own weight. He made a special four-wheel towing carriage; the wheels were driven by men standing on the carriage floor pumping handles with cranks attached to the wheels. He attached a number of coal wagons whose weight was known and he put iron weights on the towing carriage. Then he varied the weights on the towing carriage and the weight of the wagons it was hauling. He found that there was a near-constant ratio between the weight of the towing carriage and the maximum load it could haul. Hedley showed conclusively that a locomotive with smooth wheels could pull a load many times its weight. He then purchased a cast-iron boiler, cylinders and drive rods and fitted them on the towing carriage. The engine worked reasonably well but was short of steam because of the small size of the boiler.

Hedley went on to design a series of engines, each incorporating improvements and each performing better than the previous engine. Most of the engines were made in Thomas Waters' works, which built engines under licence from Trevithick. Waters was a well-known local card; once when he was having problems with an engine he held down the boiler safety valve saying 'either she or he would go'.

Hedley's later engines were so big and heavy that he was obliged to mount them on four pairs of wheels to distribute the weight. He refused to use Chapman's patent for the bogie and he devised a system of the wheels having some axial movement to enable the locomotive to go round curves. The experiment was not a success and Hedley went back to two pairs of wheels. The locomotives regularly hauled eight loaded wagons at five miles per hour. One interesting item in the colliery accounts of the time was a payment in compensation of damage to crops caused by 'the fire-throwing proclivities of the machines'. One of the Hedley engines was christened *Puffing Billy*: it was one of the first engines to pipe the exhaust steam from the cylinders into the chimney to increase the draught to the fire and provide better combustion with a consequent increase in power. For the first time, onlookers heard the distinctive chuff-chuff sound that became the trademark of the steam locomotive. Other engines were named *Black Billy*, *Wylam Dilly*, *Lady Mary* and *Old Duchess*.

The Wylam collieries were dependent on keels to transport coal down the river Tyne for transfer to seagoing vessels. In 1822 the keelmen went on a strike that lasted ten weeks. The *Wylam Dilly* had her wheels removed, was fitted with paddle wheels and mounted on a keel and put to work towing another four keels.

One Sunday, Timothy Hackworth, Hedley's principal assistant and engineer, was on his way to preach at a prayer meeting when he met a Wylam workmate who told him that he would lose his job if he didn't go to work. 'Lose or not lose, I shall not break the Sabbath', replied Hackworth. He left Wylam with its climate of innovation and policy of developing steam locomotives to go to work at Walbottle Colliery; as a result, Wylam locomotive development and innovation came to an end.

The name that towers over all others is that of George Stephenson, who achieved worldwide fame as the 'Inventor of the Railway', a title that exaggerates his importance and contribution. However, he did make a massive contribution to the development of the railway and his fame is due to his great achievements on the Stockton & Darlington and the Liverpool & Manchester railways, and in part due to Samuel Smiles's eulogistic biography. He combined the qualities of fearlessness and ambition, he was a brilliant mechanic and he had an aptitude for understanding engineering problems and finding solutions.

George Stephenson was born in 1781 in a small workman's cottage housing four families on the Blackett estate close to Wylam Colliery where his father worked as fireman of the pumping engine. As a boy he started colliery work as a picker, cleaning stones and dross from the coal. He worked at several collieries and finally joined his father as assistant fireman at Darley Colliery. When he was promoted to engineman he married and his son, Robert, was born in 1803. The family moved to Killingworth where he got a better job as an engine brakeman. George Stephenson was determined to earn as much as possible to keep and to better his family. In addition to his job in the colliery he shovelled ballast from ships, mended clocks and shoes and even cut dresses to be sewn by colliers' wives. He spent some of the additional money at night school learning to read and write; he was triumphant when, aged 19, he learned to sign his name. Wanting his son to have the best possible education, Stephenson bought a donkey so that Robert could set off to the best school in the district with his slate, chalks and lunch box on his back. In the evenings the boy would mentor his father with all that he had learned at school that day.

During his days or nights in the colliery George Stephenson became expert at maintaining the pumping engines; he would take them apart and rebuild them, and he established a reputation for running engines efficiently. His wife and daughter died in 1806 and he accepted a job looking after a Boulton & Watt engine at a spinning works in Montrose, Scotland. He walked the 160 miles there with his belongings on his back and spent 12 months running the mill's steam engine with great success. He returned to Tyneside to find his father had been blinded in a work accident and to find his conscription papers to join the army in the war against France. He thought of joining his sister's family in America, but decided to stay in England. His savings from his Montrose job together with some borrowings paid for a substitute to go to the war in his place and Stephenson went to work at the Killingworth collieries.

There were serious problems with the pumping engine which drained the mine at the High Pit Colliery. The Killingworth engineers tried all the known procedures for trimming and adjusting the engine but without success. Stephenson asked if he could try his hand and was given permission. He chose a crew of mechanics and took the machine to pieces, made a number of modifications to the boiler injector, raised the level of the injection water cistern and increased the boiler pressure. The rebuilt engine pumped the pit dry in three days and Stephenson was appointed engine-wright[2] for the Killingworth group of pits.

Stephenson often visited the nearby Wylam Colliery to look at their locomotives. Every Saturday afternoon the locomotives were taken out of service for routine maintenance and Stephenson, now a friend of Jonathan Foster, the Wylam engine-wright, often helped with the work and became enthusiastic about the use of steam locomotives replacing horses.

Stephenson asked Lord Ravensworth, the leading partner in the Killingworth collieries, for the resources to construct a 'Travelling Engine'. The locomotive had two pairs of wheels and was named *Blutcher,* Northumbrian for 'huge animal'; the wheels were driven through a series of spur gears from the connecting rods. Stephenson then made improvements to the recently devised system of taking the waste steam

2. As well as locomotives and railways Stephenson designed a miner's safety lamp that became a standard.

from the cylinders and piping it to the bottom of the chimney to force a draught for the fire, with the result that the fire and boiler generated double the amount of steam without increasing the weight of the engine. His next advance was to eliminate spur gears and to drive the wheel on the rail by joining the connecting rod to a pin fastened to one of the wheel spokes. Although the *Blutcher* hauled about 30 tons at four miles per hour the economics of running horses or the locomotive were in the balance, largely because running the heavy unsprung engine did so much damage to itself and to the railway.

Stephenson saw that the next step to speed up locomotive running and improve the economics of transporting coal to the river was to improve the rails. He is quoted as saying that he regarded the rail and the locomotive 'as man and wife', and together with a local iron founder he designed and patented a new type of chair to support the rail on the sleeper or crosstie, and a half-lap joint to replace the traditional butt joint between rails in order to give a smooth join. Stephenson constructed at least another five locomotives, each incorporating advances such as wrought-iron wheels in place of cast-iron and fitting the boiler to a separate frame. One development that failed was to mount the boiler and frame on four steam cylinders to act as springs and compensate for the unevenness of the rails. A hundred and thirty years later, the Citroën car company adopted a variation of the system for their beautiful DS cars, but with nitrogen-filled cylinders rather than steam.

The success of the Killingworth railway and locomotives was so great that the owners of the nearby Hetton colliery decided to upgrade their waggonway to a railway with locomotives to provide improved transportation of coal from the pits to the staithes, eight miles away on the river Wear. Eight miles was the longest and most ambitious line for steam-hauled trains. The line ran through hilly and undulating country, and they had neither the time nor the resources to build embankments or dig cuttings to provide a track sufficiently level to be within the capability of a locomotive. Stephenson was asked to be chief engineer; he upgraded the rails and installed stationary winding engines at the top of the two main inclines to haul loaded trains up the steep grades. There were five other lesser hills where loaded wagons ran down the grade pulling up empty wagons attached by rope. Known as *iron horses*, the five Stephenson locomotives hauled trains of 17 wagons weighing a total of 64 tons along the flat sections of the line.

Retrospectively it is not possible to define the contributions of each of the early engineers to the innovations, improvements and development of the steam locomotive. The sons of Hedley and Hackworth each wrote a biography of their father, as did one of Richard Trevithick's sons, and Samuel Smiles's *Life of George Stephenson* probably magnifies his achievements. When a Dr Lardner, lecturing in Newcastle, called George Stephenson the father of the locomotive, William Hedley objected and wrote 'I beg to say ... it was the engine on the Wylam Railway that established the character of the locomotive engine ... as an economical prime mover'. The bitterness of the rivalry between Hedley, Hackworth and Stephenson came out in a letter some years later from Hackworth's son. The letter refers to a panegyric about the development of the crankshaft by Stephenson, it was 'called by the name of some planet or star, *no doubt of the first magnitude*'; Hackworth junior does not hide his scorn.

Regardless of who was first to exhaust spent steam through the smokestack, introduce the return flue boiler or the multi-tube boiler to increase the area of heat transfer from the fire to the water, or substitute the weight-loaded safety valve with a spring-loaded one, it is clear that the rivalry of these colliery engineers stimulated a release of creative energy that resulted in the steam locomotive replacing animal traction as the reliable and economic method to transport coal.

The early 1820s was a period of great excitement and speculation about the future of railways. In 1821 George Stephenson wrote 'On a long and favourable railway I would start my engines to travel 60 miles a day with from 40 to 60 tons of goods'. In 1824 an article in *Mechanics Magazine* described a '*Proposition for a General Iron Railway*' of a six-track railway from Edinburgh to London and on to Falmouth, a distance of about 650 miles. There was to be a toothed rack in the centre of each track and points or switches to turn 'the vehicles off into their respective branch railways'. A certain William James patented a 'Mode of Propelling Railway Carriages' to avoid the need for using a rack and pinion for steep gradients and for rounding sharp curves without additional friction: 'a wheel, in effect, possesses as many diameters as there are variations in the surface of its periphery …'. Sir George Cayley, whose claims to fame included making and flying a glider, the first-ever heavier than air machine, devised the 'Patent Universal Railway'. His incomprehensible description included '… two endless chains, consisting of portions of a railway so jointed that they formed an inflexible right line when resting on the ground, but each capable of coiling round a fore and hind wheel …'. In the middle of all this hysteria, Nicholas Wood, engineer, colliery owner and later a judge at the 1829 Rainhill locomotive competition, advised moderation in making claims for the future of the railway. He even discouraged forecasts of trains 'travelling at the rate of 12, 16, 18 or 20 miles an hour; nothing could do more harm towards their [railways] adoption or general improvement than the promulgation of such nonsense'.

❖

The Stockton & Darlington Railway was the world's first public railway. There was opposition to it from vested interests and from local landowners and it failed in its first attempt to get parliamentary approval. A second attempt in 1821, which included a wide detour round the Duke of Cleveland's fox coverts, was successful. The principal promoters were Edward and Joseph Pease, a Quaker father and son who saw the opportunities of linking the collieries of the South Durham coalfield with a 27-mile railway line past Darlington to Stockton with its staithes on the river Tees. The Peases intended to lay a railway with cast-iron rails; they believed that a horse could draw a ten-ton load on iron rails as compared to one ton on a roadway. They appointed George Stephenson as company engineer and surveyor and he took on his 20-year-old son, Robert as his assistant.

Stephenson tried to persuade the Peases that a locomotive could do 'fifty times the work of a horse'. After a visit to see steam locomotives working at Killingworth, a new Bill was submitted to Parliament to give authorisation for the company to use steam locomotives and for the line to carry passengers. There was no suitable supplier of steam locomotives and the Stephensons and the Peases established the firm of Robert Stephenson

& Co's Forth Street Works in Newcastle; the firm's first order was to supply two stationary engines and winding machinery to haul coal trains up the inclines over Etherley and Brusselton ridges on the Stockton & Darlington.

The line was to have a gauge of 4ft 8½ inches; Stephenson wanted 12-ft long wrought iron rails, more expensive than cast-iron rails, but for reasons of economy it was decided to use cast-iron rails for a substantial length of the track. The railway was laid as a single track with four passing sidings every mile so that wagons and locomotives going in opposite directions could pass. The first locomotive, *Locomotion*, and the first passenger carriage were delivered by the Stephenson Locomotive Works in early September 1825. Timothy Hackworth was appointed locomotive superintendent and the Stockton & Darlington was ready for a grand inauguration ceremony for its opening.

The opening of the world's first public railway was arranged for the 27th September in the same year. An announcement in the press stated 'A superior Loco Motive Travelling Engine, of the most improved construction, will be employed with a train of convenient carriages for the conveyance of the proprietors and strangers'. The programme for the great day described the inaugural train: 'The Company's Locomotive Engine, the Engine's tender with water and coals, Six Waggons laden with coals, the Committee and other Proprietors in the coach belonging to the Company, Six Waggons with seats reserved for Strangers, Fourteen Waggons for the Conveyance of Workmen and others, Six Waggons laden with coal'. The last six wagons were to be detached at Darlington leaving the rest of the train to continue to Stockton. The locomotive was driven by George Stephenson and made a triumphant journey to Stockton. An eyewitness account: 'The signal being given, the engine started off with this immense train of carriages; and such was its velocity, that in some parts the speed was frequently twelve miles per hour ...'. Crowds lined the track to cheer the triumphal progress of the train, people ran alongside trying to keep up with the cavalcade, horsemen galloped beside the engine and a stagecoach kept up with the train for a part of the way. There were banners everywhere with the company's motto '*Periculum privatum utilitas publica*'[3]. Other banners trumpeted 'May the Stockton &

Darlington Railway give public satisfaction and reward its liberal promoters'. The local newspaper wrote up the event and the celebration and its account included 'the striking contrast exhibited by the power of the engine and horses; the engine with her six hundred passengers and load, and the coach with four horses and only sixteen passengers'. The inaugural journey was followed by a grand dinner for the proprietors and their guests. At the end of the dinner there were 23 bumper toasts, almost all accompanied by music and song and many 'three times three'. They even drank to the health of the 'Solicitors of the Railway Company' as well as to 'Other Peers and MPs who assisted the Company'.

The main business of the company was hauling coal from the collieries to the sea. *Locomotion* was joined by other Stephenson locomotives, *Hope, Black Diamond* and *Diligence*. There were problems with all of them and they spent almost as much time in the company's Shildon workshop as on the line. In 1828 *Locomotion's* boiler blew up, killing the driver and maiming another man 'whose face was black and speckled like a Dalmatian dog ever after'. The reliability of the early Stephenson locomotives was so poor that the management considered abandoning steam traction. However, they agreed to let Timothy Hackworth, who had been appointed the company's engineer, to construct a new locomotive. Hackworth's *Royal George* made its first journey in November 1827. It proved to be a great success and confirmed conclusively that steam traction was more economic than horse haulage. The Stephenson works also delivered two new locomotives; one, the *Experiment,* was modified to have an additional two wheels and was known as *Old Elbows*. As usual the Hackworth men at Shildon found fault with it.

In the early years the engine drivers working the trains were paid by the ton/mile of coal moved. They were responsible for paying their assistants, firemen, oilers and greasers. There was modest, very modest, pay if the locomotive was in the workshops. There were no brakes on the engine or tender; the fireman and the oilers had to jump down at the beginning of each downward incline and tie down as many wagon brakes as they thought necessary. The brakes had to be disengaged at the end of the

3. Private enterprise for the public good.

incline with the men walking back on the coal along the top of the train's loaded wagons and jumping from one to the next. It was customary to hang a board on the last wagon so that they could check that none had been lost. There were no grease boxes for the wheels: the engine would slow down the train, the oilers would jump off and oil each journal as it went past and then jump onto the last wagon, climb up and walk and jump along the loads back to the engine. On the early engines the piston valves had rods that had to be juggled by hand to exchange forward for reverse gear. If the change had to be done in the dark, the fireman held a lighted end of rope dipped in oil so that the driver could see while he wrestled with the rods.

The Company had to learn how to manage and run a railway. It ran a tight ship and published its *Rules and Regulations*; they included a list of fines for contraventions. In addition to the penalties for obvious misdemeanours, drivers were fined for excessive speed; one driver was fined for descending to Yarm station at 12mph, another was sacked for taking a train the 40 miles from Shildon to Stockton and back in 4¼ hours. The management disapproved of speed because of the damage it did to both track and machinery and because they felt it could only be achieved by holding down the boiler safety valve. There was a strict speed limit of 5mph to reduce the risk of fire when the train passed by a wood or plantation; the management attached boards to the chimney with the engine number so that the public could note the identity of an offending engine. The proprietors or 'Committee', as they called themselves, held fortnightly meetings with employees when fines and penalties were imposed. The employees were generally cowed when they found themselves standing in front of the seated Committee; one courageous driver who complained about a succession of unsatisfactory fireman was asked their names. He replied, 'Badger, Bullet, Baggy and Buck'.

The company built a series of passenger carriages, the *Express, Defiance* and *The Union,* which they leased to local innkeepers who competed to carry passengers. The carriages were similar to stagecoaches but fitted on wagon frames with standard flanged wheels. All the passenger traffic was horse hauled and the frames were fitted with a yoke at each end so that a horse could be harnessed to pull the coach in either direction. There was no system of signals on the line. Steam had priority over horse-drawn coal wagons but passengers had right of way over coal. When passenger carriages met head-on there was trouble deciding who should go back. Eventually the company put posts halfway between the passing sidings; whoever reached the post first had right-of-way. This did little to help the situation, as carriages from opposite directions made a mad dash to reach the post.

Timothy Hackworth was appointed General Manager of the line. It is hardly surprising that *Practical Mechanics Journal* reported 'His duties were of a most arduous and fatiguing character, such as can scarcely be conceived at the present time, considering the raw state of everything connected with railways ... almost the entire guidance and direction devolved on himself.' Within about three years the company managed to achieve a successful operating pattern. The chaos of having a large number of contractors running carriages, wagons or trains led the company to change its policy and operate all the traffic on the line. This coincided with horse-drawn wagons being withdrawn and replaced by steam traction for both passengers and coal.

Traffic increased and in 1830 the company purchased a desolate 500-acre site that had a few farm buildings. The hamlet was called Middlesborough and was situated close to the mouth of the river Tees with deep water for mooring large vessels. In the same year the Stockton & Darlington tracks were extended an additional five miles from Stockton to Middlesborough, 'the first town to owe its existence to the railway'. The inaugural train was hauled by the *Globe*, the company's first locomotive specifically designed for passenger work. The *Globe* was built by the Stephenson works largely to Hackworth's design; it was probably the first locomotive to have horizontal cylinders inside the frame driving cranked axles and the first locomotive to be fitted with reversing gear. Forty-five years later, Middlesborough had become the greatest iron-producing centre in the world.

The line from the Brusselton incline to Stockton was double-tracked to handle the increasing traffic and in 1833 the management contracted out the operations of the line to Hackworth for a guaranteed return on their investment. The arrangement lasted to 1840 when Hackworth left to establish his own locomotive design and construction works close to the

Company's Shildon works. He built locomotives for a large number of railways in Britain and overseas and made the first steam locomotive to run in Russia.

The Stockton & Darlington Railway became a successful company and became the most profitable British railway company in the 1850s, paying a mean annual dividend of 9.5%.

Robert Stephenson 1803–1859   Isambard Kingdom Brunel 1806–1859

3 The Engineer Heroes

The cities of Liverpool and Manchester are about 35 miles apart; at the beginning of the 19th century Liverpool was a great seaport well on its way to becoming the busiest port in the world with its 35 miles of quays. It was not only a seaport but a city of merchants doing business with the world and especially with the Americas. Manchester was compared to the centre 'of a 30-mile spider's web of cotton manufacturing towns'; together with its immediate neighbour Salford it was the second city of the British Isles. The Irwell and Mersey Navigation canal, the Bridgewater canal and a series of roads linked the two cities, but by the 1820s they had become inadequate to handle the rapidly increasing traffic. Merchants complained about the mountains of raw cotton piled up in Liverpool; it was said to take longer to transport a cargo from Liverpool to Manchester than to import it across the Atlantic from the United States.

In 1821 local businessmen formed a committee to put together a scheme to raise funds and to get assent from Parliament to build a railway between Liverpool and Manchester. About the same time the merchants of Liverpool issued a Public Declaration: '… new line of conveyance has become absolutely necessary to conduct the increasing trade of the country with speed, certainty and economy'. The scheme was vigorously and even violently opposed by landowners and the operators of canals and turnpike roads. The scheme's promoters were known to have visited the

Killingworth steam railway. Opponents of the enterprise said the poisoned air from the engines would make women miscarry, prevent cows grazing, hens laying and kill birds flying overhead; the landowners chorused that they would be unable to preserve foxes or breed pheasants in nearby coverts. It was even said that the smoke was as poisonous as an evil dragon's breath.

The promoters did indeed visit Killingworth to see steam traction, but they also went to meet George Stephenson, to evaluate his experience and abilities to plan and engineer their proposed new line. On their return to Liverpool they offered him the job of engineer of the projected Liverpool & Manchester Railway. Stephenson had almost completed the construction of the Stockton & Darlington; he accepted the job and moved to Liverpool.

Following two surveys, the Liverpool & Manchester Railway's promoters applied to Parliament in 1825 for the necessary powers to construct the railway. In April Stephenson was called to the witness box to be examined by a Committee of the House of Commons and their barristers. He was regarded as an ignoramus and a fool and one committee member thought him a foreigner because of his Northumbrian accent. He was even considered a maniac when he answered questions about using steam locomotives on the line. His assertions, based on his experience at Killingworth, were simply not believed. As a hands-on man with practical experience, Stephenson stumbled when answering technical queries about the survey, and the committee voted against the scheme for building the railway.

A third survey was made under the supervision of John Rennie, and another bill was submitted to Parliament. Despite talk of 'the smoke and the noise, the hiss and the whirl of locomotives', opposition was muted and the bill passed successfully through the House of Commons and the House of Lords to become law.

The proposed line from Liverpool had a number of construction challenges. The approved route for the railway ran almost due east from Liverpool, and the civil works included a 2,200-yard long tunnel, a steep and long incline past Edge Hill, crossing Whiston and Sutton ridges, a two-mile long cutting 80ft deep through the sandstone massif of Olive Mount, a nine-arch viaduct across the Sankey river, and another 63 bridges either over or under existing roadways. At the time it was considered a challenge of 'the most stupendous description'. But the greatest part of the challenge was crossing Chat Moss: 12 square miles of a seemingly bottomless sponge of vegetation and pulp that many inhabitants thought was left over from the Deluge. A man couldn't stand on this vegetable quicksand; he had to fall forward and crawl to escape the clutches of the bog. Everyone from engineer to village idiot said that it was impossible to build a railway across Chat Moss. Stephenson's plan was to float the railway on a long raft made from a matting of heath and branches. The raft was constructed much wider than the width of the two rail tracks in order to distribute the weight of the permanent way and trains over a wide area. There were many problems in executing this solution and stagecoach drivers, recognising their jobs were at risk, spread rumours, 'hundreds of men and horses had sunk and the workers completely abandoned'. The engineer himself was declared to have been swallowed up in the Serbonian bog; 'Railways were at an end forever'. Despite this wishful thinking, the line was completed in 1830.

Construction was well advanced before any decision was made about the type of traction for hauling trains. The idea of using horses had been discarded early on, and the choice was between stationary steam engines with winding gear and ropes or steam locomotives. Two distinguished engineers made a detailed study of the Killingworth railway and came back with the recommendation to build stationary engines. They claimed the initial cost was higher but the operating costs were more economic; they recommended building twenty-one engines along the line to haul the trains. Opinion was all in favour of the stationary engines but Stephenson was so persistent in advocating locomotives that the directors agreed, almost reluctantly, to stage a competition to see if they might be suitable, and they offered a prize of £500.

To be eligible for the competition, locomotives had to meet a number of conditions: speed, load, boiler pressure, fuel consumption and weight – 6 tons maximum, 4½ tons preferred – and a number of other technical requirements. The weight limitation eliminated most existing locomotives: *Locomotion* on the Stockton & Darlington weighed nearly 8 tons. Many schemes were proposed but on the day of the trials only four locomotives were considered eligible to compete: Braithwaite and Ericsson's *Novelty*, Timothy Hackworth's *Sans Pareil*, Robert Stephenson's *Rocket* and Burstall's *Perseverance*. A fifth, Brandreth's *Cycloped* was not permitted to enter; it was a three-ton machine propelled by a horse on a treadmill.

The competition required each engine to make 20 two-mile trips at an average speed exceeding 10mph along a length of line at Rainhill near Liverpool. The Rainhill Trial attracted crowds of spectators; with excitement and interest worldwide, the results of the Trial were even reported in a Boston newspaper. The *Perseverance* never went faster than six miles per hour, both *Novelty* and *Sans Pareil* had a series of mechanical failures and there were objections to the enormous amount of fuel used by the *Sans Pareil*; its blast was too strong and blew burning coke out of its chimney. The *Rocket* travelled the specified distances at 15mph, 50% greater than the required speed, and even reached a maximum of 29mph. It was the clear winner of the trial.

The success of the *Rocket*[1] demonstrated that a steam locomotive and train running on rails was a viable and commercially economic combination to transport passengers and freight. It was the beginning of the steam railway age, which was to last 150 years.

Development and improvement of locomotive design became so rapid that the *Rocket* was soon overtaken by faster and more powerful locomotives. She was taken out of service five years after her Rainhill triumph and sold to a colliery railway.

The ceremonial opening of the world's first intercity railway was on 15th September 1830 and was an occasion of immense splendour and enormous crowds. Eight Stephenson locomotives hauled about 600 dignitaries, including the Duke of Wellington, Sir Robert Peel and Mr Huskisson who had been President of the Board of Trade. There were thousands of spectators along the line who cheered the progress of the trains running at 24mph. The *Northumbrian*, hauling the Duke of Wellington's carriage, stopped to allow the other trains to pass as if in a review. Mr Huskisson, who had had a coolness with the Duke, was on the other side of the line; seeing the Duke raise his hand in what he supposed

1. The Rocket can be seen and admired in London's Science Museum.

was a gesture of friendship, he started towards him and tripped just as the *Rocket* was coming. The train ran over his leg. Instantly the *Northumbrian* was detached from the Duke's train and took Huskisson at an average speed of 36mph, to Eccles, a Manchester suburb, where he died the same evening[2] .

The next day the railway was open for business and 140 passengers were taken on the first train to Manchester in the scheduled two hours. In the following year the company was carrying the mail, had run its first excursion train, laid on special trains for taking passengers to the races and was transporting road-rail containers for Pickfords, the removal firm. Sixteen years later the Liverpool & Manchester became part of the London & North Western Railway, the LNWR.

Following the twin triumphs of the opening of the Liverpool & Manchester Railway and of the *Rocket*, George Stephenson was asked to design and engineer a short railway from the collieries at Swannington to Leicester. Stephenson declined the job and suggested his son Robert in his place: the 16-mile railway was completed in 1832.

In 1836 George Stephenson was given responsibility for constructing the northern section of the Grand Junction Railway between Birmingham and Warrington where it joined the Liverpool and Manchester Railway; his Dutton viaduct over the river Weaver, with its 20 arches, was probably his finest bridge design. Following problems and disagreement he was

---

2. A tablet erected to mark the event reads:

A tribute of personal respect and affection
has been placed here to mark the spot where on the
15th of September 1830 the day of the opening of this rail road
THE RIGHT HONble WILLIAM HUSKISSON M.P.
singled out by the decree of an inscrutable providence from
the midst of the distinguished multitude that surrounded him
in the full pride of his talents and the perfection of his
usefulness met with the accident that occasioned his death
which deprived England of an illustrious statesman
and Liverpool of its most honoured representative which changed
a moment of the noblest exaltation and triumph that science and
genius had ever achieved into one of desolation and mourning
and striking terror into the hearts of assembled thousands
brought home to every bosom the forgotten truth that
IN THE MIDST OF LIFE WE ARE IN DEATH.

replaced by Joseph Locke, one of his pupils. Stephenson was then appointed to engineer the Birmingham & Derby, the Manchester & Leeds, and the lines of a number of other companies. He was asked to make recommendations for the construction of a west-coast main line from the Liverpool & Manchester Railway to Scotland. He proposed building the line along the levels of the coast with a massive embankment across the mouth of Morecambe Bay. He reckoned that the land behind the embankment would silt up and become a valuable asset that would help defray a large part of the costs of building the line. His proposals were rejected in favour of Joseph Locke's shorter and less costly inland route over Shap summit.

George Stephenson was convinced that coal was the basis of prosperity for an increasingly industrialised Britain: 'The Lord Chancellor now sits upon a bag of wool, but wool has long ceased to be emblematical of the staple commodity of England. He ought rather to sit upon a bag of coals, though it might not prove quite so comfortable a seat.' He found several rich seams of coal when he was building the Claycross Tunnel for the Midland Railway and, together with his son Robert, developed a colliery; he was convinced that the area could supply coal to London by rail at prices competitive to sea transport from the North East.

George Stephenson bought Tapton House north of Chesterfield as his final residence. The house was a fine building with a classical façade situated on top of a hill overlooking his Claycross collieries, his Ambergate limeworks, and the Midland Railway line. He handed over his railway commitments to Robert but retained an interest in the collieries and limeworks close to his house. He became an enthusiastic gardener and horticulturist and built melon houses, pineries and vineries. His ten glasshouses were heated with circulating hot water; he devised a method of growing champion melons by suspending them in gauze baskets to relieve the tension in the stalk and allow the nourishment to flow more easily to the fruit. He was also determined to grow straight cucumbers and finally succeeded by growing them inside glass cylinders. He died in 1848 aged 67 and is buried in Trinity Church, Chesterfield.

❖

George Stephenson's son, Robert was brought up in the shadow of Killingworth Colliery and was already expert in the workings of colliery machinery and steam engines by the time he went to college in Edinburgh to study geology, chemistry and science. He learnt shorthand and took down the lectures verbatim so that he could read them to his father on his return to Killingworth. He then helped his father survey the Stockton & Darlington Railway and became a partner with him and Edward Pease in Robert Stephenson & Co's Forth Street Works in Newcastle. He designed and constructed the stationary engines for winding trains up the Brusselton and Etherley inclines on the Stockton & Darlington and built a number of locomotives including *Locomotion*. He left abruptly to accept a job as engineer and manager of a silver mine in Colombia. Possibly there had been disagreement between father and son; George Stephenson must have been very overbearing and almost certainly did not tolerate differences of opinion with his boy.

The Colombian venture had inadequate resources and Robert received criticism rather than support from the London board of directors; he decided to return to England at the end of his three-year contract. On his way home, waiting for a ship in Cartagena, he met a down-and-out Richard Trevithick and they travelled together to the United States. Their ship ran aground on the way to New York but the passengers and crew managed to get ashore. After some weeks travelling in North America, Stephenson sailed for Liverpool and went straight to the Newcastle works, which he found in chaos and short of orders. The locomotive was not yet established as the preferred form of railway traction; as late as 1829, the Act for the Newcastle & Carlisle Railway obtained Parliamentary approval only provided the line was worked by horses. Robert Stephenson made sweeping improvements to the organisation of the works and combined the latest design features in the firm's locomotives together with the reliability he had learnt from the operations of colliery locomotives and the Stockton & Darlington Railway.

The 112-mile London & Birmingham Railway, the world's first trunk line, was authorised by Parliament in 1833, with George Stephenson as engineer who handed over the responsibility for design and construction to Robert. There was the inevitable opposition from canal and coach operators and the Stephensons opened a Westminster office to make the necessary representations to Parliament. By this time landowners were generally reconciled to the idea of railways running across their land but they had to be 'conciliated' or paid off by the railway company.

The line needed to be as near level as possible because the locomotives had limited power and could not haul trains up any but the easiest gradients; this resulted in the need for a large number of expensive civil engineering works and more than four miles of tunnels. These included Kilsby Tunnel driven through waterlogged quicksand, which the 160-horsepower pumps took eight months to drain. There were massive cuttings at Tring and Blisworth. Stationary engines with winding gear were needed to lift the trains up the steep incline from London's Euston terminus to Camden where locomotives were coupled to the trains for the journey to Birmingham. The line was opened in sections, while construction at Blisworth and Kilsby was still going on and it was finally opened to Birmingham in 1838. That year the *Tally-Ho*, the fastest stagecoach, made the journey between London and Birmingham in 11 hours with up to 14 passengers; the fastest train did the journey in five and a half hours with up to 300 passengers.

Robert Stephenson was appointed engineer to the line from Darlington to Scotland. It involved two major engineering works: the 28-arch masonry Royal Border Bridge over the River Tweed into Scotland and the High Level Bridge over the Tyne between Gateshead and Newcastle.

George Stephenson had made an initial survey from Chester to determine the site of a port to provide a convenient crossing from England to Ireland. He proposed a route from Chester over the Menai Straits to the isle of Anglesey and Holyhead with a bridge across the Straits. Robert Stephenson took over the construction of the project and built the 84-mile line. The route included three important bridges. First was the bridge over the river Dee, which failed and had to be rebuilt. Next was the crossing over the Conwy Estuary for which he designed two massive 400-ft wrought-iron tubes that were floated below the masonry piers and then jacked up. Stephenson drove the first train through one of the tubes. Finally, bridging the Menai Straits presented the greatest challenge because of the width of the Straits, the fierceness of the tides and because

Admiralty regulations wouldn't permit a scaffold or falsework to be erected. The elder Stephenson couldn't envisage that length of bridge being rigid enough to support the weight and vibration of a moving train and recommended that freight and passengers should cross the bridge in horse drawn wagons or carriages. Robert decided to build the bridge with three piers supporting massive wrought-iron box section tubes. The tubes over the water were 460ft long, more than 100ft greater than the height of St Pauls Cathedral. The Britannia Tubular Bridge was a masterpiece of daring and innovative engineering and provided a link for commerce and travellers between England and Ireland for 120 years. In 1970 schoolboy vandals started a fire that destroyed the structural continuity of the bridge and it was repaired with a rail deck supported by lattice arches sprung from Stephenson's original stone piers; the Admiralty no longer had concerns about navigation in the Straits.

Robert Stephenson later designed and built the world's longest bridge, the Victoria Bridge, across the two miles of the St Lawrence at Montreal; the tubes were supported on masonry piers, and gave Montreal a direct link to the United States. Stephenson designed bridges to cross the Nile, and was consulted for advice on railways in Sweden, Belgium, Switzerland and on the possibility of cutting a canal across the Isthmus of Suez. Stephenson's health was failing in his later years, and he took narcotics and stimulants to keep himself going. His friend Isambard Brunel asked him to advise on overcoming the problems of the launch of his giant Great Eastern steamship at Millwall. Stephenson fell in the wet mud and caught a severe chill that further damaged his health, and he died the following year, 1859. He was buried in Westminster Abbey next to another engineer, Thomas Telford, the great canal builder.

❖

The combined feats, advances and innovations of the Stephensons, father and son, are only rivalled by those of the Brunels, father and son. Marc Isambart Brunel was born near Rouen twelve years before George Stephenson. Marc Brunel was very proud of his middle name because he was a great admirer of Isambart of Xaintes, a master mason who built bridges and was asked to complete the construction of London Bridge at the beginning of the 13th century. The end 't' became anglicised to a 'd' when he went to America. As a second son, Marc Brunel was destined for the church, but thanks to an influential cousin he became a naval cadet and did a six-year spell of duty in the West Indies. The French Revolution began and the revolutionaries recalled the vessel, so he returned to France and Paris, a stout royalist, and published pamphlets of support for the monarchy. He became a marked man and fled to Rouen where he met Sophie Kingdom, a beautiful English 16-year-old studying to improve her French. They became secretly engaged to be married when Brunel was obliged to flee France. He contrived to obtain a passage from Le Havre to New York, where his abilities as an engineer were quickly recognised and he was asked to survey the route for a canal from the Hudson near Albany to Lake Champlain. He was then appointed New York City Engineer and designed a number of buildings for the city, including the famous Park Theatre. In the meantime Sophie who had been interned in France finally returned to England and when Marc Brunel arrived in England, they married and settled in Portsmouth. There Brunel designed a machine for making wood pulley blocks for the Royal Navy. The blocks performed better than the ones they replaced, quality was consistent and they could be made in great quantity at low cost. However he had difficulty getting payment from the Navy and this, together with other financial difficulties, resulted in his being sent to a debtors' prison.

Traffic in London had become very congested by the early 19th century, especially on the few bridges crossing the river and a company was formed to drive a tunnel under the Thames downstream from London Bridge. It was an audacious scheme; the crown of the tunnel was to be only 14ft below the riverbed and it was the first serious attempt in the world to tunnel under water. Pilot bores indicated a thick layer of impervious blue clay below the riverbed. In fact, there were also areas of porous gravel; in some places the gravel had been dredged, reducing the distance between the crown of the tunnel and the river. The fact that the river had been an open sewer for London for 2,000 years added to the problems; curdling filth carrying disease had penetrated deep into the subsoil. Marc Brunel was aware of the intention of building the tunnel and designed and patented a tunnelling shield for boring it. In 1824 the promoters of the Thames Tunnel Company appointed him as the engineer for the project. The task was more difficult and hazardous than anyone anticipated: disease affected the engineers as well as the navvies, Marc Brunel lost his health in the tunnel, pumps were operated day and night to prevent the works from flooding, but even so there were two major collapses of the roof which resulted in the workings being flooded. Six workmen lost their lives in the second collapse and Brunel's son Isambard was nearly drowned in the filthy water after rescuing men working in the shield. The directors of the Thames Tunnel Company passed a resolution praising the young man's 'intrepid courage and presence of mind' and the way in which he had 'put his life in more imminent danger to save the lives of the men under his immediate care'. The inundation coincided with the company running out of money and the entrance to the tunnel was bricked up.

Additional money became available and digging resumed seven years later. The tunnel was finally opened in 1843 to be fêted as one of the wonders of the modern world. On the day of its inauguration 25,000 visitors walked through the tunnel and in three months more than a million people crossed the river Thames through the tunnel. Marc Brunel was knighted by the Queen, took *en avant* as his motto and lived a further six years. Approach roads were never built and the tunnel never attained its objective as a thoroughfare for horse-drawn traffic as well as pedestrians. Today it provides the link under the Thames for the underground railway between Wapping and Rotherhithe.

Marc and Sophie Brunel's only son, Isambard Kingdom Brunel, was born in 1806. Marc was determined he should become an engineer and sent him to a series of colleges in France and he served as an apprentice in Louis Breguet's workshops, famous for its scientific instruments and chronometers. Isambard returned to London to work with his father in his city consulting offices and he played a major part in the early stages of the Thames tunnel's construction. His father, whose health was failing, made Isambard host the famous 1828 banquet in the tunnel to confirm to the world that the young man was now the engineer responsible for the works. The inundation the following year badly affected Isambard's health, and he left London, first for Brighton and then for Clifton in Bristol, to recover his health. While he was in Bristol he learned of the competition to design a bridge across the gorge of the River Avon to link Clifton and Leigh Woods on the south bank. Brunel submitted a design that was rejected by the judging committee, but then argued his case with the judges and even succeeded in getting them to accept his Egyptian pylons to support the bridge's suspension chains. Shortly after, the bridge promoters ran out of money and the chains were sold to be used on a bridge over the river Tamar. The bridge was finally constructed with the chains from Brunel's Hungerford Bridge across the Thames, which had been replaced by the present railway bridge from Charing Cross still in use. During these delays Brunel was bidding for engineering a number of jobs, particularly for dock systems. They all seem to be delayed: 'So many irons in the fire and none of them hot'. In fact he did execute a number of important projects that included docks in Bristol, on the river Wear and the river Neath.

The Merchant Venturers, an association of leading Bristol businessmen, looked at the growing prosperity of Liverpool with its trade with the Americas and its railway link to the industrial Lancashire towns, and they were aware that the railway to London via Birmingham would soon be completed. They knew their city needed good communications with the capital to continue to prosper, and so they promoted a scheme for a railway to link Bristol to London and succeeded in getting Parliamentary approval in 1835.

Based on his reputation for his designs for the Clifton Suspension Bridge and his work on the Bristol Docks, the railway promoters chose 27-year-old Isambard Kingdom Brunel to make the survey for the route, and to be responsible for the construction of the line. The Parliamentary committee sat for 57 days; Brunel as chief technical witness spoke with skill, knowledge and self-assurance to win support for the Bill. As might be expected, there was opposition from landowners and other vested interests including Eton College. 'The railway would be injurious to the discipline of the school and dangerous to the morals of the pupils'.

After several changes of name the company came to be called the Great Western Railway or GWR. Brunel had a grandiose vision and ambition for the line. He was determined it would be the most splendid line ever built and running the fastest trains. It was to be 'the finest work in England', with magnificent civil works, station buildings and trains. He persuaded his board of directors to allow him to adopt a gauge of 7ft 0¼ inches (2,140mm) between the rails, nearly 50% wider than the 4ft 8½ inches of the London & Birmingham and other railways. He was contemptuous of the standard gauge and referred to it as the 'coal waggon gauge' and maintained that a broad gauge track gave locomotives and carriages a low centre of gravity to provide increased safety. It also meant engines could have bigger boilers to provide more steam and speed. He ignored the problems of interchange or through workings with the London & Birmingham or other railways and he dismissed criticism of the extra costs involved. The Great Western Railway continued to run its magnificent broad gauge trains for more than 50 years, but then adopted the standard 4ft 8½ inch gauge of all the other railways at great expense and scrapped or converted its locomotives and rolling stock.

For the 119 miles to Bristol, Brunel chose a route that ran along the Thames Valley as far as Swindon. The London terminus was a wooden building at Paddington, a village on the edge of London; it was replaced by a handsome terminus 14 years later. The most notable engineering project between London and Swindon was the Maidenhead bridge across the Thames. The bridge had to allow sufficient clearance for sailing barges but Brunel refused to build embankments to increase the height of the tracks over the river; instead he designed a bridge with two 128-ft very shallow semi-elliptical arches, supposedly the flattest bridge arches in the world. There was widespread criticism and even ridicule of the design but the bridge is still in service, carrying locomotives weighing more than three times the weight of the 1841 engines and travelling at more than 100mph. Sonning Cutting, further along the line through the northern ridge of the London Basin, was a massive undertaking. Several contractors went broke and Brunel decided to direct the civil works himself with 1,200 navvies and more than 200 horses.

Swindon was a small Wiltshire town and it was the junction between the main Bristol line and the important branch to Gloucester and Cheltenham. Eighty miles from London, it was a convenient place to change locomotives, replacing the engines with big wheels for the level run from London by engines with smaller driving wheels for the more steeply graded line on to Bath and Bristol. It was here that Brunel decided to site the railway works for building and maintaining engines and carriages. There were few local skilled workmen, so men came from the north of England and were accommodated in a model housing estate known as the Railway Village. All the necessary facilities for the growing community were provided by the GWR, including the Mechanics Institute, which was the social, cultural and educational centre. The GWR made a deal with Rigby the contractor; Rigby paid for the building of Swindon station in return for a permanent lease of the refreshment rooms and the requirement that all trains stopped for ten minutes so that passengers would patronise them. With the introduction of more powerful locomotives there was no longer any need to change engines so the GWR tried to renege on the agreement and finally bought out the lease for £100,000 in 1895; it remained a charge against the company's revenue until 1920.

The railway continued from Swindon over a series of embankments, along cuttings and through tunnels to reach Bristol. The greatest engineering feat on the line was the construction of Box Tunnel, almost two miles long, dug by 3,000 navvies. Progress was halted over and over again because of flooding and other problems. In its approach to the Georgian spa city of Bath, the railway crossed through the Sydney Pleasure Gardens; Brunel designed an elaborate stone balustrade to go along each side of the line and a series of decorative iron and masonry footbridges. He gave Bath station a handsome Jacobean façade and the line terminated in the great wooden hammerbeam train shed at Temple Meads in Bristol; the office and station buildings were an elaborate Tudor confection that was criticised in London as an extravagance. The Bristol secretary wrote back that the design was only marginally more expensive than 'a thoroughly naked assemblage of walls and windows as might be permitted to enclose any Union Poor House in the country'.

The line was opened in 1841. Brunel had designed the buildings, engineered the civil works and supervised the construction of the enterprise to the highest possible standard. It was in the matter of locomotive design that he failed. He issued specifications to contractors that were not only unrealistic but sometimes contradictory. At one point the line had only one fully working locomotive, Stephenson's *North Star*.

Brunel then took on 21-year-old Daniel Gooch, trained in the Stephenson Locomotive Works, to run the locomotive department. Gooch was shocked at the chaotic state of the company's locomotives, and found it necessary to go behind Brunel's back to complain to the directors. Brunel did not take kindly to criticism but the two men made up their differences. Gooch then drew up the plans for the famous *Firefly* class engines which were constructed by a variety of engine builders to a very tight specification. They performed brilliantly and were given splendid names: *Phlegethon* hauled the first royal train in 1845; *Ixion* ran a 50-ton train over 53 miles in less than 64 minutes and even hit a 61mph maximum speed, an amazing feat at the time; and there were *Cerberus*, *Mars*, *Lucifer*, *Harpy*, *Mazeppa* and another 50, all with exotic names. Gooch rose to glory and became Sir Daniel Gooch MP and Chairman of the Great Western Railway Company.

After building the GWR to Bristol, Brunel surveyed and engineered the Bristol & Exeter Railway, which extended the line from Paddington west through to Exeter; the first section of the line opened a year after the opening of the GWR. Brunel was also the engineer for the South Devon Railway linking Exeter to Plymouth, for which he chose atmospheric traction rather than locomotives: 'I have no hesitation in taking upon myself the full and certain responsibility of recommending the atmospheric system on the South Devon Railway'.

The idea of an atmospheric railway had been patented in 1824 and had its supporters. There were a number of possible variations; the most common was fitting a pipe between the tracks. The pipe had a narrow opening running along the top, which was kept closed by a greased leather seal. A piston, joined to the first carriage, fitted in the pipe and the air in front of the piston was evacuated so that the train was pushed forward by atmospheric pressure. When George Stephenson was asked about the feasibility of atmospheric railways, he responded 'It won't do: it is only the fixed engine and ropes over again in another form; and to tell you the truth I don't think this rope of wind will answer so well as the rope of wire did'. The first section of the South Devon opened in 1846 but the 'Atmospheric Caper' was replaced by steam locomotives two years later. There were many reasons for its failures including rats chewing the leather seal, which was lubricated with tallow.

Brunel was then retained by the Cornwall Railway to extend the railway from Plymouth to Penzance. He designed a series of timber viaducts to take the line over the many steep Cornish valleys and he also built his most magnificent and enduring monument, the Royal Albert Bridge over the Tamar Estuary. The Royal Navy Plymouth base and depot was situated on the river Tamar, and they specified a 100-ft clearance under the proposed bridge at high water. Brunel's great bridge comprised two main spans each 455ft long supported by piers on each side of the estuary and by a central pier. He had spent time with Robert Stephenson during the construction of the tubular bridge over the Conwy and he suspended the rail deck of each span from a vast oval wrought iron tube. Raising the two trusses, one after the other to keep the channel clear took 13 months. The railway company put an inscription at the top of each of the two end piers

I.K.BRUNEL
ENGINEER
1859

No man could have a finer title or a finer memorial.

Brunel's vision extended to include huge steamships picking up passengers at Bristol and continuing west across the Atlantic to America. Three years after his appointment as engineer to the Great Western Railway construction started on his design of the transatlantic steamship *Great Western*. She was the largest steamship ever built and she was fitted with engines and bunkers designed for long distance steaming. There was an accident at the beginning of her maiden voyage, when Brunel fell from the deck into the engine room and was lucky to survive. He continued to pursue his vision of transporting passengers in the swiftest and most comfortable way from London to New York with the construction of two enormous new ships. The *Great Britain*, laid down in Bristol in 1839, had an iron hull and, weighing 4,000 tons, was bigger than any other iron vessel by a factor of eight. Originally designed for paddles, she was the first large vessel to be propelled with a screw propeller. Brunel did the complicated maths and designed the propeller himself. The vessel made a successful maiden voyage to New York in 15 days. On her fifth Atlantic crossing the *Great Britain* was driven aground in Dundrum Bay, Ireland; Brunel wrote 'The finest ship in the world … is lying like a useless saucepan'. The ship was bought and sold a number of times and finally did 24 years' service between England and Australia. Then she became a prison hulk in the Falkland Islands, and finally was towed back to England and restored in the Bristol dock[2] where she was built.

Undismayed by the problems of constructing the *Great Western* and the *Great Britain*, Brunel designed the *Leviathan*, or *Great Eastern* as she became. Constructed at Millwall in London she was easily more than double the size of anything afloat. Displacing 18,000 tons, she had four funnels, masts for sails, paddle wheels and a twin screw. She was built on stocks parallel to the river, and just launching the hull in 1858 became a major engineering challenge. The best-known image of Isambard Brunel is a photograph of him at the launch dressed in a heavy shapeless serge suit, top hat, hands in his pockets and a cigar in his mouth standing in front of the massive launch brake chains. The *Great Eastern* was dogged by disaster. On her initial voyage an engine-room explosion blew off the front funnel and killed five crew. Brunel, whose health had been steadily declining, died a few days after the accident. The *Great Eastern* was finally sold for £25,000, a small fraction of her cost, and was used to lay the first telegraph cable across the Atlantic. One biographer wrote 'Brunel's great ships made an important contribution to the development of marine engineering but were disastrous for the investors who placed so much confidence in him'.

Joseph Locke also deserves the title 'Hero Engineer'. He began his professional life working for the Stephensons but unlike them he was not a polymath and he became a specialist in designing and supervising the construction of railways. He worked on the Liverpool & Manchester and then took over engineering the Grand Junction and laid out the Crewe locomotive works and the town. He engineered the west coast mainline over Shap and Beattock summits to Scotland and took over a number of failing projects, notably the London & Southampton line.

---

2. The restored *Great Britain* is open to the public.

Locke left no great memorial such as the Britannia or Royal Albert bridges but he established a reputation for giving accurate cost estimates and managing projects to budget. His method was based on making a detailed and comprehensive survey and then drawing up complete specifications and drawings of the civil works and buildings on a project. He also used large and specialised contractors; Thomas Brassey was the best known and he worked with Locke building railways in France, Holland, and Italy as well as in the UK. Locke's planning and methods of supervising construction became the template for railway construction around the world. He became an MP and died aged 55, commemorated by a statue and a park in Barnsley where he had grown up.

❖

George Stephenson, the uneducated but gritty and brilliant engineer, pioneered the evolution of the railway from a colliery ancillary to a viable and commercial transportation system for the world. He himself had little gift for innovation or invention, but he recognised these gifts in others and incorporated them to build machines that worked and structures that stand today. He became President of the Institution of Mechanical Engineers but found reading and writing difficult to the end of his life. Perhaps his most important legacy was training and teaching by example a whole generation of engineers who designed and constructed railways and locomotives around the world.

Robert Stephenson and Isambard Brunel were born within four years of each other and died within 18 weeks of each other. Both died before they reached the age of 60. Each personally, in all weathers, either on foot or on horseback, surveyed every inch of the hundreds of miles of the railway systems they designed. They superintended engineering and construction works on an unprecedented scale. Stephenson and Brunel made innovative and daring advances beyond the known parameters of the possible with tunnels, bridges and other constructions. They died young as a result of physical hardship, overwork, responsibility and anxieties. Despite a lack of precedents and paucity of knowledge about the materials they used, each designed and constructed bridges and buildings that were not only suitable for the ten- or fifteen-ton locomotives of their day but continue to support engines weighing up to ten times that weight and travelling many times as fast. Not only is the volume of work that each undertook astonishing but so is the fact that they were given and accepted such vast responsibilities when they were still in their twenties.

It is interesting to compare the work and style of Robert Stephenson with his close friend and rival, Isambard Brunel. Despite their different backgrounds they were both sons of distinguished engineers who had been recognised and honoured for their achievements. Stephenson, brought up beside a colliery, was a model English pragmatist who engineered his projects for economic and trouble-free running of the railway. His designs were often handsome and sometimes had great nobility but they were always a means to an end. Brunel had a classic Cartesian upbringing underlined by his schooling in the elitist Henri IV lycée in Paris. He was a man of vision, touched by genius. He resented criticism, and even when the South Devon Railway replaced atmospheric traction with steam locomotives, he was at first Olympian and then elusive but never admitted his judgement could have been faulty. He was splendidly dismissive of difficulty. When asked about the problems of running steam locomotives on the Metropolitan Railway under the streets of London, he responded 'I thought the impression had been exploded long since that railway tunnels require much ventilation'. And when he was asked if Metropolitan locomotives could run just on the steam and heat built up at the start of the journey he replied 'If you are going on a very short journey you need not take your dinner with you or corn for your horse'. Brunel not only had genius but he was also an artist, not just in his techniques of drawing and his designs for railway buildings but in his passion for the way everything he touched should look. Even the portals to his tunnels are elegant memorials to this astonishing shooting star of a man and an engineer.

Both Robert Stephenson and Isambard Brunel had an enormous variety of gifts and attributes: energy, fearlessness, great aptitude for engineering as well as skill, the ability to master parliamentary committees and of course a glorious gift of the gab to placate uneasy shareholders.

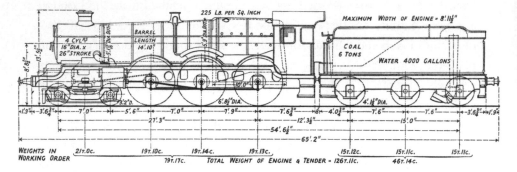

Scantlings of Charles Collett's GWR *Castle*-class locomotive

4 British Apogee and Decline

The earliest public railways were promoted and largely financed by businessmen in the regional centres of Darlington, Liverpool, Birmingham and Bristol, who saw the advantages that a railway would bring to their businesses and to their cities. However, a large part of the population of the nation lived in London and its immediate surroundings and the capital's need for convenient transportation of freight and passengers was becoming pressing.

The 3¾ mile London & Greenwich Railway was the first railway to serve London. It was constructed on nearly 900 brick arches running east to cross the Bermondsey slums and marshes and included a handsome skew bridge over the Surrey Canal. The first section, from London Bridge on the south bank of the Thames to Deptford, was opened in 1836, and it was extended east to Greenwich two years later. To draw attention to the new railway a band of musicians dressed as Beefeaters was stationed at London Bridge and another at Deptford. In the interest of economy, the Deptford band was superseded by a large barrel-organ. The music came to an end when passenger traffic became established. The company was refused parliamentary approval to extend its line further east because the Admiralty feared that vibration from passing trains would upset the Royal Observatory's scientific instruments. Three years later the London &

Croydon Railway was opened; its $8^{3/4}$ mile line branched from the London & Greenwich in a southerly direction to Croydon.

Both lines shared the London Bridge terminus. The London & Croydon platforms were on the north side of the station with their southbound trains crossing the London & Greenwich's west to east tracks; after five years of unhappy co-existence the two companies swapped platforms in the station. In time, the London & Greenwich became part of the South Eastern Railway (SER) connecting London to Dover and Kent. After an unsuccessful experiment with an atmospheric traction system, the London & Croydon Railway became part of the London Brighton & South Coast Railway (LBSCR) serving commuterland and the Sussex coast. Later the SER and the LBSCR agreed that the London Bridge terminus needed rebuilding to handle the growing traffic but they couldn't agree a plan or a design and so they built a wall to divide the site in two and then built their own separate stations each side of the wall.

With the exception of the lines running beside the river, building railways to serve London posed problems for promoters and engineers. The outer ring of the London Basin around the river Thames is formed by two massive chalk ridges extending east from Salisbury Plain. The southerly ridge is formed by the North Downs extending to the White Cliffs of Dover, the northern ridge by the Chiltern Hills stretching to the flatlands of the Eastern Counties. Generally these ridges slope gradually toward London but have a steep outward slope; they are penetrated by a series of valleys and it is along these valleys that the railway builders constructed the lines radiating from the capital.

The Eastern Counties Railway (ECR) was established to serve East Anglia; the line was opened as far as Colchester in 1843 and it served the East Coast ports and towns by working its trains on the lines of local companies. In 1862 the ECR merged with these companies to form the Great Eastern Railway. Its Liverpool Street terminus opened in 1875 and was conveniently situated on the edge of the City of London in order to generate commuter traffic. Not far from Liverpool Street station was a smaller terminus, Fenchurch Street, opened by the London & Blackwall Railway in 1841 to serve the suburbs and towns on the north shore of the Thames estuary.

Brunel's Great Western line terminated at Paddington, which was a suburban village in 1838. The first station was a modest wood building, replaced after 16 years by Brunel's magnificent triple-span arched train shed.

The LBSCR, London Brighton & South Coast Railway line from Victoria station headed south and crossed the river Thames within half a mile from the end of the station platforms. Its lines ran along a succession of embankments, viaducts and tunnels to branch through a maze of loops and junctions to serve the commuting population of south London, Surrey and Sussex. The company also ran express trains to Brighton and the south coast towns. Two years after the opening of Victoria Station, the London Chatham & Dover Railway (LC&DR) built its main terminus immediately next door. The two stations remained separate until 1924 when an arch was built in the wall separating them. The LC&DR, which also had two small central London terminal stations at Blackfriars and Holborn, competed for the Kent and the Channel Ports business against the SER operating from its London Bridge terminus and from a secondary terminal station at Charing Cross in London's West End. The rivals amalgamated in 1899.

The London & Southampton Railway, which became the London and South Western Railway, had its first London terminus at Nine Elms. It served the southwest London suburbs and Hampshire, Dorset and the south Devon coast. Nine Elms was an inconvenient location for commuters and the line was extended in 1848 to the new Waterloo terminus which was closer to the City.

To build a railway between London and Scotland was the ultimate challenge for the promoters and railway engineers. The challenge was not recognised for many years because 100 miles of heath and hills separated the industrial towns of northern England from the great cities of Glasgow and Edinburgh and because both these cities and the other Scottish centres of population were on the sea or had access to navigable rivers.

The first step to link London to Scotland was the 1838 opening of the London & Birmingham Railway from its Euston terminus to Birmingham. There it connected with the Grand Junction Railway, which had been opened a year earlier, linking Birmingham to the Liverpool & Manchester Railway. This established a through route from the capital to Liverpool and

Manchester. A number of small railway companies provided the tracks north from the Grand Junction to Carlisle on the Scottish border. In 1846 the lines on the route between London and Carlisle were amalgamated into the London & North Western Railway (LNWR) and the West Coast line to Scotland was completed with a working agreement with the Caledonian Railway to run trains on its tracks from Carlisle to Glasgow and Edinburgh. The combination of the LNWR and the Caledonian came to be known as the West Coast Route (WCR).

The rival East Coast Route (ECR) to Scotland comprised the North British Railway north of the border and a series of lines south to Doncaster, amalgamated by George Hudson, the master railway manipulator of the time, into the North Eastern Railway. Great Northern trains ran south from Doncaster to the LNWR's London Euston terminus until 1854 when the company opened its own terminus, King's Cross, less than half a mile from Euston.

Meanwhile George Hudson masterminded the amalgamation of a number of railways such as the North Midland, Midland Counties, the Birmingham & Derby and others into the Midland Railway with its headquarters in Derby. The Midland, however, had no access to London; one of its lines went as far south as Hitchin where it linked with the Great Northern over which it had running powers, and Midland expresses hauled by Midland engines ran into King's Cross by 1858. The Midland also connected with the LNWR at Rugby where it handed over its trains for London. At times the LNWR line, which naturally gave priority to its own traffic, was so congested that there was a five-mile-long tailback of Midland Railway coal trains waiting at Rugby for transit to London. The Midland operated a network of lines that was well placed to collect coal, freight and passengers, but was unable to deliver them to London without paying a heavy toll to one of its competitors. It proposed to amalgamate with the LNWR, but this was dismissed by Parliament because it was thought it would reduce competition. Finally the Midland decided to build its own line into London, and in 1868 opened a four-track line to terminate in the magnificent St Pancras station between Euston and King's Cross.

The Midland could only reach Scotland by paying expensive tolls to the LNWR for running powers from the north Midlands to Carlisle. So it proposed a bill to Parliament to build its own line north to Carlisle to connect with the Caledonian Railway's rivals, the Glasgow & South Western and the North British, to Glasgow and Edinburgh. The LNWR promptly reduced its tolls and the Midland proposed a Bill for the abandonment of the expensive project. Parliament, keen to promote competition, refused to accept the abandonment and the Midland was obliged to build a 73-mile line crossing the high hills of the Pennine Chain from Yorkshire to Carlisle. The Midland, with its longer route with more curves and gradients, could not compete on journey time against the West or East Coast Routes so it competed with price and comfort. It included third-class passengers on its crack express trains from 1872, and three years later upgraded third-class to the standard of second-class and abolished second class. Quite apart from the appeal to passengers, it simplified train formations with only two classes, each with its smoking and non-smoking sections.

The Great Central was another railway that grew and expanded from regional origins. It started as the Sheffield, Ashton-under-Lyne & Manchester Railway and became the last trunk railway between London and the north, reaching its Marylebone terminus through Lord's Tunnel immediately beside Lord's, the revered headquarters of the game of cricket. The line was a late and pale imitation of its three neighbours and was mainly used to serve country towns such as Aylesbury and Princes Risborough, with the occasional express to Sheffield and Nottingham. The company was primarily a carrier of freight, with only a quarter of its business coming from passengers, a much lower proportion than the other trunk lines. The Great Central's most memorable legacies were the fish docks at Grimsby and the 1,000 acres of the Immingham Dock rail yard.

In addition to the lines radiating from London there were a number of important regional railways. The Lancashire & Yorkshire, an intensively worked network, served the dense industrial area of the north. Other lines such as the Furness, the North Staffordshire, the Highland, the Cambrian, and many others, served their regions and gave passengers and freight access to the trunk lines. Some lines provided a specialised service, such as the Barry Railway that collected loads of steam coal from the South Wales colliery lines and took them over its 19 miles of track to the company's docks for shipment overseas. There was even an 11-mile Macclesfield, Bollington & Marple Railway, and there were many more minor feeder lines scattered across the nation.

There was no overall order or method to building a new railway. Lines were built in competition with one another almost regardless of the potential traffic, lines overlapped, some shared stations and others built their own stations next door. A porter in one station would pretend to be incapable of directing a passenger down the road to the station of a rival line. Fortunately all the lines, apart from the Great Western, were built with the same 4ft 8½ inch gauge. There seemed to be railways everywhere and still they continued to be promoted[1] and to be built. In 1846, at the height of the Railway Mania, Acts of Parliament were passed for the construction of 270 new railways though only a few of these were actually built.

The lines were built by navvies. The word came from the previous century when the men or their fathers dug the canals and were nicknamed navigators or navvies. The navvies were itinerant with no home or base, and lived alongside the work as the line progressed. When the line was completed they either followed the contractor as part of the workforce or tramped the country to find another project. They included skilled men such as masons, miners, blacksmiths or carpenters, but most were labourers who moved astonishing quantities of earth with a minimum of mechanical aids. Usually they worked in a 'butty gang' of ten or twelve men who would contract to cut and remove a volume of 'dirt'. Experienced navvies became skilled in knowing the best way to deal with the different clays and soils. Thomas Brassey, the contractor, took English and Irish navvies with him when he constructed the Paris–Rouen railway and other contracts in Europe. Three thousand navvies camped close to Corsham for the four years needed to build Brunel's Box Tunnel. The local inhabitants benefited by supplying provisions to navvy camps; at Box they supplied the 300 horses needed for the project. Drunkenness and rows with the locals were all part of camp life and there were a number of notorious incidents of violence between navvies and local inhabitants, notably at

---

1. George Stephenson was shocked by the rate of proliferation of new lines and is quoted, 'It is really shameful the way the country is going to be cut up by railways ...'.

Penrith, Edinburgh and the Battle of Mickleton where the local militia was mobilised. The work was not only hard and unrelenting but it was often dangerous, especially tunnelling where the works were lit only by candles and hundreds of tons of black-powder were used for blasting. In 1846 Parliament appointed a Select Committee on Railway Labourers after reports of the casualties and dangers experienced in building the trans-Pennine Woodhead Tunnel.

❖

Each of the many railway companies had different liveries for their express engines and carriages. Francis Webb of the London & North Western painted his locomotives black that looked blackberry black on a sunny day and supposedly was the first to say 'I shall use any colour as long as it is black.' The company had an armorial device of a seated Britannia with shield, trident and a lion painted on the wheel-splasher or the tender. Caledonian engines were a bright royal blue with a cartouche enclosing the royal arms of Scotland. Great Eastern engines were a darker blue lined in red with an elaborate design of the arms of the City of London surrounded by the arms of eight of the towns they served. The Great Northern engines were a deep green and the Great Western a Brunswick green. The Midland had crimson-lake engines with scarlet buffer beams, the North British opted for a greeny-yellow the French know as *caca d'oie* for their locomotives, and the London, Brighton & South Coast had a wonderful mustard yellow. The London & South Western had light green engines and its carriages had brown lower panels and luminous canned salmon-coloured upper panels. Every company, great or small, had its own livery and elaborate armorial device. In the 1880s, Carlisle's Citadel station, the Anglo Scottish junction for six trunk lines, was a dazzling kaleidoscope of different coloured engines and carriages.

From the beginning and even up to the present day the British gave names to express passenger locomotives as well as to trains. In the 19th century these included *Pandora*, *Lady of the Lake*, *Lord of the Isles*, *Coquette*, *Flirt*, *Herod*, *Banshee*, *Sisyphus*, *Caractacus* and *Penguin*. For a time some engines were called after towns served by the company; this was abandoned because passengers mistook the names for their destinations. In the 20th century names were duller; engines were named after kings, regiments, castles, schools, birds, steamship lines and even duchesses. The London & North Eastern was the exception to this dullness with a series of high sounding Scottish names for some of their express engines: *Cock O'The North*, *Thane of Fife*, *Earl Marischal*, *Wolf of Badenoch* and in 1964 the last mainline steam locomotive to be built for British Rail was appropriately named *Evening Star*.

The *Irish Mail* between London and Holyhead was the first named train. The *Royal Scot* on the west coast route and the *Flying Scotsman* on the east coast route were the rival express trains between London and Scotland. The west was served out of Paddington by the *Cornish Riviera Express* and the *Cheltenham Flyer*, advertised in 1931 as the world's fastest train. The *Brighton Belle* ran to the south coast and the *Golden Arrow* connected with the Dover packet to France and the *Flèche d'Or* train on to Paris. There were many lesser named trains such as the *Pines Express* from Manchester to Bournemouth, the *Red Dragon* to Wales and the *Bradford Executive*; most strange was the *Further North Express* from Inverness across the western end of the Black Isle to Dornoch.

There had been a loose understanding between the companies of the West Coast Route (WCR) and the East Coast Route (ECR) to Scotland. The ECR had a more level and marginally shorter route to Edinburgh and timed its crack daytime train for a nine-hour journey including a half-hour lunch stop at York. The WCR took ten hours including a lunch stop at Preston. Sir Richard Moon, the autocratic chairman of the London & North Western, senior partner of the WCR companies, believed 40mph to be the preferred speed for an express train to keep coal consumption to a minimum, reduce the need for locomotive and rolling stock maintenance, and to ensure a long life for the permanent way. This cosy East Coast/West Coast relationship was threatened when the Midland, with the North British and the Glasgow & South Western provided a new service between London and Scotland. Then in June 1888 the WCR, shortened its journey time by an hour and equalled the nine-hour ECR. In July the ECR timing was reduced to 8½ hours. In August the WCR matched it. The same day the ECR reduced the journey to eight hours, which was equalled by the West Coast only days later. A week later the East Coast Route reduced its schedule to 7¾ hours. The West Coast bettered it to 7 hours 38 minutes, which the East Coast then reduced to 7 hours 7 minutes. Finally the two groups agreed an ECR journey time of 7¾ hours and an 8-hour WCR journey. Competition had resulted in a substantial improvement for passengers.

Seven years later the speed contest between the West Coast and East Coast Routes reopened. The great bridge over the Firth of Forth was open and it shortened the ECR run to Aberdeen to 523 miles, 16½ miles less than the WCR. Although a shorter and more level route, the ECR went only as far as Kinnaber Junction, where it joined the Caledonian's WCR tracks for the remaining 38 miles to Aberdeen. The first train to reach Kinnaber was the first to Aberdeen.

In summer, Aberdeen was important, not only because of the fashionable grouse shooting and salmon fishing but also because the Queen and the Court moved north to Balmoral, close to Ballater station served by the Great North of Scotland Railway. Both the WCR train and the ECR train left Euston and King's Cross respectively at 8p.m.. Until summer 1895 the ECR train arrived in Aberdeen at 7.35 the next morning, with the WCR train arriving 15 minutes later. The Great North of Scotland train left Aberdeen for the Dee valley and Ballater at 8a.m.; there was not much time to make the connection if the trains from the south were delayed.

In June the WCR improved its timing to reach Aberdeen at 7.40; a month later the ECR bettered its timing for a 7.20 arrival. In mid August the West Coast train arrived at 6.47; two weeks later the East Coast train arrived at 6.25. On August 19th the East Coast line planned its schedule to arrive at Kinnaber at an average speed of 55mph, including stops for changing engines. It reached Aberdeen at 5.40 – to find the West Coast train had arrived 16 minutes earlier. Then both routes abandoned their schedules, opened their lines for the race, reduced the weight of the trains to three or four light carriages and chose their engine men for courage and skill. Patrick Stirling, Locomotive Superintendent of the ECR Great Northern instructed his lieutenants 'The London & North Western Company have expressed their intention to reach Aberdeen before us. This of course we cannot permit …'. The next three nights, trains on each route bested each other; early one morning the Kinnaber Junction signalman accepted the WCR train less than 60 seconds before he was offered the ECR racer which had to stand and watch the rival steam away into the distance. Finally, on the night of the 22nd, the WCR train reached Aberdeen at 04.32, a record average speed of more than 63mph for the 540 miles. To make peace between the companies, the West Coast called its record *An Exhibition Run*. A year later the WCR train that had taken part in the race left the rails on the sharp curve out of Preston; the accident killed the appetite for railway racing.

Another rivalry that ended in disaster happened in the South West. The Great Western line out of Paddington reached Plymouth via Bristol, on a route 16 miles longer than the London & South Western out of Waterloo. The Great Western had the mail contract for the Atlantic liners that called at Plymouth, but the London & South Western Railway competed to take the passengers to London. In order to compete, the Great Western ran faster and faster trains; in 1904 one of them, with the *City of Truro* locomotive, achieved 102mph down Wellington bank, an unofficial record that stood for many years. Then the Great Western constructed a new line bypassing Bristol that was five miles shorter than the Waterloo route. On the July 1906 day it opened, the rival London & South Western picked up passengers for London from the liner *New York* in Plymouth and took the curve out of Salisbury station too fast. The train leant so far into the curve that it tore into an empty milk train resulting in a major wreck with the loss of 28 lives.

However, it was the Anglo Scottish rivalry that held the interest of railway enthusiasts and the general public and it lasted through the 1923 Grouping of 120 separate railway companies into four main groups. The West Coast companies were amalgamated into the LMS, London, Midland & Scottish and the East Coast companies were amalgamated into the LNER, London & North Eastern Railway. In the 1930s the rivalry between these two companies increased and resulted in regular services from London to Glasgow in 6½ hours on the LMS and 6 hours to Edinburgh on the LNER. The excitement of the rivalry was all the greater for the rail enthusiast because of the two very different Chief Mechanical Engineers (CMEs) or locomotive designers of the rival companies. Nigel Gresley of the LNER and William Stanier of the LMS were both born in 1876 and both were knighted, a popular move with rail enthusiasts. Both men served apprenticeships. Thirty-five-year-old Gresley became CME of the Great Northern and then the LNER after the Grouping, a job he held for 30 years until his death in 1941. Stanier spent most of his professional life in the Great Western works at Swindon until he joined the LMS as CME in 1932. Both chiefs supervised the design of a number of different types of locomotive and in 1935 Gresley introduced his first streamlined engine for the East Coast line, which hauled the *Silver Jubilee* train, at an average speed of 71mph for most of the London–Newcastle journey. A second batch of streamliners followed a year later and hauled the high speed *Coronation* train between London and Edinburgh.

The rival LMS hesitated about responding to the challenge, which, in addition to its technical achievement, was a marvellous public relations exercise. Their priority was a general upgrading of standards, and their trains covered a much greater mileage at over 60mph than the LNER. Stanier introduced the first streamlined engine for the LMS in June 1937. The engines became known as the Duchess class. A trial run reached 114mph, a British record. However, the glory of the achievement was a little tarnished because the engineman was late shutting down steam, and the train rode the crossovers leading to the Crewe platforms at three times the permitted speed. The result was a crash of crockery and a lot of embarrassment all round. A year later the LNER took on the challenge and on 3rd July Gresley's A4 type *Mallard*, hauling seven coaches, achieved the world speed record for steam traction, 125mph[2]. The locomotive in its Garter-blue livery is still in working order in the National Railway Museum at York.

LMS and LNER enthusiasts argue endlessly over the technical qualities of Stanier and Gresley express passenger engines. Each type had outstanding characteristics, and it is a pity that the outbreak of war stopped further development of high-speed express train steam locomotives. The Gresley A4 streamlined Pacific locomotives, with their wedge-shaped fronts and the handsome line of their profile, were probably the most aesthetically pleasing locomotives ever built anywhere. The LMS

---

2. A record about 0.5mph faster than a German steam locomotive two years earlier.

Duchess's more bulbous streamlining had better aerodynamic qualities, but smoke obscured the enginemen's view ahead. Most rail buffs preferred the sight of an honest boiler, firebox and cab and a full view of the valve gear, so it was probably a matter of relief when the streamline casing was removed from the Duchesses and the side valances from the A4s to simplify maintenance during the war years.

❖

Apart from trunk lines absorbing feeder lines, there was little change in the structure of the railway companies and their systems from the 1870s until 1914, the beginning of World War I. In September 1914 it was announced that 'The control of the railways has been taken over by the Government ...'. Frequencies were reduced and schedules slowed and the railways transported the troops and equipment to the south coast for shipment to France. However, the most daunting task was fuelling the British fleet, which burnt only the best quality Welsh steam coal. The battle-cruiser squadron was based in the Firth of Forth, far from South Wales but the real problem was fuelling the Grand Fleet comprising 24 battleships and a large number of secondary ships at their home station at Scapa Flow in the Orkney Islands. The London & North Western and the Caledonian had the locomotives and experience to handle the heavy coal trains, but the Highland Railway had great difficulty on its line from Perth to Thurso on the extreme north coast of Scotland, where the coal was shipped to Scapa. The Highland was accustomed to heavy holiday traffic over its mountainous mainly single-track line during the summer and autumn and it spent the winter repairing and maintaining its engines. The problems of heavy coal trains on the line were caused by a difficult line with steep gradients, insufficient engine power, ineffective management and a shortage of staff.

After the armistice there was labour unrest resulting in a nine-day transport strike. Sir Eric Geddes, Minister of Transport proposed the Grouping of the 120 railway companies into four groups which would more or less have regional autonomy. The LMS and the LNER were to serve the North, the Great Western the West and the Southern Railway the

South. The scheme was accepted and the four companies operated the British railway system from 1923 until the outbreak of World War II. During these 16 years, cars and long-distance buses took an increasing share of passenger traffic and road transport, which combined the convenience of door to door delivery with a faster service, took away a growing amount of freight business from rail. The railways also had the burden of being classed as a Common Carrier with freight rates regulated by Parliament; they had the obligation of accepting all classes of goods, and they were also obliged to operate lines and services without regard to profitability. The roads creamed off the best business, leaving the railways with the least profitable. Apart from a few crack passenger trains the railways became run down in terms of equipment and morale. Railway methods, engines and stock were antiquated. Railwaymen joined the 1926 general strike and 13 years later the enginemen's union became so militant that it arranged a strike of its members seven days before the declaration of war against Nazi Germany. A government appeal, 'We may need you to get the children away', helped prevent the strike.

Railway managements anticipated World War II even when the Prime Minister returned from Munich in 1938 promising 'Peace for our time' and they went ahead with war contingency plans. With the outbreak of war the railways evacuated more than 600,000 children and hospital patients from London in just four days, and almost as many from the great manufacturing towns. The evacuation of troops across the Channel from Dunkerque brought 300,000 troops to the southeast ports and gave the railways the problem of dispersing them to destinations across the country. Trains were limited to ten carriages so that they could be hauled by any type of engine. Redhill, at the apex of the lines from the Channel ports, set up an operation to provide coal and water for the engines; specials brought steam coal to Redhill and carted away the ash emptied from the fire and smoke boxes. Engines didn't wait in line for the turntable but went tender-first to collect another train. Three years later, prior to Operation Overlord for the invasion of Normandy, the railways ran 250 specials a day in addition to their normal services. There were often surprises; for instance, carriages and engines assembled to pick up a couple of army divisions from the Clyde found the convoy had been switched to Liverpool at the last minute. In 1943 the railways carried 46% more tonnage than three years previously with 100,000 fewer workpeople and the same number of engines and wagons. And all this in a blackout, when even the space between the cab and the tender was sheeted over to prevent the glare of the firebox being seen from the air. The Blitz – the Luftwaffe's aerial bombardment – targeted stations and viaducts and scored hits on moving trains. This was followed by the V1 flying bombs and then the V2 rockets. At the end of the war railwaymen were completely exhausted, engines and equipment were worn out and the permanent way needed repair or replacement. The nation was in a dire economic situation; food and petrol rationing continued for three years after the end of the war, and there was not enough British coal to keep the electricity generating stations operating or to fuel the railways.

Railway nationalisation had been a plank of Labour party policy since 1908, and on 31 December 1947 enginemen blew their whistles to celebrate nationalisation of the British railway system as part of a national transport system that included major bus and road freight carriers. Sadly there was no charismatic or inspired leader to take charge, and the railways were run by committees that were victim to the partisan feeling of the old companies. Not only were the railways starved of talent, they were starved of money. The only substantial new investment was the electrification of the Manchester–Sheffield line. The Conservatives came to power in 1952 and installed a distinguished general as railway supremo. In 1955 came the Modernisation Plan, with an enormous budget. The Plan included colour-light signalling, and new freight-marshalling yards[3]. It also included replacing hand brakes on freight wagons with continuous braking, and large-scale replacement of steam engines with diesels.

A rival and possibly superior plan of electrifying some of the main lines and using steam on lines still to be electrified was rejected. Steam engines were scrapped before their working life was over and replaced with large numbers of diesels that were delivered before servicing, training and maintenance facilities were ready. Despite the massive investment, the

---

3. They were redundant almost as soon as they were completed because of the introduction of merry-go-round trains where the train, rather than a wagon, was considered as a single unit.

railways still lost huge amounts of money, and in 1961 Dr Richard Beeching was appointed Chairman of the British Transport Commission with the brief to make the railways pay their way. He proposed closing 2,000 stations and withdrawing 250 train services; many of his proposals were adopted but he resigned following disagreements with the new Labour government. Electrification of a number of commuter lines around London and Glasgow, together with the electrification of the West Coast Route from London as far as Manchester, was an important part of a new Modernisation Plan. This mainline electrification resulted in faster and more frequent trains with a consequent large increase in passenger revenue; despite this success it took another eight years to extend West Coast line electrification north to Glasgow. Electrification from London to Leeds and Edinburgh was completed in 1991. The HST, diesel-electric High Speed Train sets, were introduced on the London to Bristol service in 1976 and then started working the South Wales line; these high-speed trains not only provided shorter journey times but much better train utilisation, resulting in most train sets running 1,000 miles each day with the obvious economies of operation.

By the 1980s Mrs Thatcher's Conservative government was determined that the railways should be privatised, and a start was made by making British Rail divest itself of many of its activities such as hotels, ships and even its engineering works, which were sold at substantial discounts. Members of the Thatcher administration felt that the railways were in terminal decline; they could not or did not want to understand that a combination of fast and frequent train services and increasingly congested roads would result in an increase in railway traffic. In 1994 John Major's government transformed the state-owned railway system into nearly 100 independent and interdependent companies, each established to maximise profits for the benefit of its shareholders. Companies were established to operate regional or intercity passenger services; their franchises were remarkably similar in geographic terms to the period before the 1923 Grouping of railway companies. Three companies were designated to compete for freight business, others leased or financed train sets and other capital equipment and finally a separate company, Railtrack, was set up to own and maintain the track, signalling and control system[4].

The state undertook to pay hundreds of millions in subsidies to these companies and still British passengers have the most expensive fares in Western Europe[5]. Seventy-five years earlier before the 1923 Grouping, railways were better organised, taking responsibility for operating their own trains on their own tracks and even *then* they needed to be amalgamated into four large groups to better serve the nation.

The dangers and inefficiencies of the divided responsibilities of the layers of companies were exposed by two tragic accidents in 1999/2000. In one, a train out of Paddington passed a red signal. Clearly it seemed the fault of the engineman until it was found that the view to the signal was largely obscured and that a number of trains had previously passed the red light but without fatal consequences. It also emerged that the train was not fitted with a device to stop the train automatically if it passed a red light. The second accident at Hatfield on the east coast main line was caused by a fractured rail that broke, derailing a number of coaches of an express train. Railtrack, responsible for maintaining the line, knew the section was suspect but did not impose any speed restriction because it would delay trains, with consequent financial penalty. An initial enquiry into the accident revealed that Railtrack not only subcontracted maintenance work but also inspection. The public came to believe that there was tier after shabby tier of expensive and divided responsibility among the companies making up the rail industry.

However, there was one momentous event during this glum period: the opening of the Channel Tunnel between France and England. It was preceded by many years of muddle and prevarication, most of it from the British. In 1855 a French engineer and geologist, Thomé de Gramond, published a paper on the feasibility of boring a tunnel under the Channel.

4. As Ian Jack wrote in *The Crash that stopped Britain*, the railways had been 'sold off hastily, cheaply and carelessly, often to owners for whom "the wheel/rail interface" was a term of management rather than science (if it meant anything to them at all).' He went on to describe the result as 'a quagmire of divided responsibility and incompetence, inspired by an ideology that placed adversarial money bargaining over human and technical cooperation.'

5. A survey based on the January 2003 Thomas Cook European Railway Timetable found the following average costs for travelling 100km: UK €21.27; Germany €13.50; France €2.56; Italy €4.83. Despite the high cost, the number of passenger journeys in the UK in 2004 was the highest since 1959.

Both the British and French governments were enthusiastic but relations cooled when it was discovered that an anarchist's attempt to assassinate[6] Napoleon III had been devised in England. The South Eastern Railway obtained Parliamentary approval to sink trial shafts in 1874 and even made a 2,000-ft bore that was abandoned for 'military reasons'. In 1914 Douglas Fox & Partners, a leading firm of engineers presented a plan for the English end of the Tunnel showing the drainage headings 'for Flooding in case of Necessity'. In 1955 the British Minister of Defence was asked if there was any strategic objection to the tunnel: 'scarcely at all'; in 1957, an Anglo-French study group was formed; 1960, it issued a report recommending twin railway tunnels; 1964, the two governments gave a go-ahead; 1965, survey completed; 1973, a further estimate of costs, with the British terminal to be sited at White City for onward connections north and west; 1974, British abandon the proposed Folkestone–White City route; 1975, British Government decide to abandon the tunnel; 1978, possibility of a single-bore tunnel considered; 1982, decision for a single-bore tunnel; 1987, Treaty of Canterbury finally gave the go-ahead to the Anglo–French Eurotunnel Company to construct and operate the tunnel; 1994, the tunnel opened.

Eurotunnel has two parallel bores, each with a single track and a crossover midway. It is 31 miles long; each bore is 25ft in diameter to take heavy lorries and buses or to take cars driven onto two decks of the largest railway vehicles in the world for the 20-minute crossing under the Channel. The original plan for the rail link between England and France included a through sleeping-car service from Glasgow, Swansea and Plymouth to Paris and other European cities. The *Night Star* fleet of 139 luxury coaches was ordered and delivered but never put in service; the dream of joining England rather than London to continental Europe has not been realised[7]. The coaches were stored for some years and most of them sold for service in Canada. Direct freight trains from distant parts of England run through the tunnel to continental destinations and vice versa;

6. Ten members of Napoleon's entourage were killed and 156 injured.

7. In any case the trains would have been superseded by low cost flights from regional centres to a wide variety of destinations.

for instance, trains of Cornish china clay run through the tunnel to customers in central Europe, and Ford send trainloads of parts from England to their assembly plants in continental Europe. The new CTRL, Channel Tunnel Rail Link, a dedicated express line linking the tunnel to London, bridges the River Medway and tunnels under the Thames, and dives under east London in a 12-mile tunnel to terminate in a revamped St Pancras station with platforms extending under flat canopies beyond the existing great train shed. The opening of the CTRL line will reduce the London–Paris travel time to 2½ hours. London schoolchildren will be able to cry 'St George for England, St Pancras for France.'

❖

The first dedicated locomotive works to build locomotives, stationary engines and wagons for the new railway companies was Robert Stephenson & Co's Forth Street Works in Newcastle, founded in 1823. Its first engine, *Locomotion*, was delivered to the Stockton & Darlington in 1825. Soon, the railway companies set up their own design and engineering works starting with the Shildon works for the Stockton & Darlington. By the turn of the century there were 25 major railway company works, each building their own designs of locomotives and carriages, some of them successful, others less so.

The enormous LNWR Crewe works even had its own steel works and the company built four churches for the spiritual well-being of its employees. All the railway works employed skilled craftsmen and fitters; it is no coincidence that Rolls Royce sited two of its principal engineering offices and works in the railway towns of Crewe and Derby. Because the companies built most of their own engines there was little opportunity for independent manufacturers to flourish, other than by supplying engines to industrial or colliery lines or to overseas railways. With one or two glorious exceptions such as the Great Western *Castle*-class engine, the apogee of British locomotive design was over by the 1860s. From that time most technical advances came from overseas: Lentz poppet valves, Cartazzi suspension, Belpaire fire boxes, Walschaert's valve gear, Caprotti valve gear, Westinghouse air brakes, and finally, the work of André

Chapelon, the greatest of all steam locomotive engineers, whose innovations and designs hugely increased the efficiency of the steam locomotive.

Arrogance was a common shortcoming of the British railway company locomotive engineers and managers. The London & North Western's Sir Richard Moon opposed any new requirements by the Board of Trade and his locomotive superintendent Francis Webb was an autocrat, unable to take criticism, who masterminded the design of a large fleet of compound engines. It was not uncommon to see one of his engines trying to make a start with the rear pair of driving wheels slipping in forward gear and the leading pair rotating in reverse. Patrick Stirling of the Great Northern, refused to design express locomotives with coupled driving wheels because it would be like a 'laddie running with his breeks down'. Sir Nigel Gresley moved his design department away from the LNER Doncaster engineering works to Kings Cross. In 1925 there was a locomotive exchange; the Great Western *Pendennis Castle* ran on the LNER main line and did everything Gresley's big Pacific engines, 22 tons heavier, could do and burned 10% less coal. Gresley and his engineers could not understand or accept the result. Later in the year another *Castle* engine went to Darlington to take part in the centenary celebrations of the Stockton & Darlington; Gresley's men secretly measured the *Castle's* motion gear with its long travel valves, and reworked the geometry of the Gresley express engine's valve gear, resulting in a saving of 1½ tons of coal on the London–Newcastle run and eliminating the need for a second engine to take over at Grantham or Doncaster. Train brakes were not so much victims of autocracy but of muddle and lethargy. In 1868 the *Engineer* magazine commented 'locomotive engineers seem to sleep the sleep that knows no waking'. After the 1923 Grouping it was decided to standardise on vacuum brakes for passenger trains and then the nationalised British Rail decided to standardise on air brakes. Until 1955 only a few freight trains were fitted with continuous brakes; most freight trains had to stop at the top of a downward gradient so that brakes on each wagon could be applied manually; at the bottom of the gradient the train stopped again and the brakes on each wagon were released. Perhaps the most startling example of muddle and backward thinking was the reluctance of British

Railways to use the lower-cost and more dependable flat-bottom rail[8] in place of bull-head rail until nearly a century after it had become the standard in North America and Continental Europe.

In the late 1970s British Rail was obliged to use three locomotives to haul 3,000-ton ore trains to the Llanwern steel works. A leading Mendip quarry owner looked for a more economic solution to haul heavy trainloads of crushed stone to customers across the country. No British builder was able to meet his requirements and, after negotiations with British Rail, he placed an order on EMD, the electromotive division of General Motors, for four diesel electric locomotives. The locomotives entered service in 1986 and their operating success was so great that other quarry operators in the Mendips purchased EMD locomotives and the English Welsh & Scottish Company, operating the main British freight franchise, purchased 250 EMD locomotives built in Canada and more recently ordered 30 Spanish-built EMD locomotives.

❖

Today, Britain, the birthplace of the railway, has a Transport Minister, a Department for Transport choc-a-bloc with civil servants, a Commission for Integrated Transport, a Rail Safety and Standards Board, an Office of Rail Regulation (ORR), a Rail Passengers Council (RPC), a Rail Inspectorate, a number of passenger and freight operators, equipment leasing companies and Network Rail. But nobody takes responsibility for running the railways as efficiently as possible to serve passengers and industry and to contribute to the prosperity of the nation. However in 2004 the Government promised to set up a Committee to simplify the running of the railways and it now seems to be making some progress.

Today, American engineering companies work on upgrading the East Coast and West Coast main lines, have helped to complete a new London tube line on schedule and, together with French engineering consultants,

---

8. The importance of the flat-bottom rail was emphasised in 1901 when Andrew Carnegie, railroad mogul and founder of US Steel, gave a dinner for 80 of his most senior men ('my boys') in Pittsburgh. The black-tied men sat around a giant table in the shape of a section of flat-bottom rail.

are masterminding the building of the CTRL from the Channel Tunnel to London. Eurostar trains are designed and largely built in France, and American designed locomotives haul most of our heavy freight trains. A number of the regional passenger train franchises are owned or partly owned by overseas companies, as is the principal freight carrier. These remarks are not a sign of petty chauvinism but rather a lament. British railways lost their heart over 100 years ago and sadly have never had a leader with the necessary support to provide the vision and energy to revitalise the industry.

A 'container crane' transferring coach bodies from road to rail.

5 Across the Channel

There was great contrast between the economic and political climate in Britain and the countries of Continental Europe throughout most of the 19th century.

After 1815 and the ending of the Napoleonic Wars, Britain enjoyed a century of peace with only a few instances of social unrest. Queen Victoria was on the throne for most of the century and wars involving British arms were in the Crimea at the opposite corner of Europe or in different continents. This long period of stability, together with overseas trade and the development of manufacturing, helped Britain to become wealthy and to establish the sophisticated banking system necessary to provide the finance for the rail companies to undertake the massive civil works and construct the buildings needed for the early railways. In addition, in the early 19th century, Britain's great regional cities had the entrepreneurial spirit to take advantage of the technology developed for the early railways serving the collieries in northeast England.

By contrast there was 50 years of turbulence, revolution and political upheaval in Continental Europe. A list of the main upsets gives an indication of some of the difficulties of organising any large-scale projects. 1823: 100,000 French troops cross into Spain. 1830: revolution in France;

Belgium gains independence from Holland. 1831: unsuccessful revolts in Italy and the Papal States. 1848: revolution in France replaces the King with a republic; Hungarians, Czechs and Italians revolt against the Austrian Empire and Emperor Ferdinand flees Vienna; the Pope flees Rome and 20,000 French troops are needed to safeguard his return. 1854–56: the Crimean War. 1859: 100,000 French troops cross the Alps to Italy to fight the Austrians in the battles of Solferino and Magenta. 1861: Kingdom of Italy proclaimed. 1866: the Austro-Prussian War. 1870: the Franco-Prussian war; the unification of Germany. The climate of Continental Europe was hardly suitable for bankers to make large long-term commitments and so, unlike Britain, most European governments played a central role in the development of the railways in their countries.

The strategic importance of railways became recognised as the century progressed. The important role that railways could play in the deployment of troops was first recognised in the war in the Crimea; Russia had no railways south of Moscow and reinforcements and supplies took three months to reach the front compared to the three-week sea journey from England. The Austrians built the railway from Venice to Milan to assure military supplies to their empire in Lombardy. The Prussians attached the greatest importance to the railway network for deploying troops and supplies; at the start of the 1866 Austro-Prussian war, the Prussians advanced into Bohemia, moving soldiers and ordnance south to the front along five railway lines. The Austrians had only one single-track line running from Vienna to Bohemia and the war was concluded with Prussian victory at Sadowa. Four years later the French declared war on Prussia and found themselves at a severe disadvantage: they had only two railway lines to the front in contrast to the six lines which served the Prussians.

In 1898, Lord Salisbury, the British Prime Minister, made a speech that included the lines, 'Railways have given them [the powerful nations] the power to concentrate upon any one point the whole military force of their population and to assemble armies of a magnitude and power never dreamed of …'. In 1914, the success of the German High Command's Schlieffen Plan depended on the rapid deployment of armies. The plan was to cross Belgium, bypass the French armies massed on the Franco-German frontier and sweep south and then east to take the French armies from the rear. After what was supposed to have been a lightning victory, the German army was to board trains to fight the Russians on the Eastern front. In 1918 Ludendorff, one of the principal German generals said 'There comes a time when locomotives are more important than guns'.

❖

In France, the town of Saint-Etienne and its coalfields lie between the River Loire, which flows into the Atlantic, and the Rhône, which runs south to the Mediterranean. The first railway in France was opened in 1827 to transport coal from the mines 15 miles to the Andrézieux dock on the Loire. The line was a single track that followed the lie of the land over hills and valleys without any civil works to provide a gently graded route. Horses provided the motive power until 1844 when they were replaced by steam. The line transported passengers as well as coal and was promoted by a M. Beaunier, a local colliery owner, following a visit to look at the railways in northeast England, 'There is no need to experiment, we can learn from their experience'.

The 36-mile double track railway from Saint Etienne to Lyon on the Rhône was built by Marc Seguin, a polymath in the tradition of the Stephensons or the Brunels. Born in 1786 to a well-off textile family, he received his education from his great uncle, Joseph de Montgolfier, famous for his invention of the hot air balloon. After building bridges over local streams, Seguin and his brothers submitted a successful bid to build a bridge, the Pont de Tournon-Tain, across the Rhône '*à ses frais, risques et perils*' in return for levying a toll for 99 years. The bridge comprised two 278-foot spans from a central masonry pier and it was one of the first, if not the first, suspension bridge where iron ropes replaced chain or link suspenders. Although classified as a historic monument, the bridge was dismantled in 1965 because the deck was too low to permit modern river navigation. Marc Seguin then became interested in steam navigation. Together with his family, he established a shipyard to build boats for use on the fast flowing Rhône and fitted them with English steam engines. The enterprise ended with a major boiler explosion on the river in Lyon.

The Seguin 36-mile line joining Saint Etienne and Lyon was begun in

1826; the profile of the line was gently graded and included a large number of cuttings, embankments, bridges and tunnels. If it was not the very first railway in France, it was certainly the first modern railway although traction was with horses. Seguin visited England in 1825 and he returned in 1828 to the Stephenson Locomotive works to purchase two second-hand locomotives; his experience with these machines led him to design an innovative multi-tube boiler for a locomotive he built in 1829. The line opened in 1832. Seguin spent his later years studying and publishing papers on thermodynamics and other physical theories. He married twice, fathered nineteen children and died aged eighty-nine.

The 1830s saw a series of short railway lines linking collieries to rivers or canals, but the true start of the railway age in France began with the 1837 opening of the twelve-mile line from central Paris to Le Pecq. Largely financed by the Rothschild combine, the line was a *chemin de promenades*. It made two crossings over the winding river Seine and came to a stop at Le Pecq. The intention had been to terminate the line in the historic town of Saint-Germain on the hill on the left bank of the Seine opposite Le Pecq. The profile of the hill was too steep for the trains of the time and passengers were obliged to take the ferry and then walk or get a cab for the last two miles. Ten years later the line was extended across the Seine and up the grade to Saint-Germain and operated by an atmospheric traction system. Locomotives became more powerful and they replaced atmospheric traction in 1860. At the opening of the railway there were open wagons for the masses while the well-off travelled in *berlines fermées* or *diligences*; the elegant coach bodies were transferred from their road chassis to rail frames by a high four-leg winch very similar to the container crane used for transferring today's cargo containers.

The line to Saint-Germain triggered the government to issue an ordinance for a rail project to link the three kingdoms, France, Belgium and Britain. The line opened in 1846 and its route resembled the 1993 LGV (Ligne à Grande Vitesse) Nord line with tracks from Paris to Lille which then divided, one line continuing north to Brussels and the other west to the English Channel.

In 1839, a line branching 2½ miles from the Paris terminus of the Paris to Saint-Germain line reached Versailles by following the Seine and tunnelling under the park of Saint-Cloud, a total of fifteen miles. The following year a rival line from Paris to Versailles opened. It was shorter and more direct but it was less successful and suffered a serious setback after a major wreck at Meudon followed by a fire resulted in 55 deaths and a large number of injured. The accident happened just outside the gates of Paris and caused the death of Admiral Dumont d'Urville, a national hero; it led many to have second thoughts about the future of passenger trains. The French Parliament was debating the future of railways when the accident happened and no less a person than Lamartine summed up the debate with an emotional speech: '... Gentlemen, we know that civilisation is a battlefield where many succumb in the cause of the advancement of all. Pity them, pity them ... and let us go forward.' Legislation for the rail network was approved, defining the trunk routes radiating from Paris and a cross-country line linking Bordeaux to Marseille.

The line west to the important seaport of Le Havre opened in 1847, to the south-west and Bordeaux in 1851, to Strasbourg and the German frontier in 1852 and to Lyon in 1854 and a through line to Marseille in 1856. There was no urgency to construct the link between Paris, Lyon and the Mediterranean, the most important route in France, the *ligne impériale*, thanks to the excellent existing system of communications. The Canal de Bourgogne linked the Yonne tributary of the Seine to the Saône and the Rhône to provide low cost through freight transportation and by the early 19th century travellers could travel from Paris to Lyon in three days by stage coach; 40,000 horses were needed to provide the service.

The principal French railway companies were established by a series of national decrees between 1845 and 1859: the Compagnies du Nord, de Paris à Orléans (P&O), de Paris à Lyon et à la Mediterranée (PLM), de l'Est, de l'Ouest and the Midi.

Three British engineers played a major role in French locomotive development. William Buddicom was a locomotive engineer with the Grand Junction Railway who joined up with William Allard in 1841 to establish a works at Rouen to build locomotives for the Paris–Le Havre line. Eight years later they opened a second factory in Bordeaux and altogether they produced nearly four hundred locomotives; their designs were direct descendants of proven Stephenson designs.

Thomas Crampton spent his early professional years working beside Daniel Gooch on the Great Western designing the famous *Firefly* class engines for the broad gauge line. The width of the broad gauge engine made it possible to have a very low centre of gravity. Crampton was determined to maintain the low centre of gravity on a standard gauge engine and took out a patent for positioning the 7-ft driving wheels behind the boiler. He licensed the manufacture of the design to Jean-Francois Cail's works in Paris, which supplied locomotives to most of the main French companies especially the Nord, Est and PLM. A Crampton hauled the last train out of Paris during the siege by the Prussians and in 1890 a Crampton engine broke the world record with a speed of 89½ mph. Crampton was a man of many parts: he went on to supervise the installation of the first cross-channel cable between Dover and Calais and he engineered the Berlin waterworks.

The third engineer had the improbable name for an Englishman of Alfred de Glehn. He became the Director of Engineering at the *Societé Alsacienne de Constructions Mécaniques* in his late twenties and developed a sophisticated system of compounding – taking exhaust steam from the two high pressure cylinders to power two low pressure cylinders – that became the standard for French express passenger engines in the 20th century. Even the most individual of the British companies, the Great Western, adopted de Glehn's mechanical layout of four cylinders in their famous *Castle* and *King* class locomotives.

The authorities recognised the dangers that would be caused by competition by the various companies to establish record speeds and in 1853 an Imperial Decree was issued limiting speed to a maximum of 75mph. This Decree did not stop Napoleon III's legendary journey in 1855, when he travelled from Marseille to Paris in 8½ hours, an average speed of 62mph, the same as the crack *Mistral* express in 1951. It was indeed legendary: the link between the line from the north into Lyon had not yet been connected to the line running south.

The high point of French steam locomotive design, and probably of steam locomotive design worldwide was André Chapelon's modifications of a large locomotive originally designed by a government-appointed committee. Despite its size the locomotive was short of power and gave a bad ride and had a tendency to derail. The great French engineer together with a Scandinavian colleague called Kylala, based the improved efficiency of the locomotive on a detailed study of the physics of the behaviour of superheated steam. The result in 1946 was the world's most powerful locomotive outside the United States. Not just more powerful than any other steam locomotive but more powerful than any diesel or electric engine. Its power equalled that of a 50%-heavier American engine. It had such low fuel consumption that it was cheaper to operate than an electric locomotive. At the time, the French railway planners were trying to convince the government to invest in electrifying the main trunk lines, and suddenly having a high-performing yet economical steam locomotive was a positive embarrassment. Like Livio Porta, the great Argentinian locomotive designer, it was Chapelon's tragedy that he lived at the end of the age of the steam locomotive rather than at its beginning.

The *ligne impériale* from Paris to the Mediterranean operated by the PLM was the most important line in France. The name *route impériale* probably originated because it linked the capital to Marseille and the French overseas empire. Trains left the Paris Gare de Lyon daily to Marseille's Quai de la Joliette to connect with boats to French Africa or to the French Orient. The line as far as Dijon was also the first section of the route for the Orient-Express trains: Athens 2,015 miles and Istanbul 1,895 miles. The *route impériale* was also the link between Paris and the complex of important manufacturing towns such as Lyon, Saint-Etienne and Grenoble; between Paris and the Alpine ski resorts; Paris and Italy and it was the link between Paris and the famous resorts of the Côte d'Azur.

The crack PLM trains included the *Train Bleu*, the night train from Paris to the Côte d'Azur and San Remo. The train was originally the *Calais-Paris-Nice-Rome-Express* but as soon as the Fréjus tunnel opened trains took the more direct route under the Alps to Rome and the *Train Bleu* was relegated to serve the Italian and French Rivieras. The luxurious blue *Wagons-Lits* carriages gave it its famous name, unofficially from 1883, and officially in 1949. The fastest train to the Côte or the Riviera in the nineteen thirties was the *Aérodynamique*, a streamlined locomotive hauling a maximum of 200 passengers in three carriages and a restaurant car. In 1937 it left Paris at 11.00 and arrived in Marseille, 536 miles away, ten hours later to connect with a Bugatti autorail that stopped at the main Côte resorts to arrive in Nice just before midnight.

The *Mistral* was the crack express train connecting Paris to the Mediterranean after World War II. Its introduction corresponded with the opening of the electrification of the line from Paris as far as Dijon in 1950. It travelled to Lyon in four hours when electrification reached Lyon and it reached its height of fame in the 1950s when its routeing was extended from Marseille through to Nice and the train's rake included two restaurant cars and a voiture-salon Pullman. The *Mistral* lost a large part of its glamour when it became a part of the TEE *Trans-Europ-Express* network and it was finally displaced by the TGV.

The very idea of the LGV (*Ligne à Grand Vitesse*) was opposed by central government and especially by President Giscard d'Estaing. The French National Railways (the SNCF) was losing enormous sums of money and was held in low public esteem; besides, it was almost universally recognised that the combination of car and aircraft would satisfy the nation's transportation needs. Persistence and enthusiasm on the part of a group of SNCF managers won the day and the necessary legislation and funding were obtained. The first LGV was planned to run from Paris to the north and to the English Channel. However delays in planning and constructing the tunnel under the Channel led to the first LGV running south from Paris to Lyon. The existing line between Paris and Dijon had reached near saturation and there was popular appeal to a dedicated high-speed line that would ultimately link the three most important French cities: Paris, Lyon and Marseille.

In autumn 1981 the first TGVs (*Trains à Grand Vitesse*) with interiors and external appearance inspired by Roger Tallon, the leading French industrial designer, started running on the new LGV to Lyon at speeds of up to 162 mph. The introduction of the TGVs to the south stimulated an enormous increase in passenger demand over the last 20 years and resulted in a great increase in the number of daytime departures and a reduction in the number of overnight trains from Paris's Gare de Lyon. The frequency of the long-distance trains to the south, not only to Marseille and the Côte but to Geneva, Grenoble, Nîmes and Montpelier outstretched the capacity of the Gare de Lyon and trains for Italy together with TACs (trains-autocouchettes), have been moved to the new Gare de Bercy nearby.

Trunk links radiating from Paris were electrified by the end of the 1970s and dedicated LGVs have been built or are under construction to the main regional centres. The planners are now at an advanced stage in developing regional services around the great centres with fast, modern train sets to serve the local population and feed passengers to the high speed national network.

❖

It was only in 1870 that Germany became the Germany that is recognisable today. At the beginning of the railway age it comprised 39 different States, each with its own border controls and its own currency.

The manager of the Berlin Royal Ironworks built the first locomotive in continental Europe after visiting northeast England in 1815. He reported 'Nothing is more surprising for a traveller at the first glance than to meet in a field a long line of wagons which move without the help of any animal'.

Unlike other earlier railways, the first public railway in Germany was established to carry passengers rather than freight, although freight made a substantial contribution to its success. The line ran four miles from Nuremberg to Fürth. Since medieval times foreigners or labourers found it difficult or impossible to obtain a civic licence to reside in historic Nuremberg. Many of them, particularly merchants and artisans, settled in nearby Fürth, which became an important centre. The proposers of the railway conducted what today would be recognised as a market survey and found the Nuremberg–Fürth highway to be the busiest in Bavaria and concluded that a railway would be a paying proposition. The Ludwigsbahn, named in honour of the King of Bavaria, opened in December 1835 with an inaugural run of the *Adler*, purchased from Stephenson's Newcastle works. Traction was a mixture of steam and horses, which were phased out by 1863, and trains continued to run until 1922 when the line closed.

The link between Leipzig and Dresden, both in the State of Saxony, opened in 1840 and was probably the first German trunk line, and the completion of the 1846 Berlin–Hamburg line was the first intercity line to cross a state frontier. The 1840s to 1860s were the period of initial expansion of trunk lines and by 1862 Prussia had more than 3,000 miles of track. Despite progress in locomotive design and railway operation, average train speeds in the German states did not increase because of the demand for more and more intermediate stops. Finally in 1852 the first *Schnellzug* or express train provided a fast service between Berlin and Cologne at an average speed of 26mph.

Vienna, capital of a great empire, suffered from having no access to the sea other than down the Danube to the Black Sea. The building of a railway to the Mediterranean was a matter of urgency and the solution was to build a line southwest from Vienna to Trieste, situated at the head of the Adriatic. There were few choices for the rails to cross the Alps and the planners chose the Semmering Pass. The line was engineered with long stretches of 1 in 40 grades with tight radius bends and in 1851 the Austrian government organised trials with a prize of 20,000 ducats to find the most suitable locomotive to haul a 110-ton load up and over Semmering at a minimum speed of 7½mph. An Austrian, a German and a Belgian company supplied locomotives for the trials. The winner was the *La Bavaria* from the Maffei Company of Munich; it had massive chains to transmit power to all its seven pairs of wheels to obtain the greatest possible adhesive weight. The system provided more than enough power but was very ponderous and complicated. The judges came to the conclusion that none of the locomotives were suitable or reliable and recommended that trains should be worked by three standard locomotives. The line opened in 1854[1] but the bottlenecks caused by working trains over Semmering still exist and a tunnel is now being considered.

By the end of the 19th century European countries felt that national pride should be expressed by building the fastest steamships to cross the Atlantic or operating the fastest trains. The runs from London to Edinburgh or Paris to Calais were faster than any service in Germany. This was despite a competition (which only had two entrants) to find a steam locomotive for hauling trains at up to 95mph. German steam locomotive

1. Semmering was the first rail route across the Alps: the second, the Brenner, between Italy and Austria, opened thirteen years later.

design was focussed on developing greater thermal efficiency to increase power to haul heavier trains with lower operating costs rather than developing express locomotives. A German Councillor said 'At an average speed of 60mph the steam locomotive has reached the limit of its economical performance. Anything beyond that is ostentation.' However before the turn of the century the *Study Group for Electric High Speed Railways* was formed and in 1901 a Siemens & Halske experimental electric locomotive ran at over 100mph on a specially modified 15-mile line between Marienfelde near Berlin, and Zossen. Two years later an AEG electric railcar ran at over 130mph.

German engineers had developed a high level of expertise in diesel engine technology and their experience with building Zeppelins led to the design of the *Rail Zeppelin*, a lightweight propeller driven railcar that, in 1931, covered 160 miles on the line between Hamburg and Berlin in 98 minutes. It clocked 143mph on the only stretch of the line where its 600hp motor could reach its maximum speed. Two years later a multiple carriage diesel unit, the *Fliegender Hamburger* or *Flying Hamburger*[2] entered service between Berlin's Lehrter station and Hamburg Central Station covering the 178 miles at an average speed of 77½mph, the fastest scheduled rail service in the world; the two coach train with its shiny dark mauve and cream livery was probably also the smartest. The Reichsbahn ordered more of the two- and three-carriage train sets to link Berlin to the other regional capitals. The Berlin–Hanover and Berlin–Frankfurt services were the first in the world to be scheduled at more than 80mph start to stop. Apart from one short period these express services held the record between 1933 and 1940 for the world's fastest start to stop schedules.

In the late 1930s developments to the existing railway system were shelved and the German rail engineers were put to work to build the Autobahn road system: 2,000 miles of highway with long straight sections and curves with generous radii for high speed road traffic. Later, Hitler ordered a design study of a huge electrified railway system running across Europe from the Ukraine to the French Mediterranean. Huge, because the gauge between the rails was to be 117¾ inches in the place of the 56½

2. It took its name from the Flying Scotsman.

inches world standard, a loading gauge width of 216 inches and a height above the rails of 270 inches compared to the 168½ inches European standard. The *gigantomanie* of the carriages accommodated passengers on two decks and a contemporary artist's impression of the interior of the first class restaurant, with its 14-ft high ceiling, chandeliers and musicians' gallery, looks like the dining room of a luxury ocean liner.

The German railway system took a tremendous battering from the allies' aerial bombardment and armies during the World War II. Pre-war, the system had radiated from Berlin with trunk lines to the important regional cities. After the end of the war and the partition of Germany, West Germany had to rethink the organisation of its railway system. There was no central point but there was a need to connect its big regional cities mainly in north-south axes across ranges of high hills rather than across the level east-west routes that existed before the war. In the Eastern Zone 3,750 miles of track were removed, reducing many double and multiple tracked lines to a single track and travel times between cities became much the same as the 1860s.

In the late 1950s the Deutsche Bundesbahn, together with other European countries, joined to develop *Trans-Europe Express* trains. The trains' design and operating specification limited speed to a maximum of 70mph, a surprising decision considering that air travel had started to attract an increasing number of passengers. The introduction of Intercity trains with either diesel or electric traction speeded up train services but by 1985 it was recognised that train speeds had reached the maximum possible on the existing tracks.

A number of new tracks were built, and in 1988 the one between Fulda and Wurtzburg ran a test of the new ICE streamlined train that reached a world record of 252mph, taking the rail blue riband from the French TGV which had clocked 236mph a few years earlier. Now there are third generation ICE trains that are scheduled to provide a 200mph start to stop service on the new dedicated high speed line between Cologne and Frankfurt which opened in 2002. Eventually ICE trains will continue on to Brussels and to Amsterdam.

❖

Italy has been known as the Peninsula Italiana for the last two millennia. However it was not a single nation at the beginning of the railway age. Naples, the south and Sicily were ruled by the Bourbons, the Papal States covering almost a third of the Peninsula were ruled by the Pope, Lombardy and the Veneto were part of the Austrian Empire and independent states such as Parma owed allegiance to the Austrians. Only Piedmont in the northwest had a measure of independence. The rulers of occupied Italy suppressed the press and stamped on the emergence of political activism or any ideas of nationalism and, not surprisingly, did not encourage travel or railway construction. On a more frivolous level, the rivalry and enmity that had existed between the city states for hundreds of years did nothing to encourage travel; a Florentine in his home town would not have taken kindly to a visiting Venetian giving the eye to any Florentine girl. In any case, with only three or four exceptions, Italy's great cities had access to rivers or the sea and there was a highly developed network of coastal navigation.

The first railway in Italy opened in 1839 and ran five miles from Naples to Portici. Maria Teresa, the second wife of King Ferdinand II of the Two Sicilies, was a Hapsburg princess and persuaded him to demonstrate that he was a modern ruler by building a railway to link the administrative capital of Naples with his seaside palace at Portici. The Neapolitan aristocracy travelling to their seaside houses were the other passengers on the line[3].

Perhaps Ferdinand took his cue from the 1835 opening of Belgium's first line from Brussels to Malines which was the seat of the Archbishop; legend has it that the Belgian Cardinal Archbishop of the time recognised his duties lay in Malines but preferred society in Brussels and requested the King to build a railway to shuttle him between the two cities. King Ferdinand's example was followed by some of the other rulers of Italy; for instance, the Austrian Viceroy of Lombardy built a line from Milan to his country palace at Monza.

Piedmont with its great cities of Turin and Genoa was the only

3. Later the line's promoter, Armand Banard, drummed up business by offering discounts for 'ladies without hats, servants in livery, and non-commissioned officers'.

independent state; Cavour, the Piedmontese Prime Minister, visited England and was impressed by the benefits of the new railways and as a result Piedmont had 500 miles of track by 1859, nearly as much as the 600 miles in the whole of the rest of Italy.

Geography increased the difficulties of railway construction. The rocky Apennine mountain spine of Italy falls straight into the sea along the Ligurian coast and stretches east across the country halfway to the Adriatic. The coastal line south from Genoa to La Spezia is a dramatic example of the challenges that faced 19th-century Italian railway engineers. The tracks run in tunnels through the mountains or on sea walls in the gaps between the mountains. Thirty-one miles of the 54-mile distance are in 54 tunnels. Henri Lartilleux, editor of *Géographie Universelle des Transports*, called the line 'one of the most extraordinary railway lines on the planet'. A 19th-century traveller said that the sequence of the sensation of flashes of brilliant and luminous sunlight reflected by the sea followed by diving into the darkness of a tunnel over and over was like a '*séance de cinematographie intermittente*'. The line was opened in 1874 and provided a direct route between Paris and Rome. It was electrified in 1926 and double-tracking the entire length of the line was completed in 1970.

The great seaport of Genoa in the Kingdom of Piedmont lies at the foot of the Ligurian Alps that rise directly behind and above the city. The route to Turin, the capital, lies across the Giovi Pass. Construction of this vital and important railway line to link the cities began in 1844 and was completed nine years later. The line climbed 1,180ft in 14 miles and the grade out of the city was a very steep 1 in 28½ followed by a two-mile tunnel. The initial steep section was worked by two back-to-back coupled saddle tank engines joined together. This astonishing combination was known as the *Mastodon of the Giovi*. In 1889 a parallel, longer but easier line with a four-mile summit tunnel was completed and worked by standard locomotives which could climb the Giovi inclines with 130 tons at 25mph. Three-phase electrification had previously been installed on a 50-mile line north of Milan and been proved successful and the same system was installed on the Giovi line in 1908 and electric locomotives known as the *Small Giants* hauled 400 tons at 30mph up the Giovi grades.

Giovi was recognised worldwide as a dramatic demonstration of the advantages of electric traction over steam on a steeply graded line.

Italian railway builders not only had encountered hideous engineering problems crossing mountain ranges they also had to contend with political problems. The projected main north-south axis linking Florence and Rome to Lombardy was through the two-mile tunnel under the 3,000-ft Porretta pass. In 1851, a convention followed by a series of meetings was held between Austria, the Papal States, the Duchies of Parma and Modena and the Grand Duchy of Tuscany. The Pope refused to agree to the tunnel because he considered it would detract from the commerce and traffic passing through the Papal port of Ancona. Finally, agreement was reached and the tunnel opened thirteen years later in 1864.

Electrification of large sections of the system was an obvious choice for Italy, a country with no coal but with plentiful sources of hydro-power. In 1953, after Italy was recovering from the effects of World War II the Ferrovie dello Stato introduced the *Settebello*, the most luxurious train in Europe. It was a seven-carriage deluxe train, for 160 first-class passengers, including a 56-seat dining car, running between Milan and Rome with intermediate stops at Bologna and Florence. The six-hour journey time for the 392 miles was the same as the best pre-war service; in fact, the train was capable of much higher speeds but it had to be fitted in with the timings of the large number of trains on the busy trunk route.

Italy was the first European country to introduce tilting trains. The trains tilt up to nine degrees on curves so that they can run faster, more safely and with greater comfort for passengers. Fiat introduced its four-carriage Pendolino train, which proved itself on the tortuous 185-mile mountain route between Rome and Ancona. Pendolino train sets in single or double formation now run on a number of national and international services and are in service on the west coast line in Britain. Construction of a dedicated north-south high-speed LGV type line is well under way, running from Turin through Milan and Rome to Naples. More than two thirds of the section between Bologna and Florence will be in tunnels and most of its remaining length will be on high viaducts crossing the Apennine valleys.

❖

The great Alpine mountain chain separates Italy from the rest of Europe. The chain stretches from the French Mediterranean coast in a northern arc through Switzerland to Austria and Slovenia in the east. The first railway in Switzerland was opened in 1847 and it was not until 1871 that the first Alpine tunnel, the Fréjus, between France and Italy, was opened. In 1882 the 9-mile St Gotthard tunnel linking Switzerland and Italy was opened, the Arlberg between Switzerland and Austria followed in 1884, and the 12½-mile Simplon tunnel, the longest in the world at the time, between Switzerland and Italy in 1906.

In addition to the international links the Swiss developed their own railway system, probably the best and most comprehensive[4] in the world for the seven million inhabitants of this small country[5] of lakes and steep valleys surrounded by high mountains. In 1999 the State Railways were nationalised in a company with the State as the single shareholder. Today the company operates 1,880 miles of lines, and regional or locally owned companies operate another 1,270 miles of passenger and freight lines providing a service along the many alpine valleys. About a quarter of the lines are narrow gauge and there are sophisticated transfer stations to fit standard gauge wagons onto narrow gauge rail frames and vice versa. The 2,450 private sidings is one of the most surprising statistics for such a small rail system which runs a service to pick up a wagon at 17.00 and deliver it to its destination by 09.00 the following day with only one days notice.

During the 1950s and the following years the Swiss followed the then-current fashion of building express highways across the country. The volume of traffic rapidly increased, mainly with traffic crossing the country between Italy and Germany. Truckers filled up with fuel in Italy or Germany where it was cheaper and rolled across the country without paying any charges but leaving Switzerland with noise, pollution, damage to the roads and a steep increase in the number of road accidents. It was even found that the high concentration of CO_2 in the valleys was reacting

4. The Swiss make greater use of their trains than any other European nation, with an average 1,290 miles/year, France 770, Germany 520, Italy 500 and the UK 420 miles/year.

5. 250 miles East to West and 200 miles North to South.

with stone and causing rocks to crumble.

From 1987 a succession of five referendums[6] in Switzerland voted to limit truck traffic, especially international traffic; to reduce it by half its present volume by 2009 and to tax vehicles on the basis of pollution emission, distance and weight to pay for a large proportion of the cost of improving the international rail links. Public opinion against road transport increased following accidents and fires in the St Gotthard, the Tauern and the Mont Blanc road tunnels. These disasters resulted in immediate safety measures that included spacing the entry of vehicles and detection[7] of excess CO_2. Swiss Federal Railways are building a new 21½ mile Lötschberg tunnel below the existing bore and a new St Gotthard tunnel[8] some 1,750ft below the existing rail tunnel. They are also making a massive contribution to building two terminals in Italy and a terminal at Singen in Germany for speedy transfer of containers from road to rail and vice versa. A line to link Lyon to Turin is also being planned. These ambitious works are being largely financed by traffic tolls and taxes.

❖

The standard 4ft 8½ inches gauge between the rails throughout Europe, apart from Spain and Russia, enabled steam and diesel locomotives to cross national frontiers. The almost universal use of electric locomotives powered from an overhead line or a third rail introduced problems for international travel. Each nation had its own engineering and electrical standards and each developed its own network for powering the railways. Southern England has a third rail 600/750Vdc system, most of the rest of Britain followed France's lead and adopted 25kVac50 Hz overhead pickup. Germany, Austria and Switzerland installed a 15kVac16.7 Hz power

6. Earlier there were regulations to control the volume of lorries on the narrow or crowded roads; for instance sugar beets had to be delivered by rail if the journey to the sugar refinery was greater than 12 miles.

7. The steam and smells from the fire officers' lunchtime fondue triggered the CO_2 alarm and closed the Mont Blanc tunnel for hours in September 2003.

8. When completed it will be the longest rail tunnel in the world.

system, Belgium and Italy use 3kVdc and the Netherlands uses a 1.5kVdc power supply.

Locomotives working from Germany though Switzerland to Italy include heavy and expensive current conversion equipment, as do the Eurostar and other European international trains.

The future of transnational rail freight was recently highlighted by running a freight train from Istanbul to Mannheim. The quarter-mile-long demonstration train went from Turkey across Bulgaria, Romania, Hungary and Austria to Germany. It needed two locomotives; an electric locomotive operated the train on the different power supplies in all six countries, while a second locomotive, a diesel, was needed to haul the train for the 50-odd miles where the line had not yet been electrified. The journey was completed in 80 hours, including stops for frontier formalities, customs and crew changes – slightly more than half the time taken by road. The possibilities not only of transnational rail freight but intercontinental rail transport will become a reality when the Turkish–Japanese consortium has opened the tunnel under the Bosphorus to link the rails of Europe and Asia.

❖

By the end of the 19th century rails had been laid in almost every country around the world and railways became the standard transportation for people, merchandise and freight. Some lines were built as commercial undertakings, some were built for trade and others were built for military reasons. There were lines that were dreams such as the Cape to Cairo, the Berlin to Baghdad and the line crossing from South Australia to the port of Darwin on the Indian Ocean. Some of the dreams have been realised.

❖

The great 5,780-mile trunk line from Moscow to Vladivostock on the Sea of Japan was sanctioned in 1886 by Tsar Alexander III, who added *Most August Founder of the Great Siberian Railway* to his many other titles. The line was built in sections and travellers[9] began to make use of it before the end of the 19th century. However, they crossed Lake Baikal, which stretched across the direct route of the railway, by ferry. The lake was a serious bottleneck to getting men and supplies to the front in the Russo-Japanese war and a line skirting the southern shore of the lake was completed in 1904, enabling passengers to travel from the Baltic to the Sea of Japan without leaving their carriage. The line was built as quickly and cheaply as possible and upgrading and rebuilding was begun as soon as the initial construction work on each section was completed. The Trans-Manchurian Railway that connected with the Trans-Siberian was completed in 1901 and it enabled passengers to travel directly to Peking. From 1956 the Trans-Mongolian Railway connecting Ulan Bator from the Trans-Siberian provides travellers with an alternative route to China and Beijing.

Transporting migrants from European Russia to Siberia was the initial spur for building the railway after the 1890 famine in Europe. The railway was also used for transporting convicts and exiles and later for transporting minerals from the Siberian mines and smelters to Europe.

In 1990 a second and substantially shorter line than the Trans-Siberian was opened between Moscow and Beijing with the completion of the tracks between Almaty in Kazakhstan to Urumqi in Western China. It runs along some of the route of the traditional Silk Road through the historic cities of Bukhara, Samarkand and Tashkent.

❖

The continent of South America is divided by the great north-south mountain spine of the Andes with its 20,000-ft high peaks. The western approach rises precipitously from a narrow coastal plain to the chain of peaks, and behind them, the 10,000–14,000ft high altiplano or plateau. The mountains and the plateau are hugely rich with a wide variety of minerals, particularly copper on which the industrial world depends. By the middle of the 19th century an effective transportation system was required to satisfy the increasing demand for the mineral wealth from the Andes.

9. The 1900 Paris Exposition included advertisements for travelling on the Trans-Siberian Express that listed the many on-board facilities: French chefs, luxurious suites, a library, a church, a gymnasium, a pharmacist and even a dark room for amateur photographers.

Railways were the answer to transport the ores from the high altitude mines and smelters to the coastal ports.

A number of lines were built into the mountains and some of these lines became legends. The Central of Peru Railway was called the *Highest and Hardest* of all the South American railways. No other railway combined high altitude with steepness of climbs, sharp curves and the effects of ground movements. The line ran from Lima and its port, Callao, to the mountain smelters and mines. Henry Meiggs, an American entrepreneur, took the contract to build the line in 1870. The main line climbs with viaducts, bridges, tunnels and reversing zigzags to reach the summit of 15,673ft above sea level in the Galera tunnel to the mines and smelters at Oroya and Huancayo. A short, recently opened spur to the Volcán mine reaches 15,872ft above sea level, the highest rails in the world.

The war between Chile, Peru and Bolivia ended in 1884 with a peace treaty that ceded the nitrate rich western plain and the west aspect of the Andes to Chile and cut off Bolivia from the sea. Access to the sea was crucial to Bolivia's economy, almost wholly dependent on mineral exports. A narrow gauge line was built from Antofagasta on the coast and by 1892 it reached Oruro in central Bolivia. A spur to a copper mine just on the Chilean side of the frontier reached a height of 15,834ft above sea level. The rail spur was abandoned when the mine was worked out. The line was extended to La Paz, the Bolivian capital, a mere 12,143ft high and a branch built to Potosi crossing the 15,705ft summit at Condor and a second branch to Cochabamba where work on a connection to Santa Cruz has begun.

By 1876 the Southern Railway of Peru completed a standard gauge line from the ports of Mollendo and Matavini to Puno, a dock on the 12,500ft high Lake Titicaca. The continuation of this line from Puno to Cuzco, the old Inca capital, is probably the railway line best known to tourists and visitors to South America; they usually get acquainted with the attendant wheeling an oxygen cylinder along the train to give relief to passengers suffering from altitude sickness. After a stay in Cuzco, visitors usually continue their travels along the 3ft-gauge railway that climbs out of Cuzco with two double reversing zigzags to run along the Urubamba valley to the astonishing Inca fortress of Machu-Picchu.

Gruelling, steep and seemingly endless gradients, narrow radius curves, reversing zigzags, frequent ground movement, violent extremes of weather and the problems of braking heavy trains on downward grades all contribute to making train operation in the high Andes one of the most difficult and fascinating rail challenges of all. However the high altitude with its low-temperature boiling point enhanced the steaming characteristics of the locomotives. Until well past the middle of the last century railways did not fear competition despite the slow speeds of their passenger services. There were no locally-based planes that could fly as high as the trains.

❖

Mauritania in West Africa holds a world railway record. It has the 450-mile long line from the iron mines at Zouorate to the port of Nouadhibou on the Atlantic coast. The line is known for its regular service of what are the world's heaviest regularly scheduled trains. The trains comprise three General Motors EMD diesel locomotives hauling 200 100-ton ore hoppers and one or two passenger carriages, a train about 1¼ miles long; it takes nine minutes from start-up for the locomotives to get the train's last hopper on the move and stopping time for the train is about two minutes at its normal running speed of 30mph. The ore trains take about 18 hours for the journey from Zouorate to the coast. The line is a roller coaster of ups and downs over an endless series of sand ridges, with the bones of unfortunate dromedaries and other creatures lying beside the tracks.

The combination of blowing sand and extreme heat is the cause of most of the operating problems. There are months of constant wind and the locomotives have high-pressure air blowers to clear sand from the rails; the working life of a wheel of one of the mineral hoppers is only a third of what it would be in Europe.

Société Nationale Industrielle et Minière, owner and operator of the mines, the port and the rail line is now planning to increase the number of hoppers on each train so that the locomotives will be hauling 22,000-ton trains. The Company is proud that the line is entirely staffed by Mauritanian nationals.

❖

1869 was the year of the completion of the first transcontinental railway across the United States from the Atlantic to the Pacific oceans. The first transcontinental railroad certainly, but not the first rail link between the Atlantic and Pacific, which opened across the Isthmus of Panama in 1855 to tranship passengers and cargo the 47 miles from one side of the Americas to the other. The line was built by American businessmen and then sold on to a French consortium with the grandiose name Compagnie Universelle du Canal Interocéanique who intended to use it for the construction of the canal. Later, Panama became a separate republic and a concession and enclave was granted to the US to build and operate the canal[10]. The route of the original railroad went across what is now Gatun Lake and it was re-laid parallel and to the south of the canal. Once the canal was open the railway became largely redundant and over the years maintenance was neglected, passenger services were discontinued and finally a speed limit of 10mph was imposed under Noriega's government.

In 1998 arrangements were finalised for a subsidiary of the Kansas City Southern Railway Company and another partner to update and operate the line. The partners virtually rebuilt the line with the standard 4ft 8½ inch gauge in the place of the original 5ft gauge and started operating a double stack container service across the isthmus. Operating a railway parallel to a canal may seem anomalous but there are good reasons for it to flourish. Some container vessels are too large to traverse the canal and the containers are unloaded to cross the isthmus by rail and then reloaded for the next stage of their journey. One shipping company not only tranships but takes the opportunity of sorting and marshalling its containers for different vessels for onward shipment to their various destinations. The railway company operates a passenger service across the isthmus and it was pleasantly surprised when excursion trains became an unexpected

10. The canal had great strategic and economic importance to the US. A decision to fortify it was taken in 1908. Two 14-inch railway guns each weighing 365 tons were included as part of the defences. They were designed to travel from one side of the Isthmus to the other in a train hauled by two Panama RR locos. The train included tool cars, a powder and a plotting car as well as accommodation cars and the guns. It took 2½ hours to cross the Isthmus and much longer along military rails to reach the gun emplacements. The guns faced the Atlantic at the start of WWII and faced the Pacific after Pearl Harbour.

source of business; Colon at the Atlantic entrance to the canal has become a Caribbean cruise port of call and trains take cruise passengers to Panama City and for a view of the Pacific Ocean.

❖

Early in the 20th century the Turkish Ottoman Empire, covering South-East Europe and the lands of the Near and Middle East was beginning to experience the turbulence of nationalism that is inevitable with the decline of an empire. Militant nationalism was especially evident among the Arabs in Arabia, Syria and Jordan; today they might be recognised as freedom fighters. At the same time German influence with its *Drang nach osten*[11] politics and ambitions for a Berlin-Baghdad railway (the concession for which was negotiated by the German Emperor during his visit to Constantinople in 1898) posed a threat to British imperial interests: the Suez Canal to the west and India to the east.

There were no systems of communication in the area. Travel and movements of goods was across deserts on camels or over mountains on mules. The first road in the region from Beirut to Damascus was opened in 1863. There were no railways until the 1890s when the narrow gauge lines from Jaffa to Jerusalem and from Beirut to Damascus were opened. The latter had a laborious rack and pinion system to climb the 5,000-ft passes in the Lebanon and the Anti-Lebanon mountain ranges. The main line through Turkey connecting Constantinople to Aleppo in Syria was completed, apart from two tunnels, by 1912; passengers, freight and military supplies were obliged to make two portages over the mountains to reach Syria until 1918.

There had been a number of early projects for laying rails in the area; one promoter proposed the CC&C Railway – *Calais, Constantinople and Calcutta Railway* – as early as 1842. Another claimed to have authorisation from the Turkish Sultan and enthusiastic Pontifical approval to build a port at Jaffa and a 54 mile line to Jerusalem funded worldwide by Catholics who would 'draw their dividends in the form of feelings of

11. *Drive to the East.*

satisfaction at having assisted by their subscriptions'.

Pilgrimage to Mecca has always been a cornerstone of Islam. Traditionally an enormous caravan of pilgrims gathered at Damascus for the annual Haj, an expensive forty day journey across desert to Medina and Mecca. In 1900 the Sultan in Constantinople announced the project for building a railway from Damascus to the Holy Cities, through what is now Syria, Jordan and Saudi Arabia, that would shorten the journey time to two or three days. He also recognised that the railway would enable the Ottomans to tighten political and military control over Hijaz[12] with its Arab nationalism and unrest. The railway was funded by Moslems worldwide and by deductions from the salaries of Ottoman civil servants; as a result the line was one of the few, if not the only major railway in the world to open without debt or shareholders. Work began south from Damascus and north from Medina with German engineers and technicians under the supervision of Oberingenieur Heinrich Meissner who was awarded the title of Pasha. The 825-mile line, the Hijaz Railway, between Damascus and Medina was completed in 1908 despite the large number of culverts and bridges over wadis, the problems of obtaining supplies, equipment and water and the hostility of marauding Bedouin tribesmen who disapproved of the construction of the line and whose opposition made it impossible to continue the line south from Medina to Mecca.

A number of attempts had been made to bypass the tortuous Damascus-Beirut narrow gauge line and link Damascus with the Mediterranean at Haifa. In 1902 the Turkish government acquired the concession to construct a line known as the Yarmuk Valley Branch to Haifa. The route was south from Damascus to Dera on the Hijaz line and then a new 100-mile line west to Haifa. The line from Dera crossed the winding river Yarmuk fifteen times in 40 miles and descended 2,570 feet to just south of Lake Tiberius to cross the River Jordan 840 feet below sea level; 50 miles of the line were below sea level before climbing to Haifa and the sea.

Germany had been courting Turkey with technical support, military aid and funds; with the outbreak of war in Europe in 1914 Turkey joined the German cause against the Allies. In early 1915, Turkish columns,

---

12. Western coastal plain of Arabia bordering the Red Sea.

commanded by German officers, marched into Egypt and troops crossed the Suez Canal before being repulsed. England was scandalized by the success of the Turks: 'Are the troops protecting the canal or is the canal protecting the troops?' The Turks were determined to make a major attack on Egypt and the Canal but were unable to use the sea as a supply line because of British naval supremacy. They recalled Meissner Pasha to build a railway from the Haifa terminus of the Yarmuk Valley line along a route more or less parallel to the coast to the Egyptian frontier. Construction was pushed ahead as rapidly as possible despite a shortage of material; rails and sleepers were lifted from lines with less strategic importance; some had only been laid two years previously and a section of Damascus tram rails was lifted for the new line. A number of skirmishes and battles were fought until the Allies under their new commander, General Allenby, planned a major offensive into Palestine to capture Gaza and Jerusalem[13]. Allenby's troops were supplied by a new rail line built from Kantara on the Canal, north past Gaza to connect to Meissner Pasha's new Turkish line.

In Arabia, the Arab Revolt captured Mecca and surrounded Medina. They tore up several miles of the Hijaz railway believing the Turkish garrison would be starved into submission. The Turkish garrison included railway troops who relaid track and built diversions or timber trestle bridges to replace bridges destroyed by guerilla warfare. The Turkish commander in Medina was reported as saying that whenever he heard the detonations of railway destruction in the night, he chuckled to himself and said 'My lazy troops will not be able to loaf tomorrow'.

T.E. Lawrence's (Lawrence of Arabia) first encounter with railway construction was in 1912 when he was organising a dig for Hittite antiquities at Jerablus on the Turkish-Syrian border and a few hundred yards from the Berlin-Baghdad railway. Lawrence entertained Meissner Pasha who had built the Damascus-Medina Hijaz line and was now supervising construction of the line to Baghdad. Because of the extent of the dig there were differences over the siting of the engine shed and workshops. Lawrence mediated after site workers attacked the German engineers. When war was declared, Lawrence, with his fluent Arabic and

13. Jerusalem fell in December 1917.

knowledge of Arab culture became an intelligence officer in the Cairo HQ. His first mission 'to see what could be done by indirect means to relieve the beleaguered garrison' of Kut was not a success, but he became convinced that he could persuade and lead desert Bedouin to join the Allied cause against Turkish-German troops despite their lack of confidence in the Allies; they saw that a large part of France was occupied by a German army and knew about the Allied disaster at Gallipoli.

Lawrence landed in Jiddah to find a Turkish army corps was on its way to recapture Mecca, reinforce the Medina garrison and support troops guarding the Hijaz railway. He rallied and led groups of Arab irregulars by arranging for the Allies to supply arms and ammunition, by paying the irregulars with parcels of gold sovereigns and by his magic gift for leadership and by his deeply held sympathy for their cause. After blowing bridges, demolishing lengths of rails[14] and wrecking trains which his men looted for food and equipment, Lawrence rode into and captured Akaba at the head of the Red Sea and established a legendary reputation for himself. Not only was his reputation legendary but so was his courage; his exploits were behind enemy lines, there was a bounty for his capture or betrayal. As it was he was grazed by bullets and wounded by shards of metal from an exploding boiler.

In the following months there were a series of attacks on the Hijaz Railway and sections of Meissner's military railway with the purpose of deflecting large numbers of Turkish and German troops from confronting Allenby on his advance and cutting off supplies to Medina. Then Lawrence decided to take a group of men 400 miles north behind enemy lines to the Yarmuk Valley Branch with the intention of blowing one of the Yarmuk bridges; because it was far north of his usual sorties he felt there would be fewer defences. However the bridges were well defended and so they contented themselves by dynamiting a train carrying Jemal Pasha on his way to organise the defence of Jerusalem.

The valleys of the Tigris and the Euphrates were part of the Ottoman Empire and construction of the Berlin-Baghdad railway reached the border of Iraq in 1914, However, the Allies, mainly Indian troops, captured

14. Especially curved ones, in short supply.

Baghdad in March 1917 and the Berlin-Baghdad railway dream was finally completed in 1940.

The war in the Eastern Mediterranean ended at the end of October 1918 with the capture of Beirut and Aleppo. However the garrison commander in Medina only surrendered when his troops mutinied in January 1919, two months after the armistice that ended the World War. The Eastern Mediterranean countries of what was previously the Ottoman Empire became Syria, Lebanon, Jordan, Trans-Jordan and Saudi Arabia. Political problems and disturbances continued and often hindered effective railway operation; in 1936 Royal Navy sailors became engine drivers, firemen and signalmen on the Hijaz Railway. In the second World War, Vichy French forces blew a bridge over a gorge on the Yarmuk Valley Branch in 1941 and in 1945 Israeli saboteurs wrecked another bridge on the line. Traffic on the Hijaz line to Medina declined, with most pilgrims from overseas travelling either by air or by sea to Jiddah and making the short overland journey to Mecca. Heavy floods in 1924 together with local conflict between Arab factions closed the line south of the Saudi-Syrian border. The line never reopened despite many intentions and meetings. Discovery of phosphates and other minerals made an important contribution to traffic on the Hijaz Railway in Jordan and a spur was built to the port at Akaba.

❖

Osuke Toibata's sketch of the quarter-size Norris locomotive presented by Commodore Perry, 1854.

By the mid 1840s railways were making an important contribution to the prosperity of the world's industrial countries. About ten years later, in 1853, Commodore Perry arrived in Tokyo Bay and introduced the outside world to an isolated Japan. On his second visit, he brought a number of samples of modern industrial products and among them was a working model steam locomotive. Political upheaval in Japan followed the Perry deputation and there was no action or plan to construct railways for more than fifteen years.

In 1869 there was a failure of the rice crop in Tohoku Province and Sir Harry Parkes, the British Minister, explained how railways could transport rice to relieve the famine. The Japanese authorities also saw that a comprehensive railway system would unite the country by centralising its effective power and government. A British engineer, Edmund Morel, was appointed the engineer for the first Japanese railway, an 18-mile line between Tokyo and the port of Yokohama. He had been building narrow gauge lines in New Zealand before coming to Japan and decided on a 3ft 6inch gauge for the line and this gauge remained the standard for railways in Japan for more than ninety years. The line opened in 1872 with the Meiji Emperor attending the inauguration[15] and making the trip to Yokohama and back to Tokyo. A second short line between Osaka and the port of Kobe opened two years later and this was followed by a number of other short lines. The first trunk line opened in 1889 from Tokyo to Kobe, a distance of 376 miles; it was followed by other trunk lines linking the main centres.

Locomotives and rolling stock were originally imported from Britain; America and Germany soon followed as equipment suppliers. In 1893 Richard Trevithick, grandson of the great man, built the first Japanese locomotive in the new Kobe works, using mainly imported parts. Wheels, boiler tubes and springs continued to be imported until the early 1920s when local suppliers could meet the technical requirements.

With hydroelectric power and limited coal supplies electrification was the obvious traction choice and in the early 1900s suburban services around Tokyo and Osaka and sections of steep gradients on trunk lines were electrified. Probably all trunk lines would have been electrified if the military authorities hadn't objected because they felt overhead power lines were vulnerable from air attack.

The 1923 Great Kanto Earthquake, in which more than 140,000 people lost their lives in greater Tokyo, derailed 25 trains and killed 117 passengers. The earthquake brought down bridges, devastated stations and

---

15. In traditional Japanese style many of the inaugural passengers entered the carriages after leaving their footwear on the platform.

wrecked miles of track. It was the trigger for a shift in the population of Tokyo; large numbers of families left the city to live in the suburbs and this led to the development of a very dense and sophisticated network of suburban services.

There were a number of scenes of political violence on the railways. In 1921 Prime Minister Takashi Hara, an opponent of updating the railways to a standard gauge, was murdered by an extreme-right railway worker in Tokyo Central Station. Japanese expansion in eastern Asia began in the early years of the last century and Hirotuni Ito, who had been Prime Minister and a leading advocate of building railways, was assassinated by a Korean nationalist in Harbin station in north east China. Under the terms of the 1905 peace treaty that ended the Russo-Japanese war, Japan took over control of the railway that had been built in China by Russia. The line was reorganised as the South Manchuria Railway Company (SMR) and in 1931 ultra-nationalist Japanese army officers masquerading as Chinese troops tore up a section of SMR track near Mukden, an action that triggered a campaign for the conquest of southern Manchuria.

After World War II General MacArthur issued an instruction to organise the railways as a public corporation and as a result JNR, Japanese National Railways, came into being. The management's main task was to rebuild a railway system that had had no investment, minimum maintenance and suffered severe aerial bombardment. JNR continued as a national system until 1987 when it was privatised into six regional passenger companies and a freight carrier. These companies were supplemented by separate companies operating feeder lines or suburban services. The 1987 JNR privatisation was the first major rail privatisation programme in the world.

Two JNR sea ferry disasters, the *Toya Maru* that sank in 1954 with a loss of 1,200 passengers and crew[16], and almost a year later two JNR ferries that collided in fog with the loss of 168 lives, mostly children, triggered an official enquiry into the feasibility of constructing a tunnel to link the northern island of Hokkaido to Honshu. Construction was delayed by the problems of tunnelling through porous volcanic rock and the 35½-mile

16. A disaster second only to the *Titanic* in terms of peacetime loss of life.

Seikan tunnel, the longest in the world, opened in 1988. Other rail tunnels and bridges have also been built to join the other islands to the mainland.

Industrial growth along the eastern coastal plan between Tokyo and Osaka saturated the existing transport facilities and in 1959 construction began on the 320-mile Tokaido Shinkansen dedicated high-speed line, the first standard gauge rails in Japan. The line started operating in time for the opening of the 1964 Tokyo Olympic Games, with trains, popularly known as Bullet Trains, running at 135mph. There was great demand for extending Shinkansen lines to all the main regional centres, and by the end of the last century there were 1,600 miles of Shinkansen lines with another 500 planned.

The story of railways in Japan is an astonishing one. Although it was the last industrial nation to build a railway it became head and shoulders world leader in high-speed passenger train operation only 92 years later.

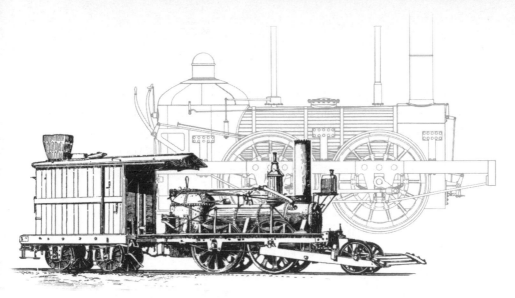

Stephenson's *John Bull* and (foreground) modified for service on the Camden & Amboy Railroad.

6 North America

There is an important difference between North American railways and British railways. The difference can be summed up in one word: scale. 2,880 miles lie between Vancouver and Montreal and the tracks continue east through another time zone to Nova Scotia. There are mountain ranges, the Appalachians, the Rockies and the Sierra Nevada; a few standard gauge lines climb to summits over 10,000ft. The Union Pacific transcontinental line climbs more than 8,000ft above sea level over Sherman Hill, close to the Continental Divide. By contrast, the Brenner, the Arlberg and the Fréjus, Europe's highest standard gauge rails are all lower than 4,500ft and Britain's highest standard gauge line, on the old Highland Railway in Scotland, reaches the summit at a mere 1,484ft. North America is criss-crossed by enormous rivers as well as mountain ranges: the St Lawrence, the Missouri, the Mississippi, the Susquehanna, the Delaware and many others.

There were not only giant geographical challenges and problems, but there were and still are giant trains. The standard gauge between the rails is an identical 4ft 8½ inches in each country but the loading gauge, that is to say the height and the width of engines, freight and passenger cars, is much larger. Maximum height to give clearance from the rails is 152 inches in the UK, and 34 inches more, a massive 186 inches, in North

America. As a result, road trailers can be piggybacked on flat cars, autos transported in three tiers of racks and there is headroom to carry two containers rather than one. Trains are heavier and longer and the bigger locomotives frequently work in multiples.

American visitors arriving at London's Heathrow Airport and travelling to central London on a Piccadilly Line tube train with its roof all of 113 inches above the rails must think the English are a race of pygmies.

Scale is not only relative to American trains and the terrain they cross, but also to the commercial buccaneering, wheeling and dealing and fraud that took place during the construction period and for years after. It was on a scale that was not even imagined, let alone practised, in Europe.

❖

By the end of the 18th century British steam engines were well known in America and were in use in a number of mines and factories. They were used to power American steamships by 1807 and the growth of the railway and the development of the steam locomotive in England were closely observed by American businessmen and engineers.

Colonel John Stevens was the first American railroad pioneer. He was a successful steamboat designer and operator. Despite this background he published a pamphlet, *Documents Tending to prove the Superior Advantages of Rail-Ways and Steam-Carriages over Canal Navigation*. Nothing came of his project to 'erect a railroad' between the Delaware and Raritan rivers, but in 1825 Stevens designed and built a small steam locomotive which ran on a circular track in one of the fields close to his New Jersey house. It was a narrow gauge line with a rack and pinion drive.

The American railroad system really began in 1828 and the next four or five years saw five or six small railroads which were the precursors of what was to become 250,000 miles of track criss-crossing a continent.

The Mohawk & Hudson line linked wharves at Albany and at Schenectady on the eponymous rivers. There was a stationary winding engine at each end to haul trains up to the high ground separating the two valleys. The line was built despite violent opposition from the supporters of the Erie Canal because the rails provided a 17-mile short cut to a 40-

mile stretch of the canal with its locks.

The Philadelphia & Columbia was built to link the port of Philadelphia with Columbia on the Susquehanna River, giving Philadelphia merchants access to Harrisburg and a large part of Western Pennsylvania. The railroad was founded by John Stevens' two sons and was incorporated under the title of the *Pennsylvania Railroad*. They also founded the Camden & Amboy Railroad that ran from Camden facing Philadelphia across the Delaware to Perth Amboy on the New Jersey shore opposite New York's Staten Island. Robert Stevens visited England and ordered iron rails to his own design and the *John Bull* from the Stephenson Locomotive Works. The *John Bull* arrived in parts and was assembled by Isaac Drips, a fitter working for Stevens. The locomotive derailed on the line's sharp curves and Drips designed and fitted pilot wheels at the front of the engine to help guide it round bends. He is also credited with devising the cowcatcher.

The merchants of Charleston, South Carolina, were aware of their northern competitors' interest in building railroads and they established the South Carolina Canal & Railroad Company to build a 136-mile line from the port of Charleston to the east shore of the Savannah River opposite Augusta, Georgia. It was the longest rail line in the world. The developers tried using horses and even sails and finally purchased the *Best Friend of Charleston* locomotive from the West Point Foundry in New York for the opening of the line in 1830. The following year the boiler exploded when the fireman held down the safety valve to save steam; the Company then instituted a policy of having a flat car loaded high with heavy cotton bales behind the locomotive to protect the passengers. The line also devised an innovative system for operating in darkness: the locomotive pushed a flat car with a sand bed and a blazing fire of pine logs.

The growth of population and towns in the Midwest exerted enormous pressure on the early American railroads to join the trading cities of the Atlantic coast – New York, Philadelphia, Boston and Baltimore – to the great river transportation system of the Midwest that finally leads to the Mississippi and the Gulf of Mexico. There was little incentive to build railroads between the coastal cities; sophisticated coastal shipping provided the necessary links and the coast is punctuated by a series of wide rivers that formed apparently insuperable challenges.

In the early years of the 19th century New York was easily the largest and most important centre of population and commerce; it was situated at the mouth of an important river to the interior and it was the only city to have a scheduled service across the Atlantic. In 1817 the decision was taken to dig the Erie Canal from Albany on the Hudson River to Buffalo on Lake Erie, which gave New York merchants access to the Great Lakes. The canal was 364 miles long and although there were no mountains or hills to cross, there was a difference of more than 500ft between the level of the river and Lake Erie. The canal was finally completed after eight years and it generated an enormous amount of profitable traffic.

East and Western Pennsylvania are divided by the Appalachian mountain chain. By the 1820s there were turnpikes through the state and across the mountains linking Philadelphia to Pittsburgh and the Ohio River. It needed four and often six draft horses to haul a four-ton load on a mountain road compared with one horse on the towpath hauling twenty tons along the Erie Canal. Clearly Philadelphia merchants were at a disadvantage and they started construction of a 394-mile canal to Pittsburgh. In fact the Main Line, as it came to be called, comprised lengths of canal, inclines with rail cars hauled by stationary engines and sections of railroad. Opened to Pittsburgh in 1834, the enterprise was never a commercial success; the changes from rail to wagon or water and the 174 locks made transportation expensive and laborious.

Although smaller than New York or Philadelphia, Baltimore had become bigger in terms of population and trade than Boston and Charleston together (even though Boston Brahmins called their city the 'hub of the universe'). The Federal Government paid for the construction of the National Road, a paved road completed in 1818 that ran from Baltimore to Wheeling, with its steamboat dock on the Ohio River. Soon, Philadelphia businesses were complaining about their loss of business to the National Road and Baltimore merchants crowed that their road was 200 miles shorter to the Midwest river system than New York's Erie Canal. However, despite being iced over a few months each year, the low freight rates on the Erie Canal maintained New York's premier position for the shipment of goods from the East Coast to the Midwest.

The Baltimore & Ohio (B&O) was the most significant of the early railroads. Significant because it was the beginning of the first attempt to build a railroad to link an Atlantic port to the Ohio River and the Mid West. On Independence Day 1828 the first stone of the Baltimore and Ohio Railroad (B&O) was laid by Charles Carroll, the only surviving signatory of the Declaration of Independence 52 years earlier. Ninety-year-old Carroll spoke: 'I consider this one of the most important acts of my life, second only to my signing the Declaration of Independence, if even it be second to that'. By 1830 the railway had been completed from Baltimore along the winding Patapsco River to Ellicotts Mills thirteen miles upstream, and the company published a timetable showing three daily passenger trains each way. The trains were pulled by horses but later in the year, Peter Cooper, a businessman from New York, designed and built the *Tom Thumb* for the run to Ellicotts Mills. The locomotive was largely built from scrap; it had a small vertical boiler with boiler tubes made from musket barrels. The locomotive convinced the B&O directors of the superiority of steam – even though the engine lost the legendary race with the grey mare on a run back from Ellicotts Mills. The B&O tracks reached the Maryland side of the Potomac river opposite Harpers Ferry in 1838. The B&O had also completed a branch south to Washington in 1835. The company bought an old boarding house as their first Washington terminal, possibly out of pique because they received no financial help from the District of Columbia.

The railroad promoters not only had to battle with the physical problems of high hills and narrow winding river valleys, but also with political railroad jealousy. The Virginia legislature imposed unacceptable conditions on the B&O for constructing their line. In 1845, the *American Railroad Journal* wrote: 'The chief obstacle which prevents the extension of the road is the unwillingness of Virginia to grant the right of way through her territory'. Finally the tracks reached Wheeling and the Ohio River in 1853.

Earlier, in 1850 the *Baltimore American* wrote: 'We see Philadelphia hurrying forward to reach Pittsburgh, and New York to reach Dunkirk (dock on Lake Erie), if they can, before we reach Wheeling; and we see Ohio and the states north and west of her, and indeed the whole Mississippi valley, stimulated to the highest enthusiasm in the railway race by that which is now running between the Atlantic Cities.' In fact, the combined tracks of ten different companies connected the Hudson River to Lake Erie in the 1840s and were merged in 1853 to become the New York Central; the Erie Railroad, opened in 1851, also crossed New York State to link the Hudson to Lake Erie. Even the Pennsylvania Railroad, a late starter, reached the Ohio River before the B&O, though it used stationary engines on one section to haul trains over some of the high mountain ridges. Later in the century two more rivals linked Atlantic ports across the Appalachians to the Mid West: the Chesapeake & Ohio with ocean dock facilities at Newport, Virginia and the Norfolk & Western joining the port of Norfolk to the Appalachian coal fields and to the Midwest.

❖

The American Civil War began in April 1861 and ended four years later. The twenty-three states and three border states of the Unionist North operated 20,000 miles of railroad and the eleven states of the Confederate South operated 9,000 miles of railroad.

Eighteen months before the outbreak of the war a B&O mail train was stopped just before crossing the Potomac at Harpers Ferry by John Brown leading an armed party of Abolitionists who had just captured the local army arsenal to hand out rifles to slaves. Later that day the train's conductor telegraphed the B&O management, 'Express train bound east under my charge was stopped this morning at Harpers Ferry by armed Abolitionists ... they say they have come to free the slaves ... and this the last train that shall pass this bridge whither east or west ...'. Management responded as only management could or can: 'Your despatch is evidently exaggerated and written under excitement ...'.

The loyalty of the Baltimore townspeople was split between North and South and at one point they even blocked rail tracks so that Union reinforcements had to travel from the north to their capital, Washington, by ferryboat. The main route west of the B&O tracks followed what was at times the border between the Union and the Confederates. B&O President John Garrett resembled the well-known Vicar of Bray; he could not decide if his business was a Northern or Southern railroad. It was staunchly

Southern after the battle of Balls Bluff, became a Northern railroad after Shiloh, Southern after the Union defeat at the second battle of Bull Run and then became Northern and stayed Northern when the Unionists repulsed General Lee at Antietam, and Garrett recognised it was in his company's interest to ship Appalachian coal to the Union factories.

The B&O and other lines such as the Louisville & Nashville were fought over back and forwards as each side lost or gained an advantage. Each time, the tracks were wrecked and bridges burned or destroyed. And each time the tracks were replaced and the bridges rebuilt. Union President Lincoln referred to the rebuilding of the bridges with nothing but the nearby trees as a miracle of 'beanpoles and cornstalks'.

The railroads were the only means of moving regiments to the front and getting supplies to the troops and there were amazing examples of rapid movement. The Confederates moved the whole of their 30,000 strong Army of Tennessee the 770 miles from Tupelo, Mississippi to Chattanooga along a single-track line in a week. The Unionists needed a roundabout route to avoid Confederate lines and moved 25,000 men and ten artillery batteries more than a thousand miles from the East Coast to Tennessee.

In 1864 General Sherman marched his army of 100,000 men to Atlanta, a city supplied from the north by a single-track railroad. As they retreated, the Confederates had a scorched earth policy of destroying tracks and bridges. As he advanced, Sherman had to rebuild the line that supplied his forces and maintain it against Confederate guerrilla attacks. The Confederates also destroyed the tracks and every railroad building in Atlanta, the rail hub of the South East; trains were set alight leaving only the wheels and axles resting on the rails. The final blow for Confederate General Robert E. Lee was when one of the last supply trains for his army was captured by General Custer as it arrived in Appomattox station to supply the hungry troops and Lee was obliged to surrender his army.

The best-known story of railroad derring-do during the Civil War was the Andrews Raid, better known as the *Great Locomotive Chase*. James Andrews, leading twenty Unionist men, intended to seize a train and put the line between Chattanooga and the Confederate supply base at Atlanta out of action. They stole the *General* locomotive and three boxcars from Big Shanty depot. They stopped frequently to try to tear up the track, cut telegraph wires and destroy bridges on their way toward Atlanta and gave instructions to oncoming trains to shunt into passing sidings because they were taking an express powder train to General Beauregard 'without a minute's delay'. Andrews and his men had been spotted making off with the *General* and were followed on foot and then on a pump trolley. The pursuers requisitioned the *Yonah*, an engine belonging to a local iron mine, to follow the *General*. It was blocked at the next station by another train. *Yonah* was abandoned and the locomotive from the train requisitioned to continue the chase. Because of damage to the track the pursuers were obliged to abandon the locomotive and commandeered the *Texas* from the next oncoming train. Each time the men on the *General* stopped to try and pull up a rail or damage a bridge, they heard the *Texas* almost on them. The *General* was running short of water when it crossed a covered wood bridge. Andrews piled up logs on the last car, detached it and set it alight on the bridge. However, the *Texas* came thundering through the smoke and flames. Andrews and his men abandoned the *General* after setting it in reverse in the path of the *Texas*, but the Confederate engine managed to move away in time and little damage was done to either engine.

❖

Victory in the 1848 Mexican–American war added California, Utah and Nevada to the territory of the United States and the discovery of gold the following year attracted enormous numbers of migrants to the west. There were three possibilities for reaching California: a 3,000-mile journey overland across the Mississippi and crossing the almost uninhabited plains and two mountain ranges; crossing the Isthmus of Panama with its dangers of disease and the problems of obtaining a passage in the Pacific; or there was the perilous 13,600-mile voyage around Cape Horn, a longer journey than from New York to Calcutta.

By 1860 Chicago was served by eleven railroad companies from the east and south and the Rock Island Railroad extended the tracks west to Council Bluffs on the River Missouri. The 1,800-mile region separating Council Bluffs from the Sacramento River and the Pacific Ocean was almost uninhabited apart from the mining villages in the foothills of the

Sierra Nevada, and Salt Lake City where Brigham Young settled with his Mormon followers in 1847. Although most of the land had been acquired from France in the 1813 Louisiana Land Purchase, there were no cities or population, no markets to serve and no sources of revenue along this vast distance; it was a commercial void. Whichever route was chosen for a transcontinental railroad from east to west, there were two mountain ranges and a desert without water and without trees and there were tribes of warrior Indians. Some merchants saw the rail line as a part of a high road for shipping goods between Europe and the Orient, but this hope ended with the opening of the Suez Canal. In fact there was little or no commercial incentive to build or operate a railroad to the Pacific. There were visionaries such as Congressman Thomas Hart Benton who said that emigrants would flock along the railroad,

> as pigeons to their roosts, tear open the bosom of the virgin soil, and spring into existence the long line of farms and houses of towns and villages, of orchards, fields and gardens, of churches and schoolhouses, of noisy shops, chattering mills and thundering forges ....

Not everyone thought the same. Senator Daniel Webster:

> What do we want with this region of savages and wild beasts, of deserts of shifting sands and whirlwinds of dust, of cactus and prairie dogs ... What could we do with the western coast line three thousand miles away, rockbound, cheerless and uninviting.

However, the political climate was beginning to put pressure on a link between east and west. The strains between the industrial north and what were to become the Confederate states of the south were starting to be felt and government recognised the need to cement a bond between the east and west of the nation.

Benton's son-in-law, John Frémont, had been a railroad surveyor in the east and, financed by St Louis businessmen, made a crude survey parallel to and about 300 miles south of the Emigrant Trail. He set off in the depth of winter to demonstrate that his proposed route was feasible throughout the seasons. After days of storms at 10,000ft in which ten of his men died and he had been rescued by friendly Indians, Frémont returned to St Louis and reported 'The result was entirely satisfactory ... it convinced me that neither snow nor winter and not the mountain ranges were obstacles...'. In 1853 Congress commissioned four surveys of possible alternative routes across the continent. The Secretary of War then recommended the southern route to Congress; however there was a problem, as part of the route crossed south of the Mexican border. Benton, who favoured a route based from St Louis, was scathing about the army surveyors: 'It takes a grand national school like West Point to put national roads outside of a country and leave the interior without one'.

The reports of the surveys were published but none was conclusive. They were read by, among others, Theodore Judah, an experienced railroad surveyor, who had just accepted a job to survey a route for the Sacramento Valley Railroad to link Sacramento with the Folsom gold mines on the western slopes of the Sierra Nevada. By the time Judah arrived the mines were worked out and the project abandoned and he found himself surveying wagon trails to the new Nevada silver mines. He became obsessed by the scheme for building a railroad over the Sierra Nevada and across the continent. He surveyed a route across the mountains, published a pamphlet, *A Practical Plan for Building the Pacific Railroad*, and lobbied in Washington and in San Francisco for support, but without success. Finally, he convinced four prosperous Sacramento shopkeepers, Leland Stanford, a wholesale grocer, Collis Huntington and Mark Hopkins, partners in a hardware store, and Charles Crocker, a dry goods merchant, to support the cost of a detailed survey for a route across the Sierra. They became known as the Big Four.

At about the same time that Judah was making his initial survey in California, Grenville Dodge was working on a survey for the Illinois Central where he met and gained the confidence of one Abraham Lincoln, the company's attorney. He then went to work for the Rock Island line where he met Dr Thomas Durant, a sharp, fast-moving railroad promoter and entrepreneur who commissioned him to do a westward survey from Council Bluffs, Iowa, across the Missouri, and along the Platte river basin west to the Rockies.

The Civil War had begun and the need for the rail link joining east and west had become urgent. In 1862 President Abraham Lincoln signed the

Pacific Railroad Act confirming the nation's support for the transcontinental railroad. A year later, the President defined the eastern terminus, 'the City of Omaha'.

Durant and his partners set up the Union Pacific (UP) to build the line from Omaha, across the Great Plains and over the Rockies to join the Central Pacific (CP) in Utah. The Big Four established the CP to build and operate the line from Sacramento over the ferociously steep Sierra Nevada and across the Nevada plateau to Utah. The deal was this: the government would give the UP and the CP ten miles of land on either side of its tracks in alternate sections of ten miles. In addition it would provide loans to pay for the construction: $16,000 a mile across the Plains, $32,000 through the Great Basin and $48,000 across the Rockies and the Sierra. The companies also negotiated favourable rates for transporting mail, government supplies and troops.

Building the CP and UP lines was a heroic nightmare. Not only were there the massive problems of organising equipment and materials and constructing the line through high mountain ranges and across deserts but both companies were always desperate for cash to meet their bills and payrolls. The weather was another frightful problem. The 1866–67 winter was the most severe in living memory; temperatures dropped to -40°F, water froze in locomotive boilers, the Missouri remained frozen to the end of March and as much as forty feet of snow blocked the passes in the Sierras. The advance surveyors were explorers; they determined the route of the track through uninhabited deserts and across high and dangerous mountains. Many died in accidents or from exposure in extreme weather conditions and there was very great privation and suffering for the construction workers. Almost all the work was manual: the steam shovel did not exist. Much of it was dangerous; working in deep snow, cutting trees to make bridge trestles or sleepers, gangs of men working together to move heavy rocks or lay rails and men using black powder to blast cuttings and tunnels. Thousands lost their lives; human lives were too cheap to count.

Neither of the railroad companies was able to attract investors and each finally solved the problem by establishing a separate contracting company; these construction companies would bill the railroad companies at an inflated price for the miles of track that had been built, and the investors

113

would have a high return. The distribution of the stock and profits of the UP construction company, the Credit Mobilier, resulted in a major financial scandal.

There were enormous problems facing the construction of the CP from the West Coast. Rails, locomotives and even hand shovels were imported round Cape Horn from the industrial cities of the east. Of the California Big Four, Stanford was the figurehead of the company and became Governor of California, Hopkins masterminded the finances and Crocker managed the construction of the great enterprise. Huntington's life was split between Boston, New York and Washington, raising money, arranging payments, shipping supplies and making friends in Congress. At the beginning, the CP headquarters and offices were on the first floor of the Huntington & Hopkins hardware store. The Big Four had another problem, a lack of workers. There were not enough people living in California to supply the thousands of men needed for the CP construction and most of the arriving immigrants came only to work in the gold and silver mines. Crocker was impressed with the quality of their Chinese workmen; they were mainly second-generation Americans who were well organised and hardworking. The Big Four then recruited thousands of workers from China to come to California and build the line to Utah. The route east from Sacramento left the Sacramento River valley to enter the foothills of the Sierra Nevada and climbed more than 7,000 feet to Summit Tunnel, which had to be bored through granite. The Chinese worked three shifts; it took four eight-hour shifts for a crew to drill a hole deep enough for the black blasting powder charge. The drill bits were used up so quickly that Huntington had to order them in 100-ton shipments. Progress was slow, less than a foot a day on each face and the tunnel was 1,660ft long. Progress on the line up to Summit was at a snail's pace; nearly fifty miles of snow-sheds had to be built to prevent the line becoming blocked and at one time half the labour force, several thousand men, were clearing snow so that the other half could lay track.

Start-up and progress was slower on the UP until an impatient President Lincoln asked Congressman Oakes Ames to solve the problems of animating the company. Ames distributed shares to his friends in Congress who then passed a second Pacific Railroad Act that included advancing payment for construcion and doubling the size of the land grants. This finally animated the promoters of the UP. Following his promotion to General in the Civil War and 'clearing' Indians from the Great Plains, Grenville Dodge joined the UP as chief engineer. The UP line followed the Platte river valley west across Nebraska. It passed the last farm 132 miles west of Omaha; there were no settlements between it and Salt Lake City. When the UP line reached a point 247 miles west from Omaha, the 100th meridian, Dr. Durant, the UP's leading backer, arranged for a party of financiers, senators, supporters and the press to inspect progress. The luxury train took the visitors to the end of the line where tents had been pitched round an enormous campfire. Half way through the feasting a party of Pawnee Indians wearing war paint whooped through the party, terrifying the distinguished visitors; it was of course a put-on show.

In fact the Cheyenne Indians did cause havoc with the progress of the line, which they rightly regarded as an invasion of their land. Further west there were battles and more carnage with the Sioux. The huge herds of Great Plains buffalo were decimated to feed the thousands of construction workers. The line crossed into the Wyoming Territory and climbed into the Black Hills and over the 8,242-ft Sherman Hill (named by Dodge after his friend General Sherman) to Laramie, a town laid out by Dodge, and across the Great Basin; one of Dodge's surveyors said the dried creeks looked like 'shallow graves of deceased rivers'. The line crossed an alkali desert; one writer said he felt like 'a cockroach struggling through a flour barrel'.

The UP construction workers lived in large rickety three-storey matchwood dorm railcars, each housing several hundred men and poised unevenly in a series of passing sidings. The men were mainly Irish immigrants and they made whoopee in the honky-tonks of the clapboard shanty towns that moved forward with the advance of the construction gangs. One writer described one of the shanty towns at the end of the line as

> by day disgusting, by night dangerous, almost everybody dirty, many filthy, and with the marks of the lowest vice; averaging a murder a day; gambling, drinking, hurdy-gurdy dancing and the vilest of sexual commerce ... a congregation of scum.

There was a need for speed and for the tracks to cover as great a distance as possible to qualify for a maximum amount of government subsidies and land at the expense of the CP. The CP also wanted to cover as many miles as possible for the same reason. Once on the empty Nevada plateau the CP crews constructed the line at the rate of four miles a day. An intense rivalry between the two companies developed as they reached the borders of Utah and finally Congress designated Promontory Summit, Utah, as the meeting point of the tracks of the two companies.

The ceremony of driving-in the last spike of the transcontinental railway was planned for 8th May 1869 but took place on the 10th May because the train with Dr Durant was delayed. He telegraphed to say the delay was caused by a track washout in Wyoming; in fact Durant was kidnapped by the line's tie cutters demanding unpaid wages. On the morning of the ceremony, Durant and Stanford quarrelled over who should have the honour of hitting the ceremonial gold spike. At noon Durant hit the spike, then Stanford missed it with his swing. The CP and UP enginemen pulled on their whistles, everyone yelled and the telegraph operators informed the world that the last spike of the transcontinental railroad had been driven in and the road was open for business.

Later the two companies settled on Ogden, east of Promontory, as their meeting point. The UP had laid 1,038 miles of track and the CP 742 miles. In November the line from Sacramento to Oakland with its San Francisco ferry was opened. The bridge across the Missouri from Council Bluffs to Omaha was opened in 1877; a continuous track of rails stretched across the continent from the Atlantic to the Pacific.

The four Sacramento businessmen became fabulously rich. Crocker went on to build railroads for the Southern Pacific and a line north to Portland. Huntington also stayed in railroads, buying, selling and amalgamating. Hopkins faded into wealthy obscurity, a luxury San Francisco hotel named after him as his only memorial. Leland Stanford became a Senator and founded Leland Stanford Junior University in memory of his son, who died young. Doctor Durant, who probably made the largest fortune of all from the great enterprise, lost most of his money in the 1873 Panic and in a number of unsuccessful mining enterprises. Oakes Ames was ruined by the Credit Mobilier scandal and General

Grenville Dodge retired to live in comfort in Council Bluffs and was reported to be the richest man in Iowa.

❖

Canada's first steam railway, opened in 1836, provided transportation between the St Lawrence and Richelieu rivers. By 1860 there was nearly 2,000 miles of track in eastern Canada. Few commercial thoughts were fixed on making a link to the Pacific on the far western horizon of the nation. However in the late 1860s there seemed urgent political reasons for building a 3,000-mile railway to link British Columbia to eastern Canada. In 1867, only some 20 years after acquiring California from Spain, the United States purchased Alaska from Russia and there seemed a real possibility that British Columbia might align itself with the Pacific States of the USA. However the province joined Canada in 1871 and Sir John Macdonald, Canada's first Prime Minister, promised to build a railway across the continent. Following the pattern south of the border the government contributed by providing land grants. However, much of the prairie appeared so dry and barren that it was considered worthless; in Alberta it was said there were 'not enough revenues to pay for axle grease from Medicine Hat to Calgary'.

The railway builders faced difficult geographic problems in addition to the problems of the immense length of the line. The line was laid to the north of Lakes Huron and Superior across the Canadian Shield, across the prairies to the Rockies and then over the high Selkirk mountains to the Pacific. The Canadian Shield is a huge undulating granite shelf perforated by lakes, muskeg and seemingly bottomless sinkholes and it was necessary to blast through hard rock for long distances. Finally a route across the mountains was agreed; the line was to climb up over three high summits, Kicking Horse, Rogers and Eagle Passes. The route over the Rogers Pass was discovered by Major 'Hells Bells' Rogers after an 18-month search. Thirty-eight men in the survey teams died before the route was defined. Construction of the railroad went through all the inevitable financial and political difficulties that affect public–private partnerships, but finally the Canadian Pacific Railway Company was incorporated in 1881. The following year the company hired a professional railroad man to mastermind the project. William Van Horne started his railroad life as a telegraph operator on the Illinois Central and rose through the ranks of a number of railroad companies to take charge and make a success of this great project.

The difficulties were enormous: 12,000 men were needed to build the line over Kicking Horse Pass. In the Selkirks, workmen had to be winched to the workings, hard rock limited tunnelling progress to six feet a day. James Ross, the mountain division construction superintendent wrote to Van Horne,

> ... snow slides on the Selkirks are much more serious than I anticipated and I think are quite beyond your ideas of their magnitude and of the danger to the line ... the men are frightened. Seven have already been buried in different slides...

The company ran out of money when construction was almost complete. Van Horne telegraphed the chairman 'Have no means of paying wages, pay-car can't be sent out ...'. Fortuitously for the Canadian Pacific Railway there was a second Riel Rebellion in Manitoba and the government was able to get troops to the trouble within a week – it had taken troops three months to reach the same spot 15 years earlier and government and opposition saw the value of the line to the nation. The government immediately passed a bill to provide the necessary funding. The east and west tracks met at Craigellachie on the Eagle Pass in November 1885; 18 months later through trains were running the 2,920 miles from Montreal to Vancouver. The westbound train was known as the Pacific Express and the eastbound as the Atlantic Express.

Other railroads were built across the continent to compete against the Canadian Pacific Railway. The Canadian Northern, opened in 1915, took a northerly route across the mountains and turned south to Vancouver through the Fraser River Canyon. The Grand Trunk Pacific built its line across the continent to Prince Rupert, a port 470 miles north of Vancouver, with the shortest sea route to the Orient. Both railways ran into difficulty and in 1923 they were amalgamated with a number of other lines into the publicly owned Canadian National Railway.

❖

The prosperity of the United States after the Civil War, combined with the opening up of the West, stimulated railroad construction across the country. Some of the railroads in the southern states had been constructed with different gauge rails; these lines were converted to the standard 4ft 8½-inch gauge. Shortly after the war, lines including the Denver & Rio Grande, the Texas & Pacific, the Santa Fe and the Southern Pacific were completed. Some companies were incorporated hardly knowing where their tracks would terminate. Cyrus Holliday drafted the charter of his railroad to run from Atchison through Topeka 'to such a point on the Southern and Western boundary in the direction of Santa Fe as may be suitable and convenient ...'. In 1883, the second transcontinental line, the Northern Pacific, was completed. Sherman called the land it crossed 'as bad as God ever made' and the land grant was increased to 25,600 acres per mile to attract investors. Jay Cooke's company, which had helped fund the Union in the Civil War, was the principal promoter of the Northern Pacific; the company's agents advertised Montana as having a mild climate which 'compared favourably with Paris or Venice' and the line became known 'Jay Cooke's Banana Belt'. Cooke's firm went bankrupt in 1873, its demise precipitating a major crisis that caused the failure of dozens of small lines and even some of the major ones. Nonetheless only ten years after the completion of the Northern Pacific there were five lines linking the Mid West or the Mississippi to the Pacific.

It took a very particular type of man to commit himself and his money to constructing a new railroad. Construction costs were astronomic, complex organisation was needed to marshal the necessary materials and thousands of workmen, especially through mountain country or across great rivers. The returns were long-term and despite all the lawyers' work on charters and influence in state legislatures, any successful line would probably face competition. As a result, many promoters tried to make money out of construction or elaborate manipulation, sometimes amounting to flagrant fraud. There was great opportunity: Charles Dow, one of the founders of the Dow Jones Industrial Average, said the railroads were 'the greatest speculative market'. However, the result of all the wheeling and dealing was a railroad system serving the nation. A contemporary railroad official stated 'the simple truth was that through its energetic railroad development, the country was producing real wealth as no country ever produced before.'

One of the more flagrant examples of commercial skulduggery came as a result of the rivalry between the Erie and its competitor, Commodore Vanderbilt's New York Central line. The Erie was completed from the New Jersey Atlantic coast to Buffalo in 1851 and then suffered every misfortune – strikes, floods, train wrecks – finally being purchased by the 'Erie Ring' led by Daniel Drew, Jim Fisk and Jay 'I don't build railroads, I buy them' Gould.

Vanderbilt had made millions with his market manipulations to amalgamate a series of railroads into the New York Central and he used them to try to buy the Erie. He bought all the available Erie stock but there was always more stock for sale. He got a tame judge to issue an injunction to stop any further stock issues. The Erie Ring, joined by the notorious William Tweed, the Tammany boss, got their tame judge to issue a counter injunction; Vanderbilt's judge ignored it and issued a warrant for the arrest of Drew, Fisk and Gould. When they learned of their intended arrest, they grabbed the company books, six million in cash and, escorted by more than 100 bodyguards, made it to the ferry-slip, where the bodyguards overwhelmed the judge's posse of sheriffs and the trio reached New Jersey where the New York judge had no jurisdiction. They holed up in the Taylor Hotel which Fisk renamed Fort Taylor. Surrounded by their bodyguards they fired off injunctions and court orders preventing Vanderbilt from appointing a receiver. Finally, Gould went to Albany, the New York State Capital, with half a million dollars in his suitcase. He was put in the charge of a sheriff who sat outside a hotel room with Gould inside, much too ill to see anyone. However, someone looking rather like Gould was seen tiptoeing around the State Senate 'with a suitcase', seeking confirmation of the legality of the issues of Erie stock. Vanderbilt tried commercial as well as legal means to acquire the Erie; he lowered freight rates to an absurdly low level to steal Erie customers. Fisk made the most of Vanderbilt's generosity and responded by having his agents buy all the cattle they could find and ship them on the New York Central to New York

City at one dollar a head.

Eventually Vanderbilt and the Ring made peace. Then Gould and Fisk turned on Drew and bankrupted him by issuing more dubious stock and bonds and making more bribes. The Erie moved its office into an ornate suite in an opera house where Jim Fisk's girlfriend, the Enchantress, performed. Gould was persuaded to leave the Erie when he was told that his departure would raise the price of the stock; he bought heavily and resigned. He continued wheeling and dealing and even brought the Union Pacific to its knees; he became its president in 1874 and went on to acquire more than 8,000 miles of railroad lines in the southwest and even the New York City elevated railways. After a coup that ruined thousands he was reported as saying 'Nothing is lost save honour'. He died a very rich man. 'Jubilee Jim Fisk, Prince of The Erie' was shot by a rival for the favours of the Enchantress. He was given a rascal's magnificent send-off with a parade of 200 bandsmen in full regalia of the Ninth Regiment, into which he had bought his way, marching behind 'Colonel' Fisk's riderless horse. Commodore Vanderbilt died in 1877; his wife played the organ at his deathbed and around him the family sang his favourite hymn 'Come all ye sinners, poor and needy'. He left about 100 million dollars.

On a few occasions commercial rivalry between companies developed into punch-ups. The Royal George Gorge on the Arkansas River was the only possible route for a railroad track to reach the rich pickings of the Leadville silver mines in Colorado. The gorge is very narrow with only sufficient space for one track beside the river and it is very deep; today it is spanned by the world's highest suspension bridge. In 1878 the Rio Grande were about to start a survey only to find that their Santa Fe rival had already begun construction along the only possible route. There was a series of stand-offs and attempts at settling their differences in the Colorado courts. Finally war broke out; a trainload of Rio Grande toughs killed and wounded some Santa Fe men. The Sante Fe hired the celebrated Marshal 'Bat' Masterson and his deputies from Dodge City to fight their corner. A bag of Rio Grande money persuaded the gun-toters to melt away. After more guerrilla warfare, the Supreme Court gave a ruling: the two companies were to share the line with the Colorado & Southern.

The Credit Mobilier scandal was the greatest and best-known railroad scam of them all. President Lincoln had become impatient with the Union Pacific's lack of progress with construction of their end of the transcontinental line and called in Massachusetts Congressman Oakes Ames, saying 'Ames, take hold of this … that road must be built, and you are the only man to do it.' Ames put a large part of his fortune and money from Boston financial houses into the Credit Mobilier. The Credit Mobilier billed the Union Pacific for track it had built, and in a few instances for track it had not built, at very inflated prices; the stockholders benefited from the huge difference between the actual and the billed construction cost. After four years Credit Mobilier declared dividends of almost 100%. It was not surprising that such enormous riches led to a quarrel[1] between Ames and Durant. The quarrel went to court and the scam became public knowledge; two separate Congressional Committees were appointed. They found that Ames had distributed Credit Mobilier stock to fellow Congressmen; the Vice President and even President Grant were implicated. Ames said in his defence 'we want more friends in Congress'; together with others, he was censured by Congress and he died a few months later.

Out west in Sacramento, the CP management had established a similar arrangement and called it the Contract & Finance Company[2]. It too was investigated by Congress and Collis Huntington was called to testify. He said that an unfortunate fire had gutted the Contract & Finance Company headquarters and destroyed all its books only a few months previously. No crimes were proved but Congress concluded that the Big Four CP entrepreneurs had trousered $63 million, that they owned most of the CP capital stock and that they controlled nine million acres of land granted by the government.

The climate of fraud and double-dealing spread north of the border to Canada. Sir John Macdonald, the Prime Minister, appointed a millionaire businessman, Sir Hugh Allan, to head up the consortium to build Canada's first transcontinental railway that later became the Canadian Pacific.

---

1. The scandal formed the basis of the plot of Anthony Trollope's novel *The Way We Live Now*.

2. It even falsified a surveyor's report and extended the Sierra Nevada several miles westward to increase the federal subsidy.

However, Allan was already a secret partner of the owners of the Northern Pacific south of the border. They were trying to delay construction of the Canadian line so that they could build a spur from their line to Canada to provide a ready-made connection to the Pacific coast. After endless toing and froing Allan deserted his furious American partners. The case became public knowledge and it emerged that Allan had provided funds for Macdonald's 1872 election campaign, possibly in return for a promise of appointing him president of the railroad company; the scandal toppled Macdonald's government.

❖

Henry Flagler and John Rockefeller were the architects of the Standard Oil monopoly. Flagler owned more than 15% of the linked series of organisations and became President of the Standard Oil Company of New Jersey. By middle age he was fabulously rich.

Florida, a peninsula of sandbank, swamp and tropical forest, was purchased from Spain for $5 million in 1822 and became a state in 1845. Key West, with the finest deep water harbour south of Virginia, had the largest population in Florida but it was an island more than 100 miles from the mainland. In the 1880s the principal east coast town between Jacksonville, situated at the extreme north, and Key West was the resort town of St Augustine with 2,300 inhabitants. In 1883 Henry Flagler and his second wife spent their honeymoon in St Augustine and two years later he decided to build an enormous luxury hotel there. He bought the Jacksonville, St Augustine & Halifax River Railroad, converted the track to standard gauge, and extended the railroad to run into Jacksonville. Thus began Henry Flagler's great Florida adventure.

He extended his railroad south to Daytona Beach in 1890 and the population jumped from fewer than 100 to more than 2,000. By 1895 Flagler had extended his line, now called the Florida East Coast Railway Company, to West Palm Beach. The same year he decided to continue building the track south to Biscayne Bay and Miami, which was incorporated as a city in 1896. Flagler tried to dredge the port to dock ocean going ships but his attempts failed and this was the main reason for his continuing the line from Miami across the ocean and the Florida Keys to Key West. The first through train from New York arrived in Key West in January 1912 with the Flagler family on board. The link between the mainland and Key West had been achieved at enormous cost both in lives and money.

Flagler's great Florida enterprise was a combination of business and philanthropy. He used his huge fortune to build churches, schools, city halls and hospitals and he twice provided new seed to the orange growers when abnormal frosts killed their trees. When he was asked about his motive for building the railroad and his other developments in Florida, Flagler replied 'I believe this state is the easiest place for many men to gain a living. I do not believe anyone else will develop it if I do not … I hope to live long enough to prove I am a good businessman by getting a dividend on my investment.' Flagler's single-handed enterprise, vision and courage were largely responsible for developing Florida as a winter resort state and for establishing its citrus fruit industry. Flagler also saw Key West with its deep harbour as an important coaling and revictualling centre for American navy ships that would need to be stationed nearby to safeguard the freedom of the Panama Canal. The railroad across the sea to Key West remained in service for twenty-three years; in 1935 a hurricane washed out many of the bridges and embankments and they later became a part of the foundation of US Highway 1, running from Maine to Key West, from the extreme north east of the nation to its most southerly point.

❖

In 1843 Congress funded the installation of a telegraph line running beside the B&O tracks from Baltimore to the Capitol in Washington. The artist turned inventor Samuel Morse transmitted the first long distance message, 'What hath God wrought!', the following year. British and other European railways made immediate use of the telegraph for running their rail systems but it was not until 1857 that the first American company, the New York & Erie, made use of the telegraph for signalling and train control. The telegraph companies installed their cross-country lines on railroad rights-of-way and granted the use of some of the lines to the rail companies. The telegraph provided the communication system that enabled railways to increase the density of traffic and increase profitability.

One of the most important advances in railway safety and operation was George Westinghouse's invention of the air brake in 1869. Westinghouse's system stored compressed air in a cylinder under each car; reducing the pressure released the brakes and a breakaway car would sever the airline and automatically apply the brakes. The railroad tycoons were hard to convince. When Westinghouse tackled Vanderbilt, the Commodore responded 'Do you pretend to tell me that you could stop trains with wind?' Not only did the continuous airbrake make a major contribution to safety, but it also enabled railroads to run faster and heavier trains.

The next step forward was in passenger comfort. George Pullman converted some passenger cars on the Chicago & Alton into sleeping cars; he then built the luxury *Pioneer* car and founded the Pullman Palace Car Company in 1867. He went on to build hotel cars, smoking-lounge cars, cars with card rooms and libraries, a barber's shop on rails and a wide variety of extravagantly decorated cars for private customers. As the business grew, Pullman established a huge works and a model village for his workpeople at Pullman, Illinois and ran the business on feudal rather than paternalistic lines with consequent labour unrest. Pullman's great competitor was Webster Wagner who founded the Wagner Palace Car Company. Wagner negotiated to use a Pullman patent for a folding berth seat cushion arrangement. The terms of the contract were supposedly broken and resulted in endless litigation that continued even after Wagner's death in a rail accident in one of his own sleeping cars.

Fresh problems arose as the rails were extended over longer distances from east to west. Philadelphia time was five minutes different from New York and there was a half hour difference between Pittsburgh and Chicago. Train scheduling became a nightmare for planners and despatchers. There are a number of versions of the origin of the vertical time zones that are now standard across the nation; Professor Dowd of Temple Grove Seminary for Young Ladies at the fashionable resort of Saratoga Springs was reputed to have put forward the original proposal, which became the standard for the railroad industry in 1883. Congress made it official nationwide in 1915.

The problems of running and scheduling trains increased as the density of traffic grew. The typewriter and carbon paper, introduced in the early 1880s, came just in time. The company could type up a schedule each week setting out what train was travelling in what direction at what time and send the copies to stations along the line.

Commentators and even officialdom recognised the carnage caused by the railroads. Washouts, subsidence in the spring thaws, bridge collapses, derailments, collisions, equipment failure and of course human error resulted in the deaths of hundreds of passengers each year of the second half of the 19th century. When a train was wrecked, the wooden passenger cars telescoped and the coal-heating fires scattered the red-hot coal and ignited an inferno. Forty-two passengers lost their lives in the Angola Horror, 80 died in the Ashtabula Bridge Disaster, 82 were killed in the Chatsworth Wreck, and 64 members of the Total Abstinence Union lost their lives in another disaster. These examples were just some of the more widely reported wrecks out of the many that took place throughout the nation. Supposedly four railroad employees lost their lives for each passenger who died and 16,000 rail workers died between 1888 and 1894 in addition to a much greater number who were maimed. Before automatic braking, trains travelled with brakemen to slow the train on downward grades. On freight trains, brakemen ran along roof walks and jumped from roof to roof of the line of boxcars, cranking closed the brake hand wheel that protruded above the roof at the end of each car. It was a perilous job especially in freezing weather and there were many fatalities. Switchman was another dangerous job, again with many fatalities and it left thousands of men with severed limbs. Cars in the earliest trains were coupled together with a chain and hook. This was replaced by a link and pin coupling; the switchman had to stand between cars as one was being backed to the other, guide the link on one car into the socket of the other and drop in a heavy locking pin. The industry finally designed an automatic coupling that snapped closed as the two halves of the coupling came in contact. The *Railway Trainman* magazine carried advertisements for manufacturers of artificial limbs; one read, 'Artificial legs warranted not to chafe stump.' In 1893, after intense lobbying led by the Reverend Lorenzo Coffin, Congress passed the Railroad Safety Appliance Act, which included a requirement making automatic couplers and air brakes mandatory. In 1901, railroads were required to report all collisions and derailments to the Interstate Commerce Commission; nine years later the ICC required reports on any injuries to passengers or employees.

❖

In contrast to England, few of the early railroads, apart from some of the very large companies, built their own locomotives. Engineering firms in the North-East built good and sound engines that combined the manufacturers' experience with their customers' requirements.

Matthias Baldwin, founder of the Baldwin locomotive works in Philadelphia, started as a jeweller's apprentice and then entered into a partnership to make presses and engraved cylinders for textile printing. The firm expanded and Baldwin designed and built a stationary steam engine to provide power for the works. Baldwin then helped to assemble a Robert Stephenson *Planet*-class locomotive for a Philadelphia company and in 1831 built *Old Ironsides* for another local rail company. This was the beginning of the firm that was to build a third of all the steam locomotives in the United States and sell locomotives around the world; in 1899 it even sold 70 locomotives to customers in England.

In 1907, the company's peak year, 18,000 men produced 2,700 steam locomotives. Its main rival, Alco, the American Locomotive Company, was a consolidation of nine US and Canadian locomotive builders that by the booming 1920s had captured half the American market. In 1933, during the Great Depression, Baldwin sold only 23 locomotives, the lowest number since 1848. Demand increased in World War II and in 1950 Baldwin merged with Lima-Hamilton, the number three steam locomotive builder, and the combined firm finally launched a line of diesel locomotives. But the company entered this new technical world too late and it shipped its last locomotive in 1956, 125 years after the first. Alco continued longer: it had an agreement with General Electric and produced a successful line of diesel switchers. Its *244* model for mainline work was a failure and despite a later and more successful model, the last locomotive rolled out of Alco's Schenectady works in 1969.

The Electro-Motive Company built its first rail auto-car in 1924 and in 1930 the company became a division of General Motors. When General Motors made the decision to manufacture diesel locomotives they established 'one fundamental policy ... Electro-Motive Corporation will build a standardised product and not undertake to build to the many different standards and specifications on which each railroad demands to purchase'. This compared with Baldwin's 1915 catalogue offering 492 different locomotive varieties and even to manufacture individual engines to customers' designs. EMD, as it came to be called, started making diesel switchers or shunting engines and in 1934 their engines powered the Burlington *Pioneer Zephyr*, which completed the 1,015-mile Denver-Chicago run in under 14 hours. This success gave GM[3] the confidence to build a green-field plant near Chicago to manufacture complete locomotives rather than locomotive power units; the first locomotive from the new works was delivered in 1936. By 1938 EMD diesel locomotives were powering some of the best-known trains including the *Wabash Cannonball*, the Illinois Central's *City of New Orleans* and the Seaboard's *Orange Blossom Special*. The diesel's improvement in efficiency and service availability was so great that railroads found it necessary to purchase only one diesel locomotive to replace two steamers.

The 1930s were the era of rural electrification and projects such as the Tennessee Valley Authority; low cost power for everyone everywhere. However the railroads found it difficult to take advantage of this new era; it was the Depression, there was not the will to provide the enormous investment required for electrification over very long distances and the majority of railroad management and staff were still wedded to the world of steam: it worked well enough and it was understood. After World War II efficient, reliable diesel locomotives became available and, apart from the North-East and some commuter lines, diesel traction became almost universal on the rails of North America.

Despite the Depression, the 1930s were the first decade of the industrial designer and of streamlining, the search for the *Ideal Form*. The Douglas

---

3. The General Electric Company also started building diesel electric locomotives and overtook GM's EMD in 1983.

DC-3 aeroplane, Buckminster Fuller's *Dymaxion* designs, cars such as the Chrysler *Airflow* and Porsche's *Volkswagen*, and Captain Buck Rogers' spaceships were all landmarks of the decade that culminated in the 1939 New York World's Fair *Building the World of Tomorrow*. American railroads followed the fashion by streamlining their crack express trains, adding glamour to comfort. Surprisingly, the first design for a streamlined train came in 1865 with the Rev. Samuel Calthrop's design of steam engine, tender and passenger car in a single tapered housing. He recognised the need for a tapered rear end to 'overcome the chief part of the resistance arising from the drag of the air behind the rear car in trains as ordinarily constructed'.

Union Pacific's 1934 *City of Salina* supplied by the Pullman Car Company and powered by a 600hp EMD diesel was the first streamlined diesel-powered passenger train to enter service and was promoted as 'Tomorrow's Train, Today!' The three-unit train carrying 156 passengers and a kitchen buffet was painted brilliant yellow with a brown roof and wheel skirting. The Chicago, Burlington & Quincy's *Zephyr* started service shortly after and on its inaugural run departed from Denver at dawn and arrived in Chicago at dusk. Unlike the brightly painted UP train, the Zephyr exterior was polished stainless steel with corrugated lower panels. The two trains, one bullet-shaped and the other with a front end shaped like a backward sloping ship's prow set the fashion for American streamlined locomotives for the next years.

A lot of ancillary equipment, air-pumps, feed-water heaters and sand domes were attached to the exterior of steam locomotives. Norman Zapf, a student, wrote his engineering thesis on the advantage of streamlining a Hudson-type locomotive. His calculations showed that an effectively streamlined engine would require 350hp less than a conventional locomotive at 75mph. In 1934 Zapf's scheme was largely incorporated in the New York Central's *Commodore Vanderbilt*, a Hudson-type locomotive that was modified with Zephyr-type shrouding to become the first streamlined steam locomotive in America. A year later the Milwaukee Road introduced their streamlined steam-hauled *Hiawathas*, named after Longfellow's 'swift of foot' Indian who could run faster than his own arrow. The Zephyr-shaped *Hiawathas* hauled nine passenger car trains at speeds up to 100mph to compete against the Burlington *Zephyrs*. They were steam-powered because sufficiently powerful diesels were not yet available to power the *Hiawatha* train combination of speed and weight. In 1940 the Seaboard line absurdly fitted streamlining to some locomotives which had been in operation since 1913; their Zephyr-type housings were painted creamy yellow and olive green with an orange waistband.

The Pennsylvania Railroad and the New York Central were traditional rivals in their 950-mile New York-Chicago service, in much the same way as the British LMS and LNER were rivals on their 400-mile west and east coast routes from London to Scotland. In British schoolboy eyes, Raymond Loewy working for the Pennsy and Henry Dreyfuss for the NYC might have been comparable to Stanier of the LMS and Gresley of the LNER. In 1938 the Pennsylvania produced Loewy's astonishing 140-foot long S-1 locomotive with a bullet nose and a protruding horizontal band housing the headlight. A few years later he designed its even larger and longer successor, the T-1 with its hideously menacing and marvellous shark's head front-end. These big locomotives hauled high-speed trains such as the *Broadway Limited* east out of Chicago through Indiana and Ohio on the first leg of their journey to New York; the T-1 wheelbase was too long for running on the curving lines through the Appalachians.

Henry Dreyfuss is famous for his streamlined *Twentieth Century Limited* trains. The Hudson type locomotive had a bullet shaped nose with a vertical ridge supporting the central headlamp, known as the 'Trojan helmet' look; the engine and the whole train were painted a shining grey with horizontal silver and white bands, a climax of chic and glamour for the railroad train. The glory of crack *Twentieth Century Limited* travel was a little tarnished as, like all NYC trains until 1937, its speed was limited to a brisk walking pace as it traversed Syracuse, NY because the tracks were laid along the city's main thoroughfare.

This was the era when some of the main railroads gave names to their trains. The Atlantic Coast Line ran *Champions* south to Florida which was also served by *Dixies* from Chicago and the Midwest. The Missouri Pacific ran *Eagles* from St Louis to Texas; the Atchison Topeka and Santa Fe ran *Chiefs* from Chicago to the west, the best-known, the *Super Chief*, covering the 2,223 miles between Chicago and Los Angeles. *Hiawathas* ran from Chicago to Minneapolis, *Zephyrs* from Chicago to Denver and on to California and *Rockets*, including the *Corn Belt Rocket* and the *Choctaw Rocket*, ran south and west from Chicago.

❖

In the last quarter of the 19th century the proprietors of the railroad companies had a very clear idea of the relationship between capital and labour. Workers' wages had been cut as a way out of a succession of crises. In 1877 four of the big eastern railroads enforced a 10% cut in wages while continuing to pay stockholders 10% in dividends. It was the second cut in eight months on the B&O and its workers went on strike; there was violence at Wheeling and the dispute spread to other lines; freight and passenger services in the North-East came to a standstill for ten days. The strike culminated with a battle in a Pittsburgh rail yard where the strikers faced the local militia; 24 people were killed, hundreds wounded, buildings burnt, 100 locomotives and 2,000 freight cars wrecked. Labour unrest continued in the railroads and 17 years later there was another depression; George Pullman tried to maintain profits by a 19% wage reduction in his Chicago plant. A committee of workmen met with him to agree a way of arbitration. 'Nothing to arbitrate', he responded and sacked three of the committee members. This led to a strike that spread to some of the nearby railroads and President Cleveland sent in federal troops, saying 'If it takes the entire army and navy of the United States to deliver a postal card to Chicago, that card will be delivered.' There was rioting and shooting; 12 men were killed and hundreds hurt.

Needless to say, the railroads became unpopular with authority; there was a combination of strikes, business failures, fraud, company amalgamations and high rates for freight shipments that incensed farmers and industry. Farmers in the prairies living far from towns and markets for their crops were outraged by the shipping charges. They formed Granges or associations to lobby the state legislatures for reasonable rates. One of the members, Shelby Cullom, became a senator and helped establish the Interstate Commerce Commission to regulate the railroads and the 1903 Elkins Act and then the 1906 Hepburn Act gave the Commission more teeth. These Acts and subsequent legislation felt to be 'essential' at the time put the railroads at a severe disadvantage when they came to compete against truckers, autos and air travel.

Rail chaos ensued when America entered World War I in 1917. More than 200,000 freight cars choked the Atlantic ports, with each rail company vying to maximise revenues. In December President Wilson nationalised the nation's railroads and they remained nationalised for 26 months. The 1930s Great Depression hit the railroads hard. At one point a third of the companies were in bankruptcy and almost two-thirds were not earning revenues to cover their fixed charges. World War II brought a revival to the rail industry's fortunes; it gave wholehearted support to the war effort and there was no nationalisation.

Decline accelerated after the war, and in 1968 the two great rivals on the blue riband New York–Chicago route, the New York Central and the Pennsylvania Railroad, merged to become the Penn Central.

The Pennsy was the bigger of the two and the senior partner in the merger. It thought of itself as 'the standard railroad of the world' but in recent years its management had become arrogant, slack and sometimes dishonest. Productivity had been ignored, the track was in bad condition with low speed limits on many sections, some as low as 20mph and even a few down to 6mph. One incident became notorious: 350 boxcars 'disappeared', were repainted and then leased to the Pennsy. Stuart Saunders, the chairman, was a star of arch-conservative Philadelphia society; one of the company's board minutes during his selection process noted 'he has a charming and capable wife who will fit into the Philadelphia picture quite well'. Saunders was openly scornful of his railroad's future, and presided over a programme of diversification that included a pipeline, property development, amusement parks, a charter airline (at a time when railroads were not allowed to own or control an airline) and a large part of Transavia, a European airline that the company purchased with money laundered through Lichtenstein. The senior executives' activities included creative accounting, insider trading and 'dates' in a company sleeping car parked on a remote siding of New York's Penn Station. By contrast, the New York Central had become a respectable but failing company after the excesses of the last years of Vanderbilt control[4] that ended in the 1950s.

It was thought that the merger would solve the problems of each railroad but it was a chaotic disaster for employees, freight customers and passengers. A year later the bankrupt New Haven Railroad was added to the Penn Central. Almost 30 months after the merger, the company filed for bankruptcy protection despite hauling more ton-miles than 10 years previously or at the height of World War II. At the time, it was the largest commercial bankruptcy in America's history and caused the collapse of the rest of the north east's railroads, largely because of the courts delaying interline payments.

The Trustees of the bankrupt company counted on abandoning thousands of miles of track and a drastic reduction in the number of employees to achieve profitability. Labour resisted with strikes and industry insisted on the retention of tracks serving factories and mines. Nationalisation was considered but this was anathema to the Nixon administration. After examining the alternatives, the Penn Central and most of the northeast railroads were incorporated into Conrail and the government became partner in a commercial business – for the first time. In 1981 Conrail became a profitable business, mainly as a result of good management resulting in a steep rise in productivity, and in 1987 Conrail stock was offered for sale on the New York Stock Exchange. 'They brought the old dog back to life, and the market was happy to have it back', said a broker.

In the early 1970s the American rail industry reached its lowest ebb since the Depression 40 years earlier. Track and equipment had been neglected through bad management or inadequate resources, there was crippling outdated regulation, a shockingly bad passenger service and labour problems and work practices which were a legacy of the change from steam to diesel traction and even from the days of the signal lantern. All this lowered the industry in the esteem of the administration, the banks and the public. The impression of terminal decline was heightened by a series of disastrous derailments of propane and toxic chemical tank-cars that incinerated at least one small town and poisoned inhabitants in other small trackside towns.

4. William Vanderbilt, son of the Commodore, famously said, 'The public be damned.'

However change was under way. Computerised central control of trains and individual freight cars was being introduced, labour problems began to be resolved, but not before the Ringling Brothers and Barnum & Bailey circus elephants, who normally travelled by rail, had to walk through the Lincoln Tunnel to their pitch in Manhattan. Piggyback rail trailers had been introduced and were beginning to be replaced by containers and then by double stack containers; the traditional railroad boxcar became obsolete. Regional container terminals were built and for the first time trucks bringing containers to the terminals co-operated with railroads rather than competed against them. And there was coal; more than half the nation's power generating capacity was, and still is, fired by coal and new tracks had to be laid to exploit the enormous Powder River Basin reserves of low sulphur coal in Wyoming and to other new coalfields.

The late 1970s were a period of deregulation. The Airline Deregulation Act and the Motor Carrier Act were followed in 1980 by the Staggers Act, which deregulated the railroads. It permitted railroads to set their own shipping rates and allowed them to refuse uneconomic business but imposed obligations in dealing with customers who had no access to competition. The Staggers Act was the beginning of an era of prosperity for the industry. From 1975 to 1995 the number of employees declined by 60% and ton-miles of freight increased by a similar percentage, resulting in a 133% improvement in the ratio of employees per ton-mile.

From the earliest days rail companies had been bought and sold and the last part of the 20th century was a period of mega-mergers or acquisitions. The Chessie system, originally based on the Chesapeake and Ohio Railway, which had absorbed a number of smaller rail companies, merged with the Seaboard Coast Line to form the CSX, supposedly designating Chessie-Seaboard-Together. The Norfolk Southern was made up from the merger between the Norfolk & Western and the Southern Railway in 1982. The Burlington Northern bought the Frisco to enlarge its territory. The Southern Pacific and the Santa Fe announced their merger but the Interstate Commerce Commission disallowed it. In 1987 the Southern Pacific was sold to the much smaller Denver & Rio Grande Western, which in turn was absorbed by the Union Pacific, which had already merged with the Missouri Pacific and Western Pacific. The Union Pacific then went on to buy the Katy, the Missouri-Kansas-Texas and the Chicago & North Western. The energetic Wisconsin Central acquired the small rail companies to the north and west of Chicago, the operating concession for the privatised New Zealand railways and the principal rail freight franchise in the UK but in 2001 it merged into the Canadian National which also purchased the Illinois Central to give it direct access to New Orleans from Canada. Earlier, Canadian Pacific acquired the Delaware & Hudson and in 1995 Burlington Northern merged with the Santa Fe to form the BNSF.

In 1996 both CSX and Norfolk Southern made competing bids to acquire Conrail but the administration was not prepared to allow such a concentration of track in the northeast in the hands of a single company. The next year the two companies put in a joint bid for ownership of Conrail; CSX acquiring 42% of the company and Norfolk Southern the remaining 58%. In 1999 Canadian National and BNSF announced their intention to merge but there was opposition from the other rail companies, customers and the administration and so the merger was abandoned.

Today, the North American railroad system is made up of about 500 feeder lines, some with colourful names: the *New Hope & Ivyland,* the *Walking Horse & Eastern,* the *Poseyville & Owensville* and the *Nittany & Bald Eagle*. They comprise nearly 30% of the nation's rail tracks. There are four big Class 1 rail companies in the US and another two in Canada. In terms of track mileage they line up with Union Pacific as the largest, then the BNSF; CSX is next, followed by Norfolk Southern, the Canadian National and the Canadian Pacific. So far none of the American lines spans the continent from the Atlantic to the Pacific. One commentator suggested things might have been different if Commodore Vanderbilt were still alive.

❖

Passenger traffic had been in decline for years and the decline in services accelerated in 1967 when the Post Office, which shipped most of its mail by rail, cancelled its contracts. Air travel made it uneconomic to have sleeping cars accommodating only 24 passengers, restaurants, parlour cars and bars hauled across the continent, and even suburban systems found it uneconomic to transport commuters packed like sardines. A large number of railroads petitioned the authorities to be allowed to discontinue their failing or failed passenger services. In 1970 Congress masterminded the formation of Amtrak. It was an impossible brief: the company was to be a with-profit company and provide a social service to the community. There were complicated financial arrangements for the rail companies to transfer their passenger cars that had been neglected for years; the first years were known as Amtrak's rainbow period because of the kaleidoscope of multicoloured liveries of passenger cars from the different railroads. There were the obvious problems of scheduling passenger trains on tracks already carrying capacity traffic; express passenger trains did not mix with mile-long freight trains. In addition there was the problem of the tracks themselves; express trains need a smooth high-speed track in tip-top condition and 100-ton mineral hoppers pound and damage rail tracks. Running Amtrak passenger expresses on freight train tracks was an uneasy compromise.

In addition to the transfer of passengers and equipment to Amtrak, the railway companies transferred many of their commuter services to local transportation boards such as the New Jersey or the Boston Metropolitan Transit Authorities.

In 1976 Amtrak took over the ownership of the tracks as well as the service of the North East Corridor line, the New Haven Boston–New York and the Pennsy New York–Washington lines. They introduced their first Acela Express trains on to the North East Corridor at the end of 2000. The 300-seat train sets incorporate many TGV features but, unlike the LGV lines, the tracks are upgrades of existing lines rather than a dedicated line. Much more work is needed on the tracks, signalling and controls before Amtrak trains can run at their design speed of 180mph and provide a journey time that competes successfully against air travel. Government subsidies were always planned to be phased out and Amtrak's future is shaky; in September 2001 it was obliged to mortgage New York's Penn Station to raise cash. The future of American passenger rail travel is in the hands of the legislators.

Canadian railways also experienced a crisis in passenger traffic. VIA Rail Canada was first established as a subsidiary of the Canadian National and became a Crown Corporation in 1976 to provide a passenger service using Canadian Pacific and Canadian National tracks. It runs a transcontinental luxury train, *The Canadian*, which alas runs through Edmonton and Jasper rather than the original Canadian Pacific route through Calgary and Banff and it operates routes linking the main centres and a high speed service between Toronto and Montreal.

There is a world of difference between the current development of the rail systems in Europe and North America. Western Europe is giving priority to upgrading existing tracks and facilities to accommodate increasing passenger traffic. Investment in new, dedicated tracks for trains running at around 200mph is resulting in a high speed passenger system covering Europe from Naples and southern Spain to London, Berlin and the Baltic. By contrast the big six companies of the US and Canada are investing in increasing their capacity for transporting freight; the Canadian Pacific built the nine-mile McDonald Tunnel under the existing higher and shorter Connaught Tunnel to increase capacity over the Rogers Pass in the Selkirks and the BNSF has reopened the old Northern Pacific line over the Stampede Pass in the Cascades. The companies working into Chicago, the most important concentration of rail traffic in the US, are combining to build an exchange system designed to handle up to 67,000 freight cars a day. Local government and the railroads jointly built the 14-mile Alameda Corridor through Los Angeles to Long Beach harbour for up to 150 double-stack container trains a day; all the Class 1 companies are double tracking a large number of existing single track lines and sometimes adding a third track to accommodate the increasing freight traffic.

A world of difference in every sense and two different views of the future of the railways.

Theodore Link's 1895 St Louis Union Station

7 Astonishing Bridges and Buildings

From the beginning of the whole railway adventure there were difficulties in engineering the route for the permanent-way. Every embankment, retaining wall, drain, culvert and bridge had to withstand the weight and the vibration of trains. Knowledge of local conditions and traditions of working masonry were allied with the empirical and increasing knowledge of the engineer for whom there were no textbooks and who seldom had any theoretical knowledge. It was said of Thomas Telford, who built canals and magnificent bridges which were the precursors of the rail engineers' great works, that 'he had a singular distaste for mathematical studies' and a friend who had recommended a young man for a job in Telford's office on the basis of his mathematical ability found that Telford 'did not hesitate to say that he considered such acquirements as rather disqualifying than fitting him for the situation'.

Engineers had to learn to use the new materials and they generally did so with wide margins of safety; occasional failures such as Stephenson's bridge over the River Dee taught important lessons that were then incorporated into the growing lexicon of engineering knowledge. The metallurgists Fairbairn and Hodgkinson provided an important new fund of knowledge about metal fatigue and stress in structures and Siemens-Martin open-hearth furnaces made steel a reliable and economic replacement for iron.

Of the many structures and buildings of the railway age, two above all tower over others in ambition and splendour: the first from the last quarter of the 19th century, the second from the first quarter of the 20th. The rail bridge over the Firth of Forth in Scotland opened in 1890 and Grand Central Terminal in New York was inaugurated in 1913. Each is a masterwork that stands up to comparison with any manmade structure through the centuries. Each is still admired and wondered at today.

❖

The east coast of Scotland is invaded by the North Sea by three large inlets or firths that inhibit north-south overland communication. Railway engineers avoided a long crossing of the Moray Firth – the most northern of the three – by building a bridge where it narrows into the Beauly River. The Firth of Tay is the second North Sea inlet. The tracks of the west-coast Caledonian Railway were inland from the Firth but had easier access to Dundee and the Aberdeenshire towns than the rival east-coast North British Railway whose access to this rich area was limited by having to cross the Firth by ferry. It was essential to try to build a bridge no more than seven or eight miles from the mouth of the Firth to give the North British direct and economic access to this important area. The company took an audacious decision. It would build the world's longest bridge. When it opened in 1878 it was more than two miles long with 88 spans. The single track ran inside trusses on high girders over the Tay's main channel, but these trusses had no braced connection to the rest of the bridge. On the 28th December 1879, a strong gale came howling directly against the bridge. A train was crossing when 13 spans of high girders collapsed. The train fell into the Firth with the loss of 75 lives. A much stronger replacement twin track bridge was opened eight years later.

The Firth of Forth, the third and most southern of the North Sea inlets on the Scottish east coast, runs past Edinburgh to the Rosyth naval base and the important docks at Bo'ness and Grangemouth. The Firth is up to 220ft deep with the small Isle of Inchgarvie in the middle, which made it possible to build a central pier for the bridge. Sir Thomas Bouch, who had been knighted for designing the Tay bridge, proposed a suspension bridge with two 1,600ft spans and construction began. However the collapse of the Tay bridge stopped site work and Bouch's design was abandoned. It was clear that after the Tay disaster the new bridge had to be stronger and safer than any other bridge in the world. Three great towers were constructed, one on the north shore, one on the south shore and one on Inchgarvie: each steel lattice tower is 342ft high and built around four massive 12-ft steel tubes. Enormous cantilevers supporting the rail deck spring from each tower. The cantilevers on the north and south shores are joined to the mainland tracks by masonry arches and a series of girder arches. The other cantilevers from the north and south towers stretch toward the cantilevers from the Inchgarvie tower; instead of joining, each pair supports a 350-ft truss that carries the rail deck from one cantilever to the next.

The complete one and a half mile long bridge is a monumental work of art that towers above the sea into the sky. The great bridge has a simple profile but the diagonal lattice braces provide a visually dense interior. The bridge, viewed from different angles, takes on quite different appearances. Perhaps the best view is from the parallel road suspension bridge, and the dense foreshortened view should be seen from one of the shores. Best of all, it should be crossed leaning out of an open window of a train, to be overwhelmed by the sensation and sound of the train travelling through the heart of the great steel structure.

The bridge was designed by the engineer Benjamin Baker. There is no architectural or decorative element; it is pure structure and it is a work of art. It was inaugurated by the Prince of Wales in March 1890 and Gustave Eiffel, whose iron tower in Paris had opened a year earlier, was at Baker's side at the ceremony. The bridge provoked wonder and admiration from around the world. But there were critics of its undecorated sculptural form: 'the supremest specimen of all ugliness' said William Morris.

❖

Construction of the magnificent Grand Central Terminal in New York City began in 1903 and opened in 1913; the *Scientific American* called it 'a monumental gateway to America's greatest city'. The 60-ft wide and 30-ft high sculpture group of Roman deities on the south façade facing Park Avenue was called 'the best piece of monumental sculpture in America'. The magnificent 200ft by 120ft Main Concourse with its marble floor, honey coloured walls with long balconies and ornamental balustrades, contains a series of short flights of stairs, each modelled on the Paris Garnier opera house, and with its astonishing blue-green ceiling with a gold-leaf astrological mural, it is one of the world's great interior spaces. Underground avenues with restaurants, including the famous Grand Central Oyster Bar, galleries and shops radiate from the concourse. The avenues enable visitors and office workers to walk directly to the elevators of the nearby grand hotels and office buildings. Designed both as a crossroads for travellers and for the people of the city Grand Central is also a potent symbol of enormous wealth and power. The tracks under the concourse and buildings are hardly evident to people using the building as a city space. Tracks on one side were designed for incoming trains, with baggage handling and cab ranks. On the other side were the tracks for the New York Central's long distance trains, the *Yankee Clipper*, the *Wolverine*, the *Empire State* and, of course, the *Twentieth Century Limited*. The tracks serving the suburbs were on a lower level and there is an important subway station with direct lines serving the principal New York boroughs. The whole splendiferous magnificent Beaux Arts style building spans Park Avenue and fronts 42nd Street, one of the main Manhattan cross-town routes, which had ferries at each end to New Jersey and to Long Island.

Gradually aircraft replaced the railway for long distance travel to many of the destinations served by the Grand Central and the automobile became the standard means of transportation for an increasing proportion of suburban travel. Grand Central went into decline; its tracks were reduced to serving the outer suburbs, advertisement hoardings almost covered the walls of the main concourse and even the directors' wine cellar was used as a lock-up. In 1954 there were plans to demolish Grand Central and replace it with I.M. Pei's hyperboloid 108 story office building. Later, a design by Marcel Breuer was considered and in 1963, the Pan Am building, now the Met Life building, was built behind the station on the site of the Grand Central offices. Its 59 stories and helicopter pad dwarf Grand Central's noble façade.

In 1967 the New York Landmarks Preservation Commission designated the exterior of Grand Central as a landmark and this ruling was later upheld by the Supreme Court. In 1968 the New York Central merged with its archrival the Pennsylvania Railroad. By 1970 the merged Penn Central railroad was bankrupt and a few years later New York State's Metropolitan Transportation Authority formed Metro-North to operate Grand Central and what was reduced to a commuter rail service. Serious repairs to the station's fabric began in 1985 and a completely and beautifully restored Grand Central Terminal was inaugurated in October 1998. Grand Central is a wonder: the best internal public space in the city, in any city. The 1913 Grand Central was a triumph; its restoration 82 years later is a triumph. It is still an important railroad station … just.

One might wonder about the economics that enabled a company to plan and construct such a magnificent and expensive building almost a hundred years ago. Commodore Vanderbilt's New York & Harlem became part of the New York Central Railroad, with its tracks spanning out to the Great Lakes and the Midwest, and it built a suitably splendid French Empire style terminal and office buildings in front of an arched train shed modelled on London's St Pancras station. To reduce smoke and dirt, locomotives were uncoupled as the train approached the station, and accelerated into a siding leaving the train to glide into the terminal with a brakeman bringing it to a smooth stop. The area north of the new terminal was chaotic with tracks and rail yards crisscrossing the roads of uptown Manhattan; steam, horses and pedestrians were a bad mixture and there were frequent accidents. Finally a series of cuttings and tunnels was dug and the tracks re-laid below the level of the roads.

Rail traffic increased and despite being enlarged and fitted with an Italianate façade, the Terminal station again became inadequate. It was still the only rail terminal in Manhattan, as *Scientific American* remarked in 1900: 'It is a remarkable fact that although New York is the second largest city in the world it has but one railroad terminal within its boundaries …'

In 1902 an accident in the smoky Fourth Avenue approach tunnel killed or injured 55 and this was the turning point. Steam traction was terminated north of the city, and the lines electrified into Manhattan down to 42nd Street. The expense of the change to electric traction was justified not only by the need to improve operating safety but also by all sorts of convoluted calculations,

> ...a person produces 0.6 cubic feet of carbonic acid gas per hour; the heavier locomotives burn about 35lbs of coal per minute, and therefore each engine destroys as much air as would 87,000 people...

Construction of the present Grand Central terminal began in 1903; the tracks running north in the cuttings were covered over and Fourth Avenue was renamed Park Avenue. The sale of land over the tracks and rail yards with their 'air rights' paid for the hugely ambitious and expensive enterprise that is Grand Central Terminal. A series of high-rise office blocks, apartment buildings and hotels were built on the site between Madison and Lexington Avenues up to 56th Street, culminating with the Waldorf Astoria Hotel in 1931. The area became one of the best-known and most expensive locations in the world.

Grand Central was recognised as one of the great crossroads of the nation with Columbia Broadcasting's *Grand Central Station* in the 1940s and '50s. Each Saturday the show began;

> As a bullet seeks its target, shining rails in every part of our great nation are aimed at Grand Central Station, the heart of the country's greatest city. Drawn by the magnetic force of the fantastic metropolis, day and night great trains rush toward the Hudson River ... then dive with a roar into the two and a half mile tunnel beneath the glitter and swank of Park Avenue and then – Grand Central Station – crossroads of a million private lives, gigantic stage on which are played a thousand dramas daily...

It is interesting to compare the two great enterprises, each the greatest of their kind. The Forth bridge was built to carry trains across an inlet of the North Sea with its ferocious conditions and gales. It is just a bridge, a necessary and utilitarian link in a communications system; but Lord Clark praised it highly in his television series *Civilization* and in the subsequent book. Grand Central was built as an extravagant, grandiose and glorious statement to surprise, amaze and impress. Each is, in its own way, a great work of art.

❖

Probably the first purpose-built railway bridge was the Causey Arch in County Durham. The semicircular masonry 100-ft bridge was built in the 1720s to take two wooden tracks for horse drawn coal wagons; the arch still stands but the waggonway has disappeared. Masonry and then brick were the materials for taking the railway across water, gullies and small valleys. As railway systems developed and extended, an inexpensive solution had to be found for bridging small spans or longer spans with intermediate piers. The most widely used solution was the timber bridge truss, which originated in New England; later the cast iron truss replaced timber, wrought iron replaced cast iron and later still steel became the standard material. A bridge truss is a self-contained load-bearing structure supporting the load and its own weight in a frame of beams. It is easily assembled on site and it became the solution for bridging thousands of roads, rivers and gullies. There were a large number of designs: the Howe, the Pratt, the Fink, and the Whipple, which was the first to bring soundly based engineering practice into truss design.

The early railway engineers were also obliged to design audaciously innovative bridges to carry rail tracks across wide stretches of water where it was not possible to build a series of piers. Stephenson's giant wrought-iron tube bridge across the Menai Straits, his High Level Bridge with its six cast iron bowstring arches supporting two decks across the River Tyne and Brunel's Royal Albert Bridge with its suspension/arch/truss combination over the Tamar are some of the best known of these astonishing structures built in Britain in the middle of the 19th century. Magnificent and beautiful masonry arched bridges such as the Royal Border Bridge with its 28 semicircular arches carrying the North Eastern line over the River Tweed between England and Scotland, and the spectacular Ribblehead Viaduct on the Midland line to Carlisle are other remarkable solutions to bridging wide valleys and rivers. By the end of the 19th century reinforced concrete had replaced masonry or brick on many bridges. Joseph Monier, a French gardener, was the first to recognise the potential of reinforced concrete when, in 1867, he made cement plant pots moulded around iron netting; eight years later he built a 52-ft reinforced concrete arch. Eugene Fressinet is one of the great names associated with the development of using concrete for vast structures and in 1930 his

Plougastel rail and road bridge in Brittany was the largest and most ambitious concrete bridge in the world with the three 592-ft segmental arch spans rising up to a height of 90ft.

The development of using coke in the place of wood for smelting iron was the beginning of the industrial revolution and in 1779 the world's first iron bridge was built. A hundred years later Gustave Eiffel was starting the construction of his masterpiece of structural art, the Garabit Viaduct, a great 540-ft iron crescent arch 400ft above the River Truyère in the French Massif Centrale. Eiffel had taken a degree in chemical engineering but a quarrel prevented him from working in the family vinegar firm. In despair he found a job as a site engineer on the construction of a cast iron bridge over the River Garonne; he then established his own iron frame construction business close to Paris. He built hundreds of structures including bridges, gasholders, train sheds and exhibition halls and in 1867 he built four viaducts for the main railway line to Vichy. His genius as a designer was evident when he won the competition to design the bridge over the River Douro near Oporto; his winning entry made an inspired minimal use of materials and was 30% lower cost than the nearest rival. The designer of the Garabit and the Paris Tower, the world's tallest structure of its time, was, according to Le Corbusier, 'inspired by not being seen as a creator of beauty ... His calculations were always inspired by an admirable instinct for proportion, his goal was elegance.'

Over the years the cities of Chicago, Illinois and St Louis, Missouri had jostled and vied for recognition as the business centre of the Mid West. Once the Civil War was over, a Missouri senator stated that a bridge crossing the Mississippi should be 'for the ages, of a material that shall defy time and of a style that shall be equally a triumph of art and contribution to industrial development'. James Eades who, with Benjamin Baker, shared the distinction of designing only one bridge, submitted a revolutionary design, the first major steel bridge. It had three 520-ft arches, each longer than any other span except a few suspension bridges. The roadway was on the upper level and the rail tracks on the lower. In 1874 14 heavy locomotives moved across the bridge as a final test. It opened on the Glorious Fourth of July for the city to celebrate Eade's triumph.

The most astonishingly situated of all the great steel arches is the 500-ft railway bridge across the Zambesi Gorge, just below the Victoria Falls. Larger, much larger, but not so spectacular, is the Hell Gate Bridge[1] with its 977-ft arch and four rail tracks[2], which can be seen by travellers crossing the Triborough Bridge on the way from JFK airport to Manhattan. Sydney Harbour Bridge, completed in 1931, with its huge 1,650-ft steel arch supporting six roadways and four rail tracks[3] spanning the beautiful harbour, is still one of the icons of Australia; the top chords of the great arch terminate just short of the stone towers, emphasising their structural function. Sadly for Sydney, the Bayonne arch bridge, completed the previous year between New Jersey and Staten Island, is just two feet longer and took the title for the world's longest arch. However the Bayonne road bridge was built for much lighter loads and its steel structure weighs less than half that of the Sydney Bridge.

The origins and principles of the suspension bridge probably date back to prehistory; from time immemorial tropical jungle vine or creepers woven and hung from each side of a river performed the role of the suspended cable to provide a crossing. James Finlay of Pennsylvania made an important breakthrough in the development of the suspension bridge by bracing the deck with trusses, a concept that was then developed in England. Thomas Telford's 1826 Menai Strait Bridge with its 580-ft suspended span for road traffic was the first major suspension bridge and from there it seemed an obvious step to adapt the suspension bridge for rail crossings. But it became evident that the weight and vibration of the railway needed the additional rigidity provided by arches or cantilevers; Samuel Brown's bridge for carrying the Stockton & Darlington over the River Tees was shaken to bits within a few months in 1826. However, John Roebling, famous for his design for the Brooklyn Bridge, completed an 820-ft suspended span across the Niagara Gorge in 1855 which remained in service for more than 40 years. It supported a single track and trains were limited to a maximum speed of three miles per hour. His family's

1. The bridge takes its name from the channel between Long Island Sound and New York Harbour; notorious for its treacherous currents.

2. Now reduced to three.

3. Now reduced to two.

spectacular and celebrated Brooklyn Bridge had three sets of tracks; one for trams, another for cable hauled trains that carried ten million passengers in their first year and the last giving the Brooklyn Rapid Transit System a toehold in Manhattan.

The 1926 Camden Suspension Bridge across the Delaware with its 1,750-ft span and massive 128-ft wide deck was built to carry both trains and autos; it was in the tradition of Stephenson's High Level Bridge across the Tyne and Eades' bridge across the Mississippi: there are obvious economic benefits in combining the two systems in the same structure. Japan has exploited these benefits on its bridge-building programme linking Honshu and Shikoku. Denmark's capital city, Copenhagen, on the Island of Zealand, is separated by sea from the Danish mainland and from nearby Sweden. Recently road and rail bridges and tunnels have been built to link the Danish capital to the mainland at Jutland and to Malmø in Sweden. The most ambitious of all bridge projects are the designs for a two-mile suspended rail/road span to be built in the future to link Sicily to the Italian mainland.

The most audacious rail crossing over sea was the Key West Extension built in 1912. Bridges and embankments joined a series of small islets or keys to form a 128-mile link between the southern tip of the Florida mainland and Key West. There were 17 miles of bridges and 20 miles of embankment. The railway closed in 1935 following a hurricane and was replaced by a road.

Every railway bridge is the product of knowledge, engineering and design as well as construction. Almost all are interesting; some are more interesting or out of the ordinary than others. The 1912 vertical lift bridge across the Willamette River in downtown Portland, Oregon with its two decks, the lower with rail tracks and the upper a combination of tramlines and road, provides a clearance of 135ft over the water level when raised. If less clearance is required, the lower deck can be raised and telescoped into the upper deck. The coastal line linking south with north Wales crosses the Mawddach estuary over Barmouth Bridge and it had the same problem of allowing vessels to pass but the designers found a different solution. One of the central spans pivoted on a pier and was opened by eight men cranking handles who became marooned on the open span until they closed it.

Nineteenth century bridges often included decoration. For instance Robert Stephenson's Britannia Bridge had massive crouching stone lions on plinths protecting the Egyptian style stone entrances[4], and many bridges and viaducts have crenellations and towers giving a fortress-like aspect of permanence that might have gone some way to reassuring nervous early passengers. Rusticated voussoirs, elaborate string courses, bands of machicolations or decorated keystones were commonplace. Sometimes rail tracks crossed the parks of aristocratic estates. A West Coast rail bridge crosses over a drive at Shugborough Park and is within sight of the Park's Grecian follies and temples. The bridge has two pairs of Ionic columns, stone balustrades on the parapets beside the tracks and running down the wing walls; the Earl's coat of arms complete with robe and coronet is at the centre of the parapet with seahorses and lions at each end. The Caledonian line was built very close to the front of Guthrie Castle and the bridge over the drive was disguised as a medieval gateway complete with castellated towers and a gatekeeper's lodge under the tracks.

Railway bridges usually carry the rail tracks over a road, a valley or a river. However, at least one bridge carrying a road over a railway merits admiration. Santiago Calatrava's Felipe II Bridge in Barcelona is a source of astonishing visual pleasure. It has two pairs of bowstring arches supporting the roadway; the outer arches are inclined toward the inner vertical arches to make a somewhat tricksy but fascinating structure.

❖

Rail companies used their principal stations to make a statement – a statement of modernism, a statement of grandeur, or a statement to emphasise the importance of the station to the city and its community – and sometimes they built the station to a design dictated by the whims and enthusiasms of the company chairman. As a result, some stations have an atmosphere of welcome for passengers and others overawe or intimidate by their scale and olympian aspect. City administrations looked on the

---

4. The tower entrances were designed by the architect Francis Thompson and the lions carved by John Thomas.

main rail station as the principal entrance to the city and there was often a quid pro quo of the city providing a suitable site and the railway erecting imposing station buildings.

Some buildings of two of the earliest stations still survive. Liverpool Road Station in Manchester was the terminus of the Liverpool and Manchester railway. The surviving 1830 buildings comprise a first-class entrance complete with handsome external wall light holders and a sun-dial, and there is a second-class entrance next door, all in a handsome rusticated stucco façade. A warehouse contemporary with the station building is on the other side of the tracks. The buildings now house the Museum of Science and Technology. The 1838 Curzon Street station in Birmingham was the terminus of the London & Birmingham and Grand Junction Railways. Its pairs of high Ionic pillars each side of the entrance and its massive entablature made it a worthy counterpart to the great Euston arch built in the same year. The station closed 16 years after it opened when the rail traffic was transferred to the much larger New Street Station.

The world's first grandiose railway terminal was the London and Birmingham's Euston station set back from the busy Euston Road. On the right side of the square from the main road was the massive propylaeum, the great Doric entrance arch to the station yard. Flanked by Grecian-style stone lodges and a screen of handsome cast iron gates decorated with the railway company's cypher, the great arch with its ten-foot diameter columns became recognized as the 'Gateway to the North'. Before the other trunk lines reached London, everyone travelling by rail to the north passed through the great arch. Beyond the arch was the station yard for setting down passengers and the grandiose buildings that housed the Great Hall and the Company's offices. Passengers waited in the Great Hall, a lofty Roman Ionic-style room with an elaborate corbelled and coffered ceiling under the gaze of a larger than life statue of George Stephenson. Behind the statue a monumental double staircase led to a marble colonnade at one end of a gallery. Behind the colonnade were three large mahogany double doors, the largest of which opened to the sumptuous baroque Shareholders Meeting Room. Around the other three sides of the gallery ranged a series of large classical-romantic painted wall panels. Behind these grand buildings were a series of very modest or even wretched iron frame sheds over the platforms for passengers' departures and arrivals. Despite protests and appeals from every quarter to every authority, British Railways demolished the magnificent and monumental buildings in 1968 to construct a mean, airport-style terminal building.

The exteriors of most London railway terminuses are visually disappointing; they expanded piecemeal to accommodate increased traffic and the enormous growth of suburban passengers. Station hotels and offices were built in front of, or even around two sides of the station so that the station itself could hardly be seen from the street. Of the 13 London terminus stations, only Waterloo, Fenchurch Street and Blackfriars did not have an adjoining hotel. At the same time the stations have been increasingly hemmed in by nearby office buildings. Indeed, at Liverpool Street, Charing Cross and Cannon Street stations office buildings have been built over the tracks with conspicuous success.

King's Cross has the most visible handsome and imposing façade of all the London stations. Two great brick arches front the 72-ft high train shed's glazed arches that span the main lines to the north and Scotland. An Italianate clock tower divides the arches and the façade is dramatic and functional. Nearby is St Pancras station with its 243-ft wide parabolic train shed arch, the largest in the world when it was built, and the pattern for a large number of stations around the world. The arch is hidden from the streets by the 1876 hotel[5] with its extravagant Gothic Revival façade.

Like St Pancras, Paddington Station is almost hidden from the street by its hotel and by railway offices. When the Great Western made the decision to build its permanent London terminus, Brunel wrote 'I am going to design, in a great hurry … a station after my own fancy … It is at Paddington.' The resulting train shed[6] is magnificent: three long arched iron and glass sheds with two transepts, the one across the concourse being known as the lawn.

Victoria Station was originally two separate stations belonging to

5. Sir Gilbert Scott, architect of the hotel, seemingly never realised the glory of William Barlow's great iron glass vault and was quoted as saying that his hotel building was 'possibly too good for its purpose'.

6. Sir Digby Wyatt was responsible for the decoration of Brunel's framework of the station; one of the rare occasions Brunel collaborated with an architect.

competing lines that were merged in the 1920s and the stations were combined to make the existing series of halls and sheds. The station is in central London and only 700 yards from Buckingham Palace so there was no space for adding tracks or platforms. The problem of providing much-needed additional accommodation was solved by extending the platforms towards the river and fitting a crossover on the track halfway along the platform to accommodate two trains simultaneously. Typically for London, most of the station, apart from a monumental Edwardian decorated entrance, is hidden by the Grosvenor Hotel.

Waterloo station, with its 21 platforms is the largest London terminus, and was built immediately after World War I. A seemingly endless ridge and furrow roof is supported on vertical columns and horizontal beams. Nicholas Grimshaw's 1993 extension for the Eurostar Channel Tunnel trains is on the north side and its beautiful curved stainless steel and glass arched roof emphasises the Parthenon-like construction of the rest of the 70-year-old station.

Liverpool Street Station, once the grimiest and most bewildering in London, has been restored; Gordon Biddle in his *Britain's Historic Railway Buildings* calls the restoration 'a remarkable and exemplary example of how to restore and to modernize simultaneously'. The whole station is light and airy and the patterns of the thin closely spaced decorated iron pillars either joined to each other in a pointed arch with filigree cast iron webs or supporting the high wrought iron train shed give the inside view of the roof a delicate and rhythmic Moorish aspect.

John Betjeman's marvellously illustrated 1972 book, *Londons's Historic Railway Stations*, drew attention to the wide variety of oddities and eccentricities under the roofs and arches of London terminal stations but none could equal Blackfriars Underground Station built in 1870 and almost destroyed in the World War II London blitz. It was a large three-storey Moorish confection with rows of friezes, balconies and windows crowned by horseshoe arches between two towers like minarets with onion domes. According to Gordon Biddle it was 'more a mosque than a railway station'.

Huddersfield Station probably has the most handsome frontage of any British railway station. High and slender Corinthian pillars support a triangular pediment over the entrance, which protrudes from the two-storey classical façade of the station building with pilasters between each set of windows. As Gordon Biddle says, 'the façade supremely combines majesty and elegance'. In nearby Halifax the local paper called their station a 'filthy dog hole of a place'. The editor probably felt that his piece in the paper was the trigger for the Lancashire and Yorkshire Railway building a new station in 1885. Not as handsome as Huddersfield but very fine and impressive.

Generally railway companies built handsome and large stations in the main regional cities. However, York station's buildings are modest and dumpy compared to its great train shed over the curved tracks and platforms. Like York, Newcastle station is built on a curve and three magnificent arches cover the tracks and platforms. The frontage has a massive drive-through portico that gives access to the station's concourse. Many consider it to be Britain's most handsome large railway station. Temple Meads Station in Bristol is next to Brunel's 1840 wooden hammer-beam roofed train shed behind its mock Tudor facade. The train shed of the present station is behind an ornate French Gothic frontage complete with a massive clock tower between two sets of twin spires covered in crockets. The clock tower was crowned with a high French chateau roof which was removed in 1935 transforming the façade from ridiculous to handsome.

In small towns and villages the railway station came only second in importance to the parish church, and stations were built to emphasize this importance. The railway companies built their small stations in a wide variety of styles. Tudor and Jacobean were common but there were Grecian, Roman, Early English Ecclesiastic, Queen Anne, Italianate, Cottage Ornée and Arts & Crafts buildings; almost every architectural style was used apart from Romanesque, which was reserved for railway tunnel entrances. Often these styles were mixed up and elaborated by seemingly playful additions that included porte cochères, decorative brickwork, iron fretwork, Dutch gables or elaborate fretted bargeboards. Platform canopies also came in a variety of shapes; generally lean-to, or ridge and furrow and were often finished with sawtooth or frilly valances. With the closure of branch lines many of these charming and remarkable buildings have fallen into disrepair or been adapted for other uses.

❖

With only a few exceptions, London railway stations give little indication of their presence from more than two streets away. By contrast, most Paris railway stations have spacious surroundings and prominent positions. The pointed arch façade of the Gare de l'Est can be seen from the Seine, more than a mile away. It is worth getting closer to see the sculpture of the nymph representing the River Seine linking arms with a very masculine River Rhine over the station clock. In the front of the next arch are two other rivers, the Meuse and the Marne, represented by two nearly naked nymphs with la Marne making definite advances to la Meuse: very bold, because a fully clothed and stern female effigy of Verdun with sword and shield looks down on them from on top of the arch.

Reynaud's original 1846 Gare du Nord neoclassical façade was dismantled and rebuilt in Lille to front the Flandre Terminus, to the anger of the city fathers who felt they were being fobbed off with a reject from the capital. The present Gare du Nord, with its façade echoing the arched sheds behind and with its 22 draped and crowned nymphs among the Ionic pilasters, dominates its whole neighbourhood. The Gare de Lyon has topless nymphs and an enormous clock tower as well as a yard to give a perspective to its handsome 1900 Beaux Arts façade and mansard roof.

Paris's busiest station, St Lazare, has a handsome façade housing its associated hotel and offices that extends round two sides of the train sheds. The large area in front of the main façade has a number of contemporary sculptures. Only the Gare d'Austerlitz is anonymous; surprising, because it is only a stone's throw from the Seine, but even it has a spacious yard in front of its handsome stone façade. Sadly the façade is invaded and pierced by an elevated Number 5 Métro line carried into the train shed on a series of trusses to run south to its Porte d'Italie terminus. During the Paris siege of the Franco-Prussian War the train shed was used to assemble hot air balloons that enabled the French Head of State, Gambetta, and his colleagues to join the government exiled in Bordeaux.

There are a large number of magnificent 19th century continental European stations. The entrance of Genoa station appears to be a merchant prince's handsome town palace; the arched end of Turin station has slender, ecclesiastic, ogival interlacing arches and there are many other handsome stations featuring variations of every architectural style. Leipzig, once the busiest station in Europe has a 1,000-ft-long neo-classical façade and a train shed with a seeming infinity of arches. Antwerp Centraal Station is quite astonishing with four huge demi-rose ecclesiastical style windows supporting a cupola over the concourse and another demi-rose window incorporated in the front façade. Looking back, under the train shed and along the platforms, the station buildings look like a giant sunburst over an elaborately decorated kitsch palace. A recent French architectural publication wrote that it was an example of an epoch when '*l'architecture éclectique peut atteindre un paroxysme*'.

The Central Station in Milan dominates a whole section of the city with its monumental and massive Assyro-Babylonian façade fronting a huge entrance that dwarfs people to insignificance. Behind the stone building are a series of handsome steel and glass arched train sheds. The building is often mistakenly taken to be a manifestation of Mussolini's megalomania. In fact, it was designed by Ulisse Stacchini in 1910 when his bombastic Art Nouveau extravagance won the design competition for the new station. The preparation of the drawings and World War I delayed building and in the early 1920s Italian Railways decided to hold another competition for a new design. Stacchini objected, claimed that he was the winner of the 1910 competition and there could be no question of organizing a second competition. He went to court, won his case and his design was built and opened in the late 1920s. Santa Maria Novella Station in Florence, designed by Michelevi and Montuori, is a building in sharp contrast to the one in Milan. Completed only a few years later in 1933, it was a trailblazer of modernism and fulfils its function with modesty and effectiveness. It provided a template for Rome's glorious Termini station, famous for its wave-shaped roof and for incorporating a small section of the Emperor Aurelian's second century Roman walls in its structure.

In continental Europe almost every big regional city boasted proud and sometimes eccentric railway stations. For instance, Metz, built after the Franco-Prussian War, has a Germanic Romanesque clock tower, arch and façade. Limoges station, built in 1925, is an eclectic muddle of all the railway styles of the previous century; its large copper dome over the concourse is an echo of Byzantium and its heavy clock tower could be a lighthouse on a rocky northern coast. The train sheds at Tours are framed by massive towers with statues that might have formed an entrance to Imperial Rome. Adolphe Dervaux's Rouen station opened in 1928 is a strange mixture of decorative architectural styles combined with pure eccentricity. Deauville station, serving the chic seaside resort, resembles a cross between a golf clubhouse and a racing stable.

Small town stations had less variety than in Britain but usually had distinct national characteristics. They had glazed tile interiors in Portugal and Spain, wood shutters in France, sometimes an improbably large stone Hermes dominating station buildings in Italy and window boxes with cruelly brilliant red geraniums in the Black Forest and Bavaria. However there are happy examples of worthwhile eccentricity: Konstanz with its high tower, reminiscent of the Palazzo Vecchio but crowned with a spire; Nara, the ancient capital of Japan has a station with its central block suitably hardly distinguishable from a Buddhist shrine. Perhaps the most enviable of all railway buildings is the crossing-keeper's old house almost in the shadow of the Château de Chenonceaux spanning the River Cher in France's Loire Valley. It is a small building with alternating bands of silvery stone and faded red brick. The first floor has a single mansard window with crockets and an elaborately carved pediment, splendid convoluted bargeboards and a fretted valance. It is a doll's house of French renaissance palace and Art Nouveau fantasy.

The Swiss Federal Railways have perfected what seems a particular and satisfactory formula for all but their largest stations. The stations are designed so that there is no barrier, actual or implied, between the station platform and the street. The station and the railway seem as much a part of the town as the streets and shops and buildings, passengers can walk straight from the street to the platform and to the train.

❖

Building a new railway line is an opportunity for designing new stations. In Japan the New Tokkaido line was routed to new stations close to the existing town stations and there was little scope for innovative station design. Building the dedicated LGV lines in France was an opportunity to think about the role of the station in the 21st century. One of the LGV lines bypassing Paris has a station at Roissy below Charles de Gaulle airport's Terminal 2 building. The station platforms are below ground but they have glazed roofs letting in natural light. These roofs are supported by novel inverted U trusses which the designer called 'croissant beams'. Beside the station are two tracks for the RER express suburban service to Paris. The next main LGV stop on the way to Marseille was designed by Santiago Calatrava and is integral with Lyon's St Exupery airport. The roof leaps across and above the centre of the long concourse and is shaped like a gigantic butterfly whose wings are great glazed dihedral fans reminiscent of Saarinen's famous JFK Airport TWA terminal. To quote architectural historian Steven Parissen;

> The result can only be called one of the world's greatest stations, a monument which is a fitting symbol of the revival in railways' fortunes and a highly public testimony to the late twentieth century's rediscovery of the splendour that can be achieved in a great railway station.

There are three further stops in the next 200 miles of the LGV line to the Mediterranean: Valence, Avignon and Aix-en-Provence. Each stop serves not only a medium-sized town but also a large hinterland. The stations are a logical development of the British Rail Parkway concept: a new station on the edge of town combined with a large parking lot, the first of which opened in Bristol in 1972. The LGV takes the concept a stage further: handsome and convenient stations, escalators instead of steps, retail shops, car-washing and service centres, car rental offices, lock-up garages, enormous landscaped parking lots, all beside main roads giving speedy access to the area served by the station.

❖

It is generally recognised that the French left a legacy of good cooking and delicious bread in their former colonies. The legacy the British left to their former empire includes bureaucracy, botanic gardens and some magnificent railway stations. Kuala Lumpur's 1911 station is a glorious

Moorish-Indo-European confection with seven minarets and hundred foot high onion domes. Paul Theroux wrote that it has 'the general appearance of Brighton Pavilion, but twenty times larger'. Calcutta's 1906 red brick Howrah station was described by Jan Morris in *The Stones of Empire* as 'a huge ... conglomerate of mixed Tibetan monastic and English penal suggestion'. It's a grim and forbidding building with few concessions to local vernacular. Most dazzling and most magnificent of all the railway buildings left by the British is Bombay's main station. The great building was inaugurated on Jubilee Day 1887 and named after the Queen Empress Victoria. Designed by F.W. Stevens, the exterior, according to architectural historian Steven Parissien, is 'a breathtaking fusion of English Gothic, Romanesque and Moghul, its two huge wings stretching out in the manner of a French Renaissance palace ...'. Astonishing sculptural decorations, spires, tympana, foliated capitals, piers, jambs, quoins, gables, arches and medallions cover the exterior which is dominated by a large tower with a high dome topped by a 14-ft statue, *Progress*. The main gateway has a massive stone Indian tiger on one side and a British lion on the other. This magnificence was built for the Great Indian Peninsula Railway. The authorities thought it extravagant and proposed it should be shared with the Bombay, Baroda & Central India Railway. The directors of the Great Indian Peninsula disregarded the suggestion partly because the façade included a series of cartouches and carved medallions with the portraits of the self-same directors. Stevens then went on to design the Bombay, Baroda & Central India (BB&C) station and corporate headquarters building: not as large and not as glorious as the Victoria Station building, it has more of an Indian Saracenic and Punjab Baroque appearance. The BB&C management were anxious about the escalating costs of their building; they vetoed the cost of installing a hydraulic lift. 'Europeans who will use the lift are comparatively very few in number and only ascend probably once a day and the exercise is extremely good for them.' They also deleted the expense of installing any fire fighting system: 'it is the rarest thing to hear of a fire except in connection with a cotton mill or some such inflammable and well insured institution ... '. Six years later the building caught fire from the fireworks and illuminations to greet the Prince and Princess of Wales on their state visit. The building was restored the following year by F.W. Stevens' son.

The station in Maputo, Mozambique, is one of the last of the colonial railway stations. Opened in 1910 it was the Lourenço Marques, now Maputo, terminus of the line from the coast to the Transvaal. The station has a very handsome façade with an arcade and a first floor colonnade. There are pavilions at each end with egg and dart decoration and splendidly pompous little balconies. At the centre is the tower, rather too large and imposing for the rest of the building. It supports a copper dome topped by an open globe. The handsome building was recently restored by South African Railways; walls are painted peppermint green and the ornate plasterwork is picked out in white. Behind the façade under a small shelter is *Gaza*, a preserved 1898 tank engine.

It is probable that the most extensive and magnificent railway stations of the future will be built in China. Recently Arep, the architectural services company of the French SNCF has won the contracts to design the new stations at Shanghai and Nankin and the Xijhimen station in Beijing. The designs are soaringly and hearteningly ambitious and on a staggering scale and will play a major role in each city's commercial and daily life as well as being centres for urban and continental communications.

❖

Grand Central in New York would still have a close rival for splendour in the same city if Pennsylvania Station had not been demolished in 1963. Sadly, the site and air-rights were sold off to a company for the construction of a new Madison Square Garden arena. The new Pennsylvania Station's ratty concourse, with its low ceilings, its few rexine-covered chairs, a maze of undersized underground passages and a series of very modest shops leading to the rail tracks, resembles an overblown version of a departure lounge of a shabby, small town airline terminal.

The management of the Pennsylvania Railroad had always been envious of the New York Central tracks running into mid-town Manhattan. Travellers on the Pennsy from Philadelphia, Washington and the south or from Chicago had to leave the train in New Jersey and transfer to ferry terminals to cross the Hudson to Manhattan. The Pennsy had acquired the

Long Island Railroad in 1901 and passengers from the suburbs also had to leave their trains and take the ferry at Long Island City across the East River to Manhattan. In addition, the Pennsy envied the New Haven's tracks handling the traffic from New York to Boston and New England.

Alexander Cassatt, chairman of the Pennsylvania had always puzzled about how to make his company's tracks reach Manhattan. He saw the possibilities of using electric traction in long tunnels when he went to the opening of the Gare d'Orsay in Paris, with its trains hauled by electric locomotives. He launched an ambitious plan: trains from the south and west would change their steam for an electric locomotive at Harrison, New Jersey and continue in a twin-bore tunnel under the Hudson and under the streets of Manhattan to a magnificent new railway station to be called Pennsylvania Station. The plan was much the same for the Long Island Railroad. Steam locos would be detached from Long Island trains in the Sunnyside rail yard and passengers would continue their journey to Manhattan by electric train in one of the four bores under the East River to the same magnificent station between Thirty-first and Thirty-third Streets and Seventh and Eighth Avenues. In addition, the plan included building the Hell Gate Bridge from Long Island to the tracks of the New York, New Haven & Hartford Railroad so that Pennsy passengers from the south could travel north to New England without changing stations.

Both Charles McKim, the famous New York architect, and Cassatt shared a great interest in classical antiquity and each had seen and admired the third-century Baths of Caracalla in Rome. In particular they admired the enormous tepidarium of the Baths. The result of their admiration was Pennsylvania Station, an enormous and gloriously romanticised neoclassical building in central Manhattan. Opened in 1910, the main façade on Eighth Avenue was fronted by 80 huge Doric columns with a double layer of columns in the centre, gigantic pavilions at each end and with a high balustrade running along nearly its full length. Set back from the façade and rising above it was the building housing the great Main Waiting Room. This impressive hall, 150ft high was longer than the nave of St Peter's in Rome, and its vaulted ceiling was decorated with 10-ft square coffers. The grand staircase was 40ft wide, all polished granite and travertine marble. Because the tracks were below street level the train shed over the tracks was concealed from the street. The shed was a lofty and complex series of glass and steel vaults supported on narrow lattice columns. The Pennsy management wanted to build a hotel over the station. McKim dissuaded them, saying that the railroad owed the city a 'thoroughly and distinctly monumental gateway'.

The most grandiose of the great 19th century American stations still standing is St Louis Union Station, which opened in 1894. Steven Parissien describes it '… Gothic gone mad: a fantasy village complete with a 200 foot high Alpine church tower – equipped with an asymmetrical bartizan; a pyramidal roof and battlements – and a grossly inflated pastiche of the Abbot's Kitchen at Glastonbury Abbey'. The Grand Hall, an enormous space covered by a huge bow vault, is a fantasy of elaborate patterns. An arcaded double gallery at one end runs above a 50-ft-long stained glass window depicting three draped nymphs representing San Francisco, St Louis and New York. St Louis is seated in the centre looking ahead and the other two look up at her with admiration. The other end of the hall has sumptuous Gothic floral frescoes, and nymphs supporting flaring electric lamps. For decades this great building was a symbol of the *Gateway to the West* and it was only superseded in this role by Saarinen's enormous and beautiful arch beside the Mississippi, at 630ft more than twice as high as the torch of New York's Statue of Liberty.

Union Station, Washington DC, was opened in 1906 and it was a significant building in the style of the City Beautiful movement. Designed by David Burnham, who masterminded the building of the 1893 Chicago World's Fair and designed Selfridges store in London, this magnificent building[7] included state reception rooms for receiving visiting royalty and grandees, a nursery, a bowling alley and a hospital, in addition to the usual restaurants and shops. One of the most familiar of all American railway photographs is the *Twentieth Century Limited*, probably the world's most famous train, departing from Chicago's La Salle Street Station with its platforms stretching out from beyond the arched train shed. The concourse behind the shed had a massive grand staircase to the waiting room, all mosaic, marble and mahogany. Following the merger between the Pennsy

---

7. The colossal 760 x 130ft station concourse is now a shopping mall.

and the New York Central, mainline operations were transferred to Union Station. La Salle Street is now a small commuter station. Cleveland Union Terminal, all marble magnificence, was opened in 1930 just at the beginning of the Great Depression. The terminal lobbies were on top of the underground tracks and the whole station was a part of an ambitious development that included three large office buildings and the Terminal Tower housing a department store and a 920-bed hotel.

Union Station[8], Cincinnati, Ohio is the most remarkable of the more recent American terminal stations. The tracks of the seven railroads serving the city were re-routed to enable the station to be sited as near as possible to the down-town area. Started in 1928, the station was opened in 1933 when passenger traffic was reducing. The station's limestone façade is a massive 200-ft diameter single arch with projecting buttresses with large bas-relief Moderniste figures. The ground slopes away from the arch with a stepped water cascade ending in a formal garden area. Most glorious was the semi-circular lobby to the concourse under a demi-spherical dome with stepped friezes each painted a different colour with an effect like a rainbow. The lobby was lined with ticket offices and enquiry booths; above them is Winold Reiss's huge mural of historical figures in the foreground of the great Ohio River city complex. The concourse lobby is reminiscent of the circular building that was once the Pan American Seaplane Terminal at New York's La Guardia airport.

Los Angeles Union Station with its 860-ft frontage and marble floors was built to a design that combined Californian Spanish Mission with Art Deco and Moderniste styles and was the last of the great American terminals; it has a certain grand simplicity but no great interest.

A number of architects specialised in designing railroad depots; among the best known was Henry Richardson, who studied at the Paris Beaux Arts. He returned to America in 1866 and became known as Romanesque Richardson because of his enthusiasm for heavy rounded arches. He designed station depots as far apart as New England, California and Oklahoma. The exterior of his Union Station in Ogden, Utah could almost be mistaken for a Provençal basilica; each of the two porches is supported

8. Designed by Roland Wank and won him the American Institute of Architects Gold Medal.

by slim columns with acanthus capitals, the brick façade has decorative stone machicolations along its length and the whole is topped by a traditional red clay tile roof.

During the early days of American railroad construction, small town stations or depots were just wooden shacks built beside the track. The wheel has turned full circle with the arrival of the Amshack, a prefab glass and plastic panel box installed by Amtrack at its minor train stops.

As business developed, stone or brick buildings replaced the wooden sheds, which, in any case, often caught fire from the sparks of a passing locomotive. As a town gained in importance the passenger and freight depots were separated into different buildings. The addition of a clock-tower was another indication of the increasing importance of the station. Small depots were built to an almost universal pattern. They were single storey with an occasional second storey for the agent's accommodation. A large bay window, sometimes topped with a witch's-cap roof, made it easy for the agent, beside his telegraph receiver, to see all arriving and departing trains. This window had a sliding pane so that the agent could pass instructions to the train crew without leaving his post.

❖

Inns or stopping places have existed ever since man first began to travel along established routes for trade, on pilgrimages or on imperial business in the great empires of antiquity. The Inn of the Bethlehem Nativity changed history and 1,400 years later the Tabard Inn of Chaucer's *Canterbury Tales* was a hostelry on a pilgrimage route.

Hotels have been the adjuncts of railways from their beginnings and the concept of the Victorian Grand Hotel springs from these buildings. At one time British railway companies owned 110 hotels. Possibly the first railway hotel was the 1827 Railway Tavern built for passengers by the Stockton & Darlington. The hotel at Euston was the first large hotel to be built by a railway company and it opened in 1839, a year after the opening of the rail terminal. In 1852 the Great Western opened their Great Western Royal Hotel at Paddington; with 103 rooms, it was the largest in the country. Ten of the 13 London terminal stations had their own hotels, either built or operated by the railway company. One included a Masonic Temple, another a cycle track on the roof and the Midland Grand that opened in 1873 at St Pancras was the apogee of High Gothic Victorian architecture. There are rows of windows with quatrefoils, ornate iron balconies, stone machicolations and decorative trimmings on the red brick walls that rise to a stone balustrade, and a steep roof with two tiers of Gothic dormer windows and seemingly innumerable chimneys, crockets, towers and spirelets. At one end of the façade is a 270-ft-high Gothic tower, possibly inspired by a Rhenish cathedral, complete with spire and clock.

The main regional capitals all had their railway hotels; the Adelphi in Liverpool, the Queens in Leeds and the Midland in Manchester were well known and *the* most fashionable hotels in their cities. The railways also opened resort hotels: among them were three next to championship golf courses, at St Andrews, Turnberry and at Gleneagles, which was one of the most luxurious resort hotels in Europe. The Great Western opened several holiday hotels in Cornwall and the LMS hotel opened at Stratford-on-Avon and at seaside resorts served by the railway.

Although the railway companies in Continental Europe built and operated railway hotels they were never on the same scale as Britain. However, the most luxurious, splendid and ornate of all railway hotels was the Hôtel Palais d'Orsay above the Paris Gare d'Orsay railway station on the left bank of the Seine. The magnificent ballroom, in a riotous Louis XIV style, had pairs of columns between large areas of mirror with convoluted cntabulatures. The columns supported an elaborate gilded frieze and a vaulted ceiling painted with the loves of Jupiter and the other inhabitants of Mount Olympus. Marble statues of standing, lying and seated nymphs under lighted swags and elaborate candelabra completed this magnificent confection of a room. The room was used as the setting for performances by the Renaud-Barrault Classic Theatre Company in the 1970s and Orson Welles shot a part of his film of Kafka's *The Trial* in its interior.

Station hotels were usually situated immediately beside the terminal station. The Pera Palace in Istanbul was an exception. Passengers disembarking from the Orient-Express at Sirkeci Station beside the Topkapi Palace gardens had to cross the Golden Horn to Galata to reach the hotel. The Pera Palace was operated by a subsidiary company of the

Compagnie des Wagons-Lits and was the last word in luxury, considered the *only* place to stay in Istanbul during the early years of the last century. It was the Istanbul base of Kemal Ataturk's[9] late years and was the stage for a number of dramas that included an anarchist's bomb in the lobby and a fatal shooting in the Orient Bar that almost ruined the barman because the clientele fled the bar before paying for their drinks. The hotel was restored to its original glory in the 1950s but has now sunk into shabby but alluring decay.

Van Horne, the general manager of the Canadian Pacific Railroad, built two great and famous hotels. The Banff Springs Hotel, which opened in 1887 in Banff National Park was one of the most monumental resort hotels in the world. It was soon matched when in 1893 the Canadian Pacific launched the construction of the Château Frontenac in Quebec City. The brick and stone keep, with its four rounded corner towers and its steep green copper roof pierced by four layers of dormer windows, dominates the city's Haute Ville and the St Lawrence River.

At about the same time that Van Horne was building the CPR's monolithic hotels in Canada, Henry Flagler was building hotels along the east coast of Florida to create passenger business for his railroad. The Ponce de Leon in St Augustine, a few miles south of Jacksonville, opened in 1888. It was a 540-room luxury hotel designed to lure the richest guests. It was built, regardless of cost, in a Spanish colonial style and embellished with Italian Renaissance external decoration and Louis Tiffany was responsible for decorating the interior. Flagler said: 'I had rather spend $5,000 too much than $5,000 too little ... I tell my friends that when they stop at the Ponce de Leon it will cost them a good deal of money, but guarantee them that they will get its full return in value'. In the 1890s the hotel went through hard days and the manager asked permission to fire a French chef and the dance band. Flagler wired back 'Hire another cook and two more of the best orchestras.' Before the Ponce de Leon was open, Flagler started to build the Alcazar only a block away. Its façade was based on the Alcazar in Seville, and though it was a less luxurious hotel it had a 120ft long swimming pool with a balcony at one end with a dance floor and two bands.

9. His room in the Pera Palace Hotel is now a museum.

When Flagler's railroad tracks reached Palm Beach, he built the world's largest resort hotel and the world's largest wooden building, the Royal Poinciana Hotel. It opened in 1894, only nine months after construction began, with more than 500 rooms. After the wings were completed it had 1,150 rooms and capacity for 2,000 guests. As sea bathing became increasingly popular, Flagler built the Palm Beach Inn on the ocean shore; it burnt down but has since had a renaissance and was renamed The Breakers to become one of the world's most fashionable hotels.

Henry Plant, a Yankee speculator, established himself as a rival to Henry Flagler by building a railway to Tampa on the Florida Gulf Coast. In 1891 he opened the splendiferous Tampa Bay Hotel, a 1,000-ft-long Moorish building with silvered minarets and domes and horseshoe shaped windows. Flagler was unmoved by the competition and continued building his line south to Miami. When he arrived for the first time, he settled on the site for his rail terminus and the site for the Royal Palm Hotel. It opened in 1897 with 350 rooms and the following year became the American army headquarters for the duration of the Spanish-American War.

Inspired, perhaps by the Royal Poinciana Hotel, the Brooklyn Rapid Transit Company built an enormous wooden hotel, the Brighton Beach, on the Coney Island seafront. Unfortunately it was too near the sea and a high spring tide invaded the reception rooms and nearly swirled away some of the guests. Undaunted, the BRT jacked up the structure over some rails and used Long Island Railroad locomotives to move it back to a safe distance from the sea.

❖

Passenger stations or depots formed only a small part of the infrastructure of a railway serving a town. There were sheds for stabling locomotives, water towers, coal storage, storage for ash and there were carriage sidings. In addition there were the facilities needed for commerce: sidings for delivering coal to local merchants, yards for transferring cattle and other animals and buildings for storing goods and parcels waiting to be transferred to drays whose horses needed stables. Large towns also had an engine roundhouse rather than a shed, sidings for assembling trains, facilities for cleaning carriages and specialised warehouses for grain and other commodities, sometimes even a fish market.

The most surprising ancillary railway building is the CN Tower, opened in 1976 by an affiliate company of Canadian National Railway and situated beside Lake Ontario in Toronto. Its hexagonal concrete core is braced with three broad radial ribs, each extending 90ft to give stability to the tower. The ribs extend up to the 1,150-ft-high revolving restaurant; from there the core continues a further 360ft to an eagle's nest observation platform and the communications spire antenna reaches a height of 1,816ft. It is the tallest man-made structure in the world.

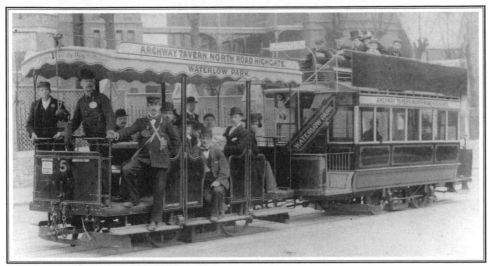

Highgate Hill cable tram *c*.1884

8 Rails in and under Cities

Rail systems in, under and out of cities come in all shapes and sizes. There are tramways and trolleys, elevated or overhead lines, Light Rapid Transit lines, Metros or subways or Undergrounds, monorails, Train-Trams and even People Movers. Classification into one or other category is not possible: for instance, some Paris Métro trains cross the Seine at the Pont Mirabcau on elevated iron columns high above the road traffic and another Métro line on stilts has trains rumbling for nearly a mile and a half over the traffic of the Boulevard de la Chapelle. Tube trains that cross central London in deep tunnels travel on the surface to reach their suburban terminuses. New York subway trains tunnel under Manhattan and under the centres of another three New York boroughs before travelling in the open to Coney Island, Far Rockaway, or across the Harlem River. Some tramways have been upgraded to Light Rapid Transit lines and some LRTS have been downgraded to tramways. Whatever the name, the function remains the same: transporting large numbers of urban or suburban people to work, to school, for visits or entertainment and then bringing them back home. The best collective name for these diverse transport systems is *metro*, derived from metropolitan – of the city – rather than from the type of system.

❖

London streets have always been crowded and congested. A late 18th-century print of crowds crossing a Thames bridge shows an almost intolerable chaos of congestion. People are jammed together shoulder to shoulder, men pushing their way through with barrows, carters driving wagons loaded with coal, water or night soil, bully-boys forcing through sedan chairs and the occasional carriage with its servants ahead trying to clear the way. The main streets were cobbled and deep with horse muck and there were crossing sweepers in the more genteel sections of town. The lesser streets were littered with both horse and human refuse and there was little or no provision for drainage. Improvements only began after 1827 when John McAdam was appointed Surveyor-General of Metropolitan Roads.

The population, apart from a small minority, walked. They walked to work, they walked to the market and they walked to church. Public transport for the well-off probably began in the mid-17th century with the introduction of Hackney carriages and the two-passenger cabriolet or cab which was introduced from Paris in 1823. In 1829 the first omnibus ran from Paddington Green to the Bank of England. Advertisements for this service of communal travel boasted 'a person of great respectability attends his vehicle as conductor ...'. George Shillibeer, the omnibus entrepreneur, went broke, not surprisingly as the bus probably carried no more than 14 passengers and progress on the unmetalled road was slow and uncertain.

A remarkable American adventurer, George Train, who had spent most of his life travelling and doing business between England and America, introduced horse trams to England in 1860. He had seen the success of street trams in New York and Philadelphia and thought that Liverpool, which he regarded as the most progressive British city, should have trams. The city fathers did not share Train's enthusiasm, so he crossed the River Mersey and introduced his ideas to the town of Birkenhead. His four-mile-long Birkenhead Street Railway was a success and he inaugurated it with a monumental banquet. His account of the banquet lists those who were invited and they included the Emperor Napoleon, the King of Prussia, the Tsar and just about every duke and noble lord in the peerage, but it does not list the guests who actually attended the celebration. His horse trams running along smooth rails carried double the number of passengers and gave them a quicker and more comfortable ride than the rival omnibuses running on the roads.

After a public hearing, and despite fierce opposition from the road omnibus companies, Train built and operated a line with stepped rails above the road surface in London from Marble Arch along the Bayswater Road. In his memoirs, *My Life in Many States and in Foreign Lands,* Train claims the rival bus drivers 'tried in every way to wreck their vehicles on the rails ...'. Finally there was an accident in which a youth lost his life and the Bayswater Road enterprise came to an end. George Train's first London tram ran in 1861 and trams continued to run in London streets for more than 90 years. The indefatigable and colourful Mr Train claimed he built tram lines in Geneva and Copenhagen, became a partner in the Credit Mobilier in New York, played an important role in the 1870 French Commune, stood for the US presidency and went round the world in 60 days (to show Jules Verne). He finally died in New York 'in reduced circumstances'.

The first steam trams ran in Philadelphia and Cincinnati in the 1860s and were followed by New York and New Orleans. This aspect of the age of steam innovation and enterprise did not reach British streets until 1880. In fact, British manufacturers had supplied steam trams to a number of overseas countries, and in 1877 even supplied 46 steam trams for the Paris tramway system. Some of these trams were still working a shift of early morning duty towing 20-ton wagons loaded with fruit and vegetables to the central wholesale markets as late as the mid-1930s.

The early steam trams combined the boiler, engine and passenger accommodation in a single unit but this was soon superseded by a separate tram engine towing passenger carriages. In Britain, legislation defined a number of technical requirements for tram engines: there should be no visible smoke or blast, no engine clatter, all working parts had to be concealed and exhaust steam had to be condensed rather than exhausted into the atmosphere. As a result there were skirts that stretched around the wheels almost to the rails and an ornamental tin grille on the sides of the roof to hide the spaghetti of condenser pipes. The resulting tram engine looked like a passenger carriage with a four-foot chimney coming out of the roof. A small number of manufacturers specialised in making tram engines and they were soon joined by manufacturers of steamrollers and agricultural machinery. One manufacturer received a proposal, 'these tram engines frighten the horses – why not make them in the shape of a natural animal? For instance they might be formed like a swan, the long neck being eminently suitable for enclosing a chimney.'

Steam tramway operators had problems with the rails, which had been laid for lighter horse trams rather than heavy tram engines. The rails also filled with grit because all road vehicles preferred running on the smooth area around the rail rather than on the stony road surface. The steam train had its heyday in Britain from about 1880 to 1902 and the last steam tram ran between Wolverton and Stony Stratford; it closed with the 1926 General Strike and never reopened. Steam trams continued in service until the 1930s in Holland, Italy and France.

❖

Werner von Siemens demonstrated the world's first electrically powered train at the Berlin Industrial Exhibition in 1879 and he installed the first commercial electric tramway at Lichterfeld four years later. The same year he demonstrated the first electric tramcar with an overhead trolley power pickup at the Paris Exposition. In Britain two tourist lines were opened in the early '80s: Magnus Volk's line along the Brighton sea shore, which continues to operate, and a line taking visitors to the Giant's Causeway in Northern Ireland.

The breakthrough to large-scale commercial city tramcar operation was made by Ensign Frank Sprague of the US Navy. He was stationed in London and regularly travelled on the steam-hauled Metropolitan Railway and he imagined how electric traction would improve the system. He returned to America, left the navy and in 1885 developed an experimental electric locomotive for the 34th Street branch of the New York elevated railway. Two years later with little experience and great courage he took a contract to install and operate an electric street tram system in Richmond, Virginia. His Richmond electric tram system combined innovation with sound engineering practice and it gained sufficient operating experience to become the precursor of city and suburban tramway systems worldwide. Sprague was a gifted engineer and organiser and he overcame many of the early technical problems. He reduced the size of the motor to fit alongside the transmission under the tram floor, he increased the motor's power up to about 12hp and he designed effective protection for the motor from the water and dirt on the roadway. His trams were sufficiently powerful to be fitted with a snowplough to clear the rails; a clear advantage over horse- or mule-drawn trams. However thunderstorms were an early hazard; the trolley poles had to be disconnected to prevent lightning flashes burning out the motors.

Sprague continued to introduce technical advances that included an effective sprung trolley pole, motors driving each axle for rapid acceleration or to overcome icy conditions, and he designed a motor controller to enable the motorman to provide smooth acceleration. The Sprague control system continued giving reliable service on Paris métro trains and probably elsewhere until the mid-1980s. Within ten years of the opening of the Richmond tramway there were nearly 15,000 miles of tram tracks with more than 40,000 electric tram cars in North America; it was claimed that tram cars or trolley cars carried six times as many passengers as the steam railroads at one quarter the cost per passenger/mile. There were even funeral cars taking the dead and their mourners to the cemetery often situated at the end of the line.

The tram or trolley car helped define the shape of North American cities. Its explosive success and adoption coincided with the period of phenomenal growth of cities. The technical problems of constructing the high-rise office building had been overcome with the introduction of the steel skeleton frame, the automatic elevator, central heating and fire protection. As a result the business centre of the modern city was a series of high-rise buildings compressed into a few blocks of the downtown area. By contrast city workers lived in generously sized property lots in the suburbs sometimes as far as twelve miles from the city centre; electric trams or trolley cars linked the spread-out suburbs to the central downtown business area.

In 1910 a group of civic-minded businessmen from Utica, New York, decided to visit towns in Ohio and the Midwest to see what lessons could be learned and to find business opportunities. They chartered a trolley car from the local Onieda Railway Company and set off from Bagg's Hotel on Main Street on a 2,000-mile odyssey that took fifteen days. They took their trolley car from one urban or interurban system to the next and visited Detroit, Indianapolis and travelled as far south as Louisville, Kentucky. The trolley pilgrims returned to a Utica covered in bunting with crowds in the streets, and, of course to a banquet at Bagg's Hotel.

Overhead trolley lines were the standard power source for almost all trams or trolley cars. However, in New York, London and a few other cities the overhead lines were found to be unacceptable and a number of other systems were used. The most common alternative was to pick up current from a cable in a conduit buried in the centre of the tramway. Budapest probably had the most advanced conduit system and its principles became the standard for the streets of New York. Blackpool, with the earliest electric city trams in Britain, started operation with conduit power pick-up but the conduits filled with salt and sand from the seashore and the system was changed to overhead lines. A few tramlines operated with cables from a winding engine; the tramcars had detachable grippers that clamped the cable as it progressed along in a conduit. The San Francisco cable car system was established in 1871 by a Scotsman who was horrified by the suffering of the horses toiling up the steep hills. Parts of the system continue to operate and are an important tourist attraction. Some other American cities used cable systems; on the first day's operation in Pittsburgh a tram set out for a round trip scheduled to take about an hour but took a week to complete the circuit. Cable systems were used in Edinburgh, on a Glasgow metro line and up London's Highgate Hill but they were all replaced by electric traction. A number of other methods, including batteries and pick-up studs which energised when the tramcar passed over the stud, were tried but with no lasting success.

The adoption of electric trams made a slow start in the UK with only about 30 miles of electrically operated track in service up to 1895. The 1870 Tramways Act had draconian requirements: tram operators were responsible for the upkeep of the roadway between and outside the rails, a total width of eight feet, and only a maximum drop of only seven volts in the return circuit was permitted, to avoid the possibility of electrolytic damage to nearby metal utility pipes and telegraph wires. Finally the Act laid down that the municipality had the right to purchase the system after 21 years at the net value of the assets. Electric trams only started to take off when J. Clifton Robinson, an experienced American tram operator and engineer, came to Britain and oversaw the building and operation of the first electric trams in Bristol and Dublin in 1895. City fathers became enthusiastic about electric tram systems; they could keep their street lighting supply generators running during daylight hours to power trams.

In London electric trams became the standard for transport south of the river and in the boroughs in the north that were not served by the Underground. Trams took children to school, their parents to work, crowds to football matches and they took families to Epping or Greenwich for a day out in green countryside. In the early days, tram rails did not cross the Thames bridges but electric trams finally beat the taboo and linked north and south London. One line of double-decker trams even clattered through more than half a mile of the Kingsway tramway tunnel from the Thames embankment to Holborn. However there had always been prejudice against trams in Britain. At the end of the 19th century, an article in *Electric Tramways in Great Britain* ended, 'The tramway is still the poor man's carriage in Great Britain and it will take years before it will reach its proper estate and be recognised as our indispensable convenience by all classes'. The prejudice continued half way into the last century: '... poor little shops standing cheek by jowl with poor little shops and miles upon miles of silver ribboned tramlines heralding the passing of rocking juggernauts ...'.

In 1886 Daimler and Maybach patented their petrol-driven horseless carriage and the first petrol engine bus, a Daimler, arrived on London streets in 1899. It was the beginning of the end for London trams. A 1931 Royal Commission reported 'Tramways, if not an obsolete form of transport, are at all events in a state of obsolescence and cause much unnecessary congestion and considerable danger to the public ...'. The last London tram ran from Woolwich to New Cross in July 1952. Glasgow had the last British big city tramway system and it closed ten years later. Buses replaced trams in British cities. In Continental Europe trams, many of them elderly and needing replacement, and almost all single deck, continued to rumble along city streets.

Worldwide, 5,198 different tram systems have been counted, with over half – 2,742 – in North America. The peak year for American tramways was 1918 and then the number started to decline. Los Angeles had the world's most extensive interurban tram or trolley system that operated more than 1,000 miles of track. In 1939, Pacific City Lines, owned by General Motors and Standard Oil of California, purchased one of the tramway companies with the intention of 'motorizing' the electric system. Two years later, together with Firestone Tyre they took over the management of the company, tore up the rails, dismantled the trolley wires and introduced GM buses fuelled with Standard Oil diesel and running on Firestone tyres. In the San Francisco Bay Area, one of the local tram companies operating a rail link across the Bay with a right-of-way on the San Francisco–Oakland Bay Bridge was bought by General Motors. Two days after the purchase General Motors announced that streetcars would be replaced by buses. In 1958 they removed the rails from the lower deck of the six-mile long Bay Bridge. This was at the time when BART, Bay Area Rapid Transport, was starting to make plans for a metro to serve the area. Because there were no more rails on the bridge and therefore no more right-of-way, BART was obliged to spend millions to drive a tunnel under the bay.

Earlier, General Motors had been involved in replacing more than 100 tram or interurban trolley systems with buses in cities that included New York, Chicago, Detroit and many others. In 1949, a Chicago federal jury convicted General Motors of 'having criminally conspired with Standard Oil of California, Firestone Tyre and others to replace electric transportation with gas or diesel powered buses, to monopolize the sale of buses and related products to local transportation companies throughout the country'. Naturally, big business won out; the court imposed a sanction of $5,000 on General Motors and convicted and fined a Mr Grossman, the General Motors treasurer, just one dollar.

Recent years have seen a renaissance of the tram in Continental Europe. Existing tramlines have been expanded and updated to serve agglomerations or regions rather than just cities. This renaissance is not only in Europe but all around the world, with progressive cities such as Toronto, Los Angeles, San Francisco, San Diego, Salt Lake, Sydney and many others operating glittering modern trams that have become LRTS, Light Rapid Transit Systems.

There are many sound reasons for the return of rails to cities. Streets, roads and highways have become saturated at peak times with petrol- or diesel-fuelled traffic. Economic forecasters in every nation predict increasing growth in the number of cars and see only very limited possibilities for increasing road capacity. Economists are only now beginning to recognise that the costs of city traffic should include the costs of road accidents and to recognise the costs to the community of stalled or very slow-moving traffic. It has become generally recognised that atmospheric pollution from dense road traffic, the air townspeople breathe, is sometimes dangerous and is almost certainly the main cause of the increasing incidence of asthma and other bronchial disorders. Public transport is the alternative. But why rails with their high initial cost rather than the bus or the electrically powered trolley bus? Rails enable the tram and its trailing cars, possibly as many as six or seven, to follow the configuration of the road and make safe turns. Multi-car trams carry several hundred passengers; three or four automatic opening and closing doors in each car speed loading and unloading and reduce journey time; low-floor cars also provide easy access, especially for children and the disabled. And, of course, in addition to the other advantages, electric traction does not create pollution in the city. Many cities give trams an immediate green 'go' light at road intersections to ensure they keep moving. Finally, trams road-run in city centres and then speed up on dedicated tracks to take passengers to their suburban destinations. The German city of Karlsruhe was the first to go a stage further: they have adapted their tram traction motors to run on both 250Vdc and 15kVac so that they run in the city streets and then speed along Deutsche Bahn rail tracks into the countryside.

In the 1980s, Californians voted for increased spending on city rails in preference to new freeways. Recent surveys in France show that people, school children especially, prefer riding in trams rather than buses. And it comes as no surprise. The leading tramcar suppliers and operators have focussed a large amount of engineering and design effort on track, suspension and controls so that passengers are given a smooth gliding ride through the city or on dedicated tramways. Seats are comfortable, many trams are air-conditioned and some have deep windows down to within a few inches of the floor so that passengers feel they share in the hustle of the pavement, shop window displays and the excitements of city centres.

Some city tram rails are not only used to transport people; in Zurich trams collect waste from a series of pick-up points and ferry it outside the city for disposal. In Dresden five-car trams transport parts from factories and the railway yard across the city to a Volkswagen assembly plant; their destination board reads *CarGoTram*. France is leading the way to try to reduce the capital cost of installing tramlines and three cities or regions are experimenting to combine the advantages of road and rail: the tramcars run on pneumatic wheels on the road with a steel guidance wheel riding on a central single sunk rail and conduit. The trams follow the guiding rail or can be steered manually when the guidance system is disengaged.

Cities, especially those with wide boulevards, are considering BRT, Bus Rapid Transit, as a cost-effective alternative to the tram. One study has shown that the capital cost is about one-thirtieth of the cost of laying tramlines, provided there is enough space on the roadway for the 80-ft megabus with its two articulated trailers. Curitiba in Brazil has led the way, operating more than 100 megabuses, each designed to carry 260 sitting or standing passengers. Bogota has followed Curitiba's lead, and European manufacturers are beginning to introduce megabuses and megatrollies of almost the same size as those in South America, but with capacity for only 180 or 200 passengers; perhaps they believe that Europeans are less prepared to be treated as sardines in a tin.

It would be a mistake to suppose that trams disappeared altogether from the UK. Blackpool's trams have run without interruption since 1885 and even the public horse tramway in Douglas, Isle of Man, which opened in 1876, continues operating every summer to this day with its 40 horses; its principal technical innovation is to provide the horse with galoshes. The revival of rails in British cities came with the 1980 opening of the Tyne and Wear Metro linking both sides of the Tyne estuary and helping revitalize Newcastle; there is no road-running and it is more an LRT than a traditional tramway. The Docklands Light Railway opened seven years later to link the City of London with the new Docklands commercial centre built over the old dock system of the Isle of Dogs. Again, with no street-running, it is an LRT rather than a tramway. Manchester Metrolink, opened in 1992, was the first new tramway to combine road-running along the main shopping streets in the city centre with speeding along dedicated tracks to outlying towns such as Bury and Altrincham. The two-car articulated trams can be operated as multiple sets with automatic coupling or uncoupling from the driver's cab. The Sheffield Supertram system opened in 1994 with three-car trams and extensive city centre street-running and dedicated tracks in the suburbs. The Midland Metro links Birmingham and Wolverhampton. In south London, the Croydon Tramlink with its low floor trams, modelled on Cologne tramcars, links Wimbledon to Beckenham and New Addington and road-runs through Croydon's business area and its animated shopping centre. Nottingham is just the most recent example of introducing trams onto British city streets and across the Channel even the Serenissima City of Venice will soon have purple and gold painted trams[1] on a 12-mile line serving Venice from Mestre.

❖

Many fanciful ideas were put forward for the first underground metro systems. In London, Joseph Paxton, designer of the Crystal Palace, proposed the *Grand Girdle Railway and Boulevard under Glass* and William Mosley proposed the *Crystal Way*, a luxury shopping mall over double tracks with pedestrian walkways beside the tracks. In New York, Alfred Ely Beach, who produced the world's first practical typewriter, proposed a pneumatic subway. He used his fortune to drive a tunnel from the basement of Devlin's Clothing Store on the corner of Murray Street and Broadway. The work was done furtively with the spoil being carted and dumped at night to avoid opposition and obstruction from Tammany Boss Tweed who was also chief of the Department of Public Works. When the line stretched just over 100 yards to Warren Street it was inaugurated with a party in its only station, which was fitted with fountains, a grand piano, a huge fish tank and wall paintings; it was presented to New Yorkers

1. Running on pneumatic wheels with a steel guidance wheel in a central conduit.

as a fait accompli combining a brilliant technical advance with a solution to overcoming street congestion. The single passenger car was a tight fit in the nine-foot diameter tunnel and was propelled by a Roots Patent Force Blast Blower nicknamed *Western Tornado* that would propel the car 'like a boat before the wind'. When the car reached Murray Street, it tripped a lever to reverse the blower, which sucked the car 'like soda through a straw'. The system was the talk of the town for a short time and there were battles between Beach and Boss Tweed in the Albany Legislature but Beach failed to raise the funding to build an extended system.

❖

Paddington Station, the London terminus of the Great Western, is nearly five miles from the City, the commercial and financial centre and principal destination for daily commuter passengers. The Great Western, the City Corporation and others subscribed the necessary capital to build the Metropolitan Railway, an underground railway from Paddington in the west in a northern arc round central London to Farringdon Street on the edge of the City. Two years later it was extended to Moorgate Street close to the Bank of England at the heart of the City.

There was general enthusiasm for the line but there were exceptions. *The Times* thought it 'an insult to common sense to suppose that people would ever prefer to be driven amid palpable darkness through the foul subsoil of London'; another opponent of the underground railway opined 'if London is to be cut up in such style, London will have to move elsewhere', and a Dr Cuming claimed 'The forthcoming end of the world would be hastened by the construction of underground railways burrowing into the infernal regions and thereby disturbing the devil'. The Company responded by providing gas lighting in the tunnels and boasting 'Gas will supply the place of the sun'. The Company PR people worked over journalists who visited the railway with such effect that one wrote about the tunnels which '… instead of being close, dark, damp and offensive are wide, spacious, clean and luminous, and more like a well-kept street at night than a subterranean passage through the very heart of the metropolis'.

The line was dual gauge, 7ft 0¼in for through Great Western trains and

4ft 8½in for the shuttle Metropolitan Railway trains and later for Great Northern trains to join the tracks at King's Cross. The line was built by the 'cut and cover' technique: a deep trench was excavated in the street, the rails laid and then covered over to make a tunnel. The initial part of the line, the world's first underground railway, to Farringdon Street opened in January 1863. Shortly after, the Metropolitan Railway was extended to Hammersmith to the west and Whitechapel to the east. Later a suburban extension was built 30 miles northwest to the towns in the Vale of Aylesbury.

A year after the opening of the first section of the Metropolitan, a new company was established to build an underground railway along a southern arc around the centre of London from South Kensington, under Chelsea, Westminster and the new Victoria Embankment to the City. It was named the Metropolitan District Railway Company (known as the District), and opened its first stations in 1868. In 1884 the northern arc of the Metropolitan Line and the southern arc of the District Line were joined at their west and east extremities to form the Inner Circle and provide a link round central London and connections between the mainline railway stations[2].

The Metropolitan and the District were obliged to cooperate to work their trains around the Inner Circle but Sir Edward Watkin, the Metropolitan chairman was openly scornful of the less profitable District. A flamboyant chairman of three railway companies, 'Nimble Ned' Watkin even funded an initial bore for a Channel Tunnel, and, after hearing of the success of the Eiffel Tower in drawing tourists, started construction of a tower[3], 15ft higher, beside the Metropolitan tracks at Wembley.

Under his leadership the Metropolitan became a large scale property developer. It was good business to sell property plots and then railway season tickets to the new commuters. The 1920s saw the introduction of house mortgages for the middle market and the Metropolitan launched a campaign to attract customers to Metro-land, its rural arcadia. There was a Metro-land magazine that included descriptions of building lots, ' This is

---

2. An interesting detail: uneven wheel wear was and still is one of the consequences of running trains in the same direction on the Inner Circle; to overcome the problem, a different train is taken each day to the Whitechapel spur and reversed in order to travel round the Circle in the opposite direction.

3. The Tower was never completed and was dismantled in 1907.

a good parcel of English soil in which to build home and strike root, inhabited from of old … the new settlement of Metro-land proceeds apace …' and 'jaded vitality and taxed nerves are the natural penalties of modern conditions, nature has, in the delightful districts abounding in Metro-land placed a potential remedy at hand.' Large parts of Metro-land, the countryside idyll, became a drab suburban sprawl.

Watkin was an enthusiastic public speaker and on one occasion addressed his shareholders about the iniquities the Metropolitan suffered from its suppliers: 'Clodd, the great railway contractor, Plausible, the great railway engineer and Vampire, the great railway lawyer'.

The Metropolitan and the District steam locomotives were designed to consume their own smoke and condense waste steam back to water but the systems were not effective and travelling in the Metropolitan with its 500 trains a day was like entering a dirty smoky hell. This was despite frequent open cuttings to ventilate the line between the tunnels. One journalist wrote 'I had my first experience of Hades today, and if the real thing is to be like that I shall never do anything wrong … the atmosphere was a mixture of sulphur, coal dust and foul fumes from the gas lamps above; so that by the time we reached Moorgate Street I was near dead of asphyxiation and heat'. The *Scientific American*: 'What is at first merely unpleasant soon becomes unhealthy and eventuates in a subtle poison …'. An inquiry following the death of a young woman in a train to King's Cross found that 'sulphurous and carburetted gases had gone on accumulating in the tunnels of the railway till the air had become dangerous to breathe'. In 1898 the Board of Trade formed a committee to investigate the conditions in the tunnels. The Metropolitan's General Manager had the effrontery to inform the members that smoke-filled tunnels were not only harmless to humans but positively beneficial and went on to say that the platforms of Great Portland Street station were 'actually used as a sanatorium for men who had been afflicted with asthma and bronchial complaints'.

The first deep London tube line was the City and South London Railway, which opened in 1890; it later became a section of the Northern Line. It ran from the City, under the Thames and after 3½ miles and four intermediate stations terminated at Stockwell. The tunnels were bored about 40ft deep using James Greathead's tunnelling shield pushed forward through London clay by hydraulic rams. The tunnels were below the level of sewers and followed the routes of the streets above to avoid the slightest possibility of causing disturbance to buildings. Where the streets were narrow the tunnels were bored one above the other rather than side-by-side. The original intention was to use cable traction but in the event they used electrically powered locomotives running on current generated by British adaptations of Thomas Edison's dynamos. Each train comprised three wooden carriages, heavily upholstered and with small high-up windows, and they became known as 'padded cells'; they were single-class carriages, possibly the first in Britain. The stations were easy to recognise from the street because each had a cupola to house its passenger-lift winding gear.

The Central London Railway, opened in 1900, ran from the City west to Shepherds Bush. It was largely financed by European and American money and much of the equipment was supplied from the US including the power generators, GE electric locomotives and Sprague supplied the 48 lifts for the line. The Central was probably the first railway line to site each of its stations on the top of a gradient: the climb up to the station helped reduce speed and brake wear and the downward grade helped the train accelerate with minimum power consumption. From Marble Arch, the line followed the path of Oxford Street and it played an important role in developing Oxford Street into London's best-known shopping area and establishing theatreland along Shaftesbury Avenue.

Whitaker Wright was an English adventurer who returned to London with a mining fortune. He financed the beginnings of what became the Bakerloo tube line but he became over-extended, tried to rig the market and fled the country leaving chaos and unpaid contractors. His money antics were considered criminal, he was arrested, sentenced to seven years and committed suicide while still in the Law Courts. Charles Yerkes was an American financial adventurer who had served a jail sentence in Philadelphia and hurriedly left Chicago after building a financial pack of cards for the construction of the Loop. He arrived in London and established Underground Electric Railways of London Ltd, which took over the District Line, and negotiated rights for other semi-built or unbuilt lines. Yerkes's role with the Underground was universally welcomed. However he soon outwore the welcome; one Member of Parliament said that he doubted 'whether for a long time, if ever, such a very dirty transaction was ever done by parties coming before Parliament'. Yerkes found the money on the basis of unrealistic undertakings to share and bond holders; he died in 1905, leaving a chaos of debt and complication and in 1908 the company was narrowly saved from liquidation.

From then on, there was prudent management, leading in 1933 to the formation of the London Passenger Transport Board (LPTB), which took over the operation of London's buses, trams and the Underground railways. Prudent management seldom builds new underground railways and it is doubtful if the Bakerloo or the Piccadilly lines would have been built if it had not been for the ambitions of Wright and Yerkes. Yerkes not only left his mark on underground London but also in many of the streets with his stations, such as Gloucester Road and Russell Square, with their distinctive plum-coloured glazed terracotta façades and arched first-floor windows.

The years of prudent management did produce one star, Frank Pick, who joined the Underground in 1909 and became vice-chairman 24 years later. He extended the tracks of the different tube lines into the suburbs and, with his architect Charles Holden, built a series of remarkable and handsome stations that became landmarks in each of their suburbs and became some of the most admired buildings of the 1930s. Arnos Grove and Southgate stations are possibly the best known. Holden then went on to design 55 Broadway, the LPTB's headquarters building which was completed in 1929 and was one of the first modern English buildings to have sculptures by well-known artists that included Henry Moore, Eric Gill and Jacob Epstein added to its façades. A contemporary art lecturer wrote of Epstein's *Day and Night* 'they are not in any sense human, more nightmares'.

Tube stations became vitally important to thousands of Londoners during World War II despite notices at the beginning of the War: 'The public are informed that, in order to operate the railways for essential movement, underground stations cannot be used as air-raid shelters ...'. The Luftwaffe's blitzkrieg on London began in September 1940 and a crowd forced their way past police to spend the night on the platforms of Liverpool Street tube station. By the end of September it was estimated that more than 170,000 spent their nights sheltering in tube stations. The authorities responded by organising tiers of steel bunk beds, sanitation, sick bays with nursing facilities and special trains calling at stations in the early hours with refreshments. Communities grew in many stations and elected officials to make life tolerable and sleep possible. Some of the shelters even published news bulletins – the first issue of *De Profundis*: 'Greetings to our nightly companions, our temporary cave dwellers, our sleeping companions, somnambulists, snorers, chatterers and all who inhabit Swiss Cottage Station of the Bakerloo from dusk to dawn ...'.

There were a number of high-explosive direct hits on stations causing casualties and there were other disasters such as a direct hit on a water supply main, which cascaded water and debris through a station and caused heavy casualties. On VE night in 1945, 12,000 were still sleeping in tube stations, mostly families who had been bombed out of their houses. Babies had been born in the tube and some children had never slept in a house. The greatest tragedy on the Underground, and possibly the worst civilian disaster of World War II, occurred during an air raid when a young mother holding her baby fell down the stairs in the dark at Bethnal Green station and 173 people lost their lives in the ensuing chaos and panic. In addition to providing refuge to Londoners sheltering from the bombs, a tube tunnel under Goodge Street station in Bloomsbury became General Eisenhower's headquarters for planning the Normandy invasion.

Thanks to the combination of over-cautious management and the delays caused by two world wars, it took 62 years to open the new tube lines, the Victoria Line in 1968 and the Jubilee Line 11 years later. In Roland Paoletti, the Jubilee Line found an astonishing combination of visionary, teacher and architect combined with the discipline and knowledge gained by having designed 37 stations for the Hong Kong Mass Transit Railway. Paoletti commissioned and worked together with some of the most distinguished architects to build 11 astonishing stations for the Jubilee Line's extension from central London under the river through the Isle of Dogs business centre to link with the Stratford interchange with its Central Line and high speed Channel Tunnel line station. An arts correspondent wrote that the stations 'are public works to compare with those of the Romans at their best, with those of the medieval cathedral-builders, with the stupendously self-confident engineering of the Victorians'.

Apart from the new Victoria and Jubilee lines, the London Underground has suffered from lack of investment and from lack of leadership. One of the new Mayor of London's first acts was to publish *The Mayor's Transport Strategy* in July 2001 in which the Underground is the cornerstone for an integrated transportation system for the whole of Greater London. Sadly, the various factions of government have regarded the underground as a fiscal item, and an expensive one, rather than part of a grander plan for providing Londoners and visitors with 'seamless' transportation around London.

❖

Several entrepreneurs put forward schemes for a Manhattan subway line to relieve street congestion. All the schemes were blocked either at a local or a state level by entrenched interests largely dominated by Tammany Boss Tweed. However Charles Harvey obtained the city's approval to build an elevated line on single iron columns along Greenwich Street. The passenger cars were propelled by gripping a moving cable between the rails; the cable was hauled by a series of stationary steam winding engines at 500-yard intervals. The first trial took place in 1867 and there is a photograph of a top-hatted Harvey sitting on a small flat board with four large wheels and holding the cable gripper as if for dear life. Within a few years the line was extended north along Greenwich Street and its continuation, Ninth Avenue. There were frequent problems with the cable breaking or jamming, and in 1871 steam locomotives replaced the cables; in the same year a passing loop was built at West 12th Street station enabling trains running in opposite directions to use the line. The line was extended to 42nd Street with its Hudson River Railroad Terminal and two years later business had become so good that the company double tracked the line.

In 1878 the Third Avenue elevated railway or el opened and was then extended north as far as 129th Street. A third track was added for express trains; it was used in just one direction for peak hour traffic. The Sixth Avenue el opened in 1879 and the Second Avenue el opened a year later. Over the next years the four north–south els were extended north through the Bronx and they had east or west shuttles running to the East River and Hudson river ferry terminals.

The early locomotives were scaled-down, standard four-wheel railroad engines but they were not suitable for frequent stops with the need for fast acceleration and effective braking. They were replaced by locomotives specially designed by Matthias Forney, which successfully hauled the seven car trains. Smoke, dirt, noise and oil and hot ash dropping on pedestrians and horses meant that steam traction was far from ideal. Following a number of experimental systems the first electric train went into service on the Second Avenue el in 1901; two years later the last steam locomotive to run on the els was withdrawn from the Ninth Avenue line. However, there were not only objections to steam but to the whole principle of the els. In 1886 the *New York Times* said: 'It may be taken as a settled fact that the problem of rapid transit for this city has not been solved by the elevated railroads and that these structures cannot be permitted to remain permanently in the streets.' The last extension to the els was completed in 1920. From then on services were gradually discontinued and the last el train ran in 1955; the demolition of the el structures was completed the following year.

New York was not the only city to have an el. Chicago has a network of elevated railways leading to the Loop around the downtown area round which trains ran 'on sight' without signals. Liverpool had the Overhead and Wuppertal in Germany has its eight-mile long Schwebebahn. Instead of riding on rails the passenger cars hang from the rails with roof-mounted bogies; the system was recently modernised and is still rolling today, more than a hundred years after its opening.

A reorganisation of the New York Rapid Transport Commission was heralded in 1894. With William Parsons as chief engineer, a new plan for the future of transportation in New York was formulated. He travelled to Europe to study the metro systems in Budapest, Paris, Berlin, and of course, London. A part of his report on his London visit reads: '... however, the air in the tunnels is extremely offensive ... The best condition of the atmosphere is just in advance of a locomotive, where there are no passengers, and the worst is just behind the locomotive where the passengers are ...'.

The Commission decided to run electric trains in shallow subway tunnels constructed with cut and cover technology learned from the building of the Budapest metro. The trains incorporated Frank Sprague's Multiple Unit System for smooth and fast accelerations: a single control in the front cab controlled traction motors not only in the leading car but on the axles under the trailing cars; the system was in already in use with great success on Chicago's South Side el. Ground was broken in 1900 with the City responsible for construction and the IRT, Interborough Rapid Transit Company run by August Belmont, a well known New York financier, responsible for operating the system. The nine-mile long line from City Hall to 145th Street opened with great celebrations in 1904. From the beginning, the line was laid with four tracks along most of its distance with eight-car express trains making only a limited number of intermediate stops and five-car locals stopping at each station. The IRT Manhattan station entrances with steps down to the ticket halls and platforms were protected from the weather by 20-ft-long steel and glass kiosks with surprising Islamic style roofs. They were derived from the kiosks built for the Budapest metro, which had in turn been inspired by Kushk, Turkish summer-houses: Kushk became Americanised into kiosk.

The IRT was extended north under the Harlem River to the Bronx and by 1908 the line was extended under the East River to Brooklyn. New subway lines were constructed up to 1920 under the 'Dual Contract' system, one between the City and the IRT and another between the City and what became the BMT, Brooklyn Manhattan Transit. In 1912, while digging the new BMT Broadway subway line, construction workers bashed through brickwork to find themselves in the forgotten station built by Alfred Beach for his pneumatic railway more than 40 years previously. They were amazed by the rotting splendour of the station fixtures and a memorial plaque in honour of Alfred Ely Beach was fitted to a wall in the BMT City Hall station. In 1932 the City built a third group of subway lines; neither the IRT nor the BMT bid to operate it, so the City operated the system itself and named it the IND or Independent. Separate companies tunnelled tracks under the Hudson to link New Jersey and its commuter dormitories to Manhattan; after a series of financial problems the Port Authority Trans Hudson Corporation, PATH, took over the operation of these rails under the Hudson.

The New York City subways and many of its bus routes were combined and, in 1953, the NYCTA, New York City Transit Authority was formed to take overall control. Partly as a result of expanding beyond the City boroughs and partly because of financial problems, the NYCTA became a public benefit corporation, the MTA, Metropolitan Transportation Authority. The system became run down until, in 1981, the New York State Legislature, declared a 'transportation emergency' and voted massive funds to modernise the equipment and its operating methods.

Recent investment and re-organisation have made the New York subway a fast, inexpensive, effective and efficient system and even crime and graffiti on the subway have been reduced. Now the main complaint seems to be noise, particularly the deafening screeches at South Ferry station where the trains make a hairpin turn, a trifling problem when compared to those faced by metro systems elsewhere.

❖

Paris had a large and growing population crammed into a small area limited by its 18th-century city walls. In the 1870s, the City Council asked eminent architects and planners for proposals for a city transit system. One of them, Louis Heuzé, who must have been an Anglophobe, put forward a proposal for a covered system of overhead walkways and rail tracks, arguing that underground travel might be suitable for people 'used to the fogs of London' for whom 'the obscurity of a tunnel is not a change', and adding that Parisians would not accept 'descending by long staircases into veritable catacombs' and would not tolerate a '*Necropolitan*'.

The 1900 International Exposition galvanised the Paris politicians into action. Unlike London or New York the municipality planned a complete metro system from the beginning. The city authorities were to be responsible for building the infrastructure of stations and tunnels and to solicit bids from companies to lay the tracks, buy the equipment and operate the system. A consortium of companies which formed the Compagnie de Chemin de Fer Métropolitan de Paris (CMP) put forward the successful bid. To economise, the city specified a narrow-metre gauge between the rails. This was rejected by national government, which specified the standard 1435mm, 4 ft 8½-inch gauge; however it neglected to specify the loading gauge and métro cars are narrower than mainline stock which cannot be used in the Paris Métro.

In July 1900 the first Métro line opened along the right bank of the Seine with terminuses at the Porte de Vincennes, a traditional city gateway in the east and the Porte Maillot, a gateway in the western city walls. The line runs in a tunnel, apart from Bastille station where it crosses the canal St Martin. The municipality chose a gifted and committed engineer, Fulgence Bienvenüe, to mastermind the Métro's construction. Bienvenüe became known as the Father of the Métro and retired in 1932 aged 80; Montparnasse-Bienvenüe station was named in his honour. There were no major setbacks or delays to the construction of the city's metro lines apart from Line 4 which was built in two sections, one on the right bank and one on the left. However, the difficulties of tunnelling under the Seine were resolved with only little delay and the complete line was opened in 1910. Its six and a half mile length is now the busiest in the system.

While the municipality was building its tunnels and stations, it let a concession to a consortium not only to operate but also build metro lines. Generally known as the Nord-Sud, the company built what is now Line 12 from Montmartre to Montparnasse and Line 13 from St-Lazare to the Porte St Ouen. The lines were built to the same standard as those built by the municipality but the Nord-Sud stations were generally more spacious than those of the CMP and had more decoration.

There was great expansion of the inner suburbs between the two world wars and most of the Métro lines were extended beyond the line of the city walls to provide a service to these suburbs. The Métro was run by the Vichy government during World War II and was the only means of transportation for the inhabitants as there was no fuel for bus services. After the war ended, the Métro, Paris buses and local SNCF services were amalgamated into the RATP, Régie Autonome des Transport Parisiens. Then followed a long period of lack of investment. Finally, there was a major management shake up, investment and the construction of the new RER (*Reseau Express Régional*) express lines linking the new outer suburbs to a series of interchange stations on the Métro.

The principal Métro lines reached their capacity by the end of the 1940s and forecasts indicated that traffic on the lines would continue to increase. The RATP were unwilling to undertake the expense of lengthening station platforms to accommodate longer trains and their solution to increase line capacity was to build new trains fitted with pneumatic tyres to provide better acceleration from the closely spaced stations, most only about a third of a mile apart.

The initial trials were considered a success and Line 11 was fitted with continuous concrete strips outside the conventional rails to support the pneumatic tyres of the load-bearing wheels and narrow vertical strips for the small pneumatic horizontal guide wheels. The bogies also housed conventional flanged wheels that drop onto the rails in the event of a failure of one of the rubber tyres. The first 'pneu' train entered service in 1956 and the pneu system was then installed on the Métro's two busiest lines, 1 and 4, in 1963 and 1966. The pneu system was considered a success and the RATP consultancy arm helped install pneu metro systems in Montreal, Sapporo, Kobe, and Mexico City. Over the following years there were advances in the design of the drives and suspension of conventional rapid-transit trains that substantially reduced the advantages of the pneu system. However Line 6 was also converted to pneu; half the line is in the open and the high cost of installing the pneu system was justified on noise and environmental grounds. Surprisingly the only new métro line, Line 14, the Météor (*Métro Est Ouest Rapide*) is a pneu system and it also operates the first driverless train in Paris.

Amongst many other things, the streets of Paris are famous for their Art Nouveau entrances to the Métro. In the late 19th century when the Métro was being planned, Charles Garnier, the most famous architect of the day and designer of the monumental Paris Opéra, proposed that the entrances should be stone, marble, triumphal columns, finials and sculptures. The CMP board rejected these grandiose ideas and unexpectedly chose unknown 32-year-old Hector Guimard as their architect. Guimard had won an architectural travel scholarship, and instead of treading the Beaux Arts path to Rome, he chose to study in Belgium under Victor Horta, the founder of the Art Nouveau school. Lines 1 to 8 still have more than eighty delicate and delicious Guimard dragonfly entrances or *édicules* with their wonderful balustrades and convoluted lettering of which *Le Temps* wrote

'These disorderly hieroglyphs are dismaying to little children trying to learn their alphabet in school ...'. A Guimard *édicule* is in the collection of the New York Museum of Modern Art and recently a facsimile *édicule* was erected as the entrance to Van Buren Street subway station in Chicago. Other facsimile Guimard métro entrances have been installed in Mexico City, Montreal and Lisbon.

The Métro is maintaining its reputation for decorative or artistic innovation. It recently commissioned artist Jean-Michel Othoniel to design a new entrance to the Palais Royal station. Instead of a conventional Métro entrance there is Le Kiosque des Noctambules; the stairway is crowned by two metal cupolas and a series of large brilliantly coloured glass spheres – a splendid fantasy before going down to the platforms. The RATP has also brought some innovative interior decoration to the platforms of some of the stations. The first was at Louvre, which has replicas of some of the more famous exhibits from the museum. Concorde is tiled with an alphabetic puzzle on the theme of the *Rights of Man and the Citizen*, Chambre des Députés has large anonymous silhouettes of faces in the place of the advertising panels and there are many other stations with decorative themes.

❖

Many of the world's largest cities now have metro systems. New York has the largest system with the most stations; London is next in mileage but with fewer stations than Paris. London is sixth in terms of volume of passengers, fewer than Moscow, Tokyo, Mexico City, Paris and New York.

Immigrant train; crossing Canada

9 Passengers

The Oystermouth Railway, later known as the Swansea & Mumbles, was the first British railway known to have a charter to carry passengers when in 1807 it made an arrangement with a contractor to run a horse drawn 'waggon or waggons for the conveyance of passengers'. The Stockton & Darlington, promoted and built to transport coal, encouraged independent contractors to run passenger services until the ensuing chaos obliged the company to run its own passenger service. The Liverpool and Manchester was built to transport freight but the carriage of passengers provided more than half its revenue from its earliest days. Possibly the main reason for this unexpected revenue was that the railway almost immediately put road coaches out of business and passengers had little alternative to rail; however it took the railways many years to reduce freight traffic carried by canal and coastal shipping.

The railways had to learn how to carry passengers and travellers had to learn how to be train passengers. An early log recording accidents includes 'Injured, jumped out after his hat', 'fell off riding on the side of a waggon', 'skull broken, riding on top of the carriage, came in collision with a bridge' and 'fell out of a third class carriage while pushing and jostling with a friend'. Most early passengers' accounts of travelling by train indicated that they were delighted by the experience. Fanny Kemble, the actress, was clearly enchanted by a locomotive and called it 'a snorting little animal' which she was 'rather inclined to pet'. Following her first railway journey she wrote, 'You cannot conceive what that sensation of cutting the air was; the motion is as smooth as possible too...When I closed my eyes this sensation of flying was quite delightful, and strange beyond description.' However, not everyone enjoyed train journeys; Thomas Carlyle, the sage of Chelsea, travelled from Windermere to London in 1847. 'Once swallowed into the belly of the rail-train, there was of course nothing more to be said or thought; nine hours of tempestuous deafening and nightmare, – like hours of Jonah in the *whale's* belly, I suppose, – and one was flung out in Euston Square, glad to have escaped, but stupefied for a week to come'. In 1829, the year of the Rainhill Trials, Carlyle wrote that the era was not a 'Heroical, Devotional, Philosophical or Moral Age but above all others, the Mechanical Age. It is the age of machinery in every outward and inward sense of the word.'

Even reading a railway timetable had its difficulties: a Great Western timetable from the early 1840s included the note, 'London Time is kept at all the Stations on the Railway, which is 4 minutes earlier than Reading time; 7½ minutes before Cirencester time; 11 minutes before Bath and Bristol time.'

First, second and third class were unknown terms until the coming of the railway. Stage-coaches designated their passengers as Mail, Inside, Outside and Waggon; early steamships carried either Cabin or Deck passengers. At the beginning, First Class referred to the speediest trains rather than to the degree of comfort and then the Liverpool & Manchester offered passengers first and second class travel on the same trains; not only did they have separate carriages, but they also had separate booking offices and waiting rooms in the main stations. Some railways herded passengers into open wagons and called it third class. An accident with eight fatalities on the Great Western at Sonning alerted Parliament to the dangers of increasingly speedy travel in open wagons and in 1844 a Parliamentary committee laid down minimum standards of safety and comfort. An enormous number of people could no longer walk to work since railways built into the centre of towns destroyed large areas of tenement buildings and the occupants were rehoused in the suburbs. A number of companies introduced workmen's trains with cheap tickets in the early morning for 'persons of the labouring classes' or 'mechanic population' to enable them to get to work. There were also cheap train fares when the South Eastern Railway introduced hop-picker specials from London to the Weald of Kent. Later other companies also ran special trains for pickers to the hop fields. As late as 1936 the Great Western issued instructions 'only third-class carriages of the oldest type must be used; in no circumstances containing lavatories or first-class compartments'.

Most companies followed the example of the Midland when it upgraded its third class to a second class standard and abolished second class. In 1893 the West Coast Mainline companies introduced their Anglo–Scottish Corridor Express with just first and third class accommodation and with a restaurant car available to all passengers. Critics claimed that the different passenger classes perpetuated the divides between the social classes. The novelist R.S. Surtees wrote that railways 'annihilated the prejudice against public conveyance. They have opened out the world to everyone'.

Up until the 1960s there were still a large number of passenger carriages in service with separate compartments and no corridors, each compartment accommodating 12 seated passengers and, during the rush hour, a number of standing passengers trying to find room for their feet. This supposed preference for separate compartments was mocked by continentals and Americans as an indication of English reserve and taciturnity in the style of Mr Phileas Fogg.

Today, one of the regrets of high-speed rail travel is that it has become more like travelling in an airliner than in a train. An announcement is made just after leaving the Channel Tunnel and heading toward Paris in a Eurostar; rather than saying 'This is your captain, we have now reached our cruising altitude of 30,000ft', it says 'This is your conductor, we have now reached our cruising speed of 300km/hour.' And, rather as travelling on Concorde used to be, there is little sensation of speed. The interior of a Eurostar carriage even looks like the inside of a passenger plane and first class restaurant service is brought to the passenger's seat on a plastic tray. A good way of getting from A to B in comfort; luxury it isn't, glamour it certainly isn't. The Thalys and TGV trains have interiors like a medium-priced Renault car; the Cisalpina trains between Milan, Switzerland and

Southern Germany are more pleasing and railway-like and they have the glorious facility of a window at the end of the last passenger carriage that looks along the track: a marvellous experience travelling along Lake Como and climbing up to the St Gotthard tunnel on the way from Milan to Zurich. Japanese Shinkansen express trains are comfortable but spartan whereas the German ICE first-class carriages have space and luxury with a modern version of the American parlour car and a separate dining car with a kitchen and real food.

Traditionally railway lines were routed to go through as many towns as possible and so went past factories, rows of houses, waste-treatment plants, station platforms with people, suburban trains and all the paraphernalia of operating a railway system. The LGV or other dedicated super express lines are routed to go from A to B in an arc bypassing human habitation or activity and what activity there is seems part of a very distant and uninteresting backdrop. A glorious exception to this tedium of high-speed rail travel is the Tokaido Shinkansen line from Tokyo to Osaka with the symmetrical and perfect Mount Fuji visible for a large part of the journey and then houses and activity, with tea and mandarin plantations almost reaching the tracks.

❖

A 150-strong Sunday School outing to Liverpool in 1831 was the first train excursion to be organised, a year after the opening of the Liverpool & Manchester Railway. In 1840 two Scottish railway companies organised excursions for horseracing enthusiasts to go to Paisley racecourse. In the same year the Leeds Mechanics Institute arranged an excursion to Hull for 1,250 passengers. Four years later there was another Leeds–Hull excursion taking 6,600 passengers in 240 carriages; known as 'The Monster Train', in fact it was probably a succession of trains.

Thomas Cook, a wood-turner by profession, organised his first excursion from Leicester to Loughborough for a temperance fête in 1841; he sold all the tickets and travelled with his customers on the train. During the following years he organised summer excursions to Scotland and to the Welsh holiday coast but by 1846 he was bankrupt. His capable son John helped pick up the pieces and devised a system of coupons to pay for hotel accommodation: the first package tour. They organised tours overseas and in time the Thomas Cook Company had offices in the main cities around the world and they even organised the visit of the German Kaiser, Wilhelm II, to Palestine in 1898; escorting the Kaiser, John Cook caught dysentery and died. Thomas Cook's grandchildren sold the business in 1928 and since then it has been owned by a succession of banks. London's 1851 Great Exhibition provoked an increase in the demand for excursion trains. There was no telegraph to provide warning of extra trains and the Great Northern Railway, in their temporary London Maiden Lane terminus, was in a state of near chaos with the arrival of unexpected excursion trains. The return north was equally chaotic; on one evening there were 3,000 would-be passengers but trains for only 1,000. A crowd of Yorkshire men took over the Lincoln train despite the foaming, furious efforts of Edmund Denison, the Chairman of the Board, trying single-handed to eject them forcibly. Finally he had to be restrained and some cattle trucks were shunted in, presumably for the Lincoln passengers.

Calling them charters or calling them excursion trains probably depends on the passengers' purpose. Going on a special train for a day at the seaside sounds like an excursion; pre-1914 sporting Oxford undergraduates organising a train to take them and their horses to a meet of foxhounds and wait to return them when the sport was over could be considered as either, and J.P. Morgan, the American banker, organising a train of luxury Pullman cars to transport Episcopalian bishops to a meeting in San Francisco almost certainly sounds like a charter. Penniless Queen Marie of Romania visited the United States in 1926 and her coast-to-coast charter train was the best-ever charter bargain; she was charged just $1 by each of the railroads. In August 1963, 21 charter trains from across the nation brought 30,000 participants to the great civil rights march in Washington. This march of more than a quarter of a million people was largely inspired by A. Philip Randolph, President of the Brotherhood of Sleeping Car Porters.

An 1896 excursion ended in disaster. In order to drum up passenger business the passenger agent of the Missouri-Kansas-Texas Railroad, the Katy line, convinced his management to stage a railway disaster to bring in the crowds. Excursion trains brought passengers to a fairground and a city of tents beside the Katy tracks between Waco and Hillsboro, Texas. Two hundred deputy sheriffs were needed to control the crowd as it tried to press close to the track. Two retired locomotives, one painted red the other green faced each other by a sign: 'Point of Collision'. They drew back and then went forward and just touched like boxers before a contest. Then the two trains, each pulling six cars of sleepers and hoardings advertising fairs and circuses, reversed for about a mile. At a signal, the throttles and whistles were lashed open, the enginemen jumped off and the trains hurtled toward each other. Fireworks and exploding signal crackers had been laid along the rails to add to the excitement. The engines met, reared up and toppled sideways with a thunderous crash and clouds of steam. The crowd felt they had had their money's worth. Then the engines' boilers exploded showering the crowd with heavy shards of metal; two spectators were killed and a number injured. A flying bolt hit photographer J.C. Deane as he was taking a picture of the colliding trains; from then on he was called Joe One-Eye Deane.

'Sunday, October 18, 1936 was written up as an unforgettable day in the land of châteaux and good wine', according to a local French paper. An excursion named *Le Train du Vin et de la Chanson* left Paris at 07.00 and arrived at Rouvray in the Loire Valley wine country for the celebration of the *vendange*, visits to the cellars with prolonged wine tasting and a mammoth lunch. The excursion continued to Saumur for more wine and an enormous dinner. The fare included a non-stop supply of Loire wine during the journey, and singing and dancing to the train's Radio Bacchus. The excursion was scheduled to return to Paris just before midnight. In California, the Napa Valley Wine Train advertises Brunch, Lunch and Dinner; the brochure makes no mention of dancing to Radio Bacchus.

In the mid-1930s the French Nord company installed a public-address system in some of its trains. Trains taking schoolchildren to summer camp or for an excursion to the countryside used the *train-radio* to endlessly harangue and lecture the children on how to behave on the train and whilst they were away.

Regular excursion trains were organised for pilgrims to visit sites of religious importance. Following the canonisation of St Theresa, the État company organised excursion tickets that included the train fare, lunch in Lisieux and entrance to the shrine's Diorama. Lourdes in the foothills of the Pyrenees was the principal and best-organised centre of pilgrimage in Europe. In 1908, 525 excursion trains from all over the continent transported more than 300,000 pilgrims to Lourdes. There were special chartered *trains des malades* to take the infirm to Lourdes. Not only was the train accommodation specially arranged for pilgrims on stretchers or in wheelchairs but each compartment was dedicated to and named after a particular saint. Doctors were in attendance and so were priests to administer the last rites if required. Pilgrims were the passengers on the first railway in Iran and the Middle East. The five mile line that opened in 1887 between Tehran and Rey shuttled pilgrims every Friday to the shrine of Shah Abdul Azim.

❖

Queen Marie-Amélie of France was the first monarch to travel by train[1]. Her husband King Louis-Philippe wanted to inaugurate the first French passenger service but his ministers considered him too august and too precious to undergo the hazards of travelling by train.

Queen Victoria made her first railway journey in 1842, from London to Windsor. After she married, she and the Prince Consort travelled by rail throughout the country meeting her subjects and performing the duties of a dutiful monarch. Extreme care was taken and elaborate arrangements were made for transporting Her Majesty; even the coal in the tender was whitewashed and the speed limited to 40mph so that she could work and attend to state papers; during her travels she sent or received telegraph messages at stations along the route. In addition to her state duties, the Queen used the railway to travel to her two private residences, one at Osborne on the Isle of Wight, 85 miles from London and the other at

---

1. The Queen's train was delayed and she arrived late for the inaugural banquet. The chef had already finished cooking the potatoes and been obliged to put them to one side. When he heard the royal party arrive he hurriedly put them back in the stove. Convinced they were an inevitable disaster, he was amazed and delighted to find they had expanded and become crusty and delicious. The combination of the chef and the Queen's late train gave birth to *pommes soufflées*.

Balmoral, 600 miles from London. King Edward VII preferred to travel more quickly and he travelled widely by train on royal business and for weekends with grandee friends to shoot or to watch sporting events. During World War II, with its aerial bombardments, the King and Queen made extensive use of the royal train, and it was often parked in a secluded siding for the night. In 1965 British Rail refurbished the royal train for Queen Elizabeth, but by this time royalty did most of their travelling by air or by car.

King Edward VII had a luxurious series of royal carriages built for him in 1903 for travelling to Paris to further the Entente Cordiale, for visiting his nephew Kaiser Wilhelm, and for visiting the Emperor Franz Joseph in the south of France or in Marienbad. The King's first meeting with President Loubet of France was planned to take place in the refurbished Bois de Boulogne station to avoid the Paris crowds. The King's carriage was supposed to be at the rear of the train, however the train was reversed when it transferred from the main line to the *ceinture* to reach the Bois de Boulogne, and the King was at the front rather than at the rear of the train. The President and the dignitaries as well as the red carpet were at the wrong end of the platform. They raced up to the front and a very out of breath President greeted an impatient Monarch. Fifty years earlier Napoleon III felt that the Gare du Nord was not a sufficiently splendid entrance to Paris for Queen Victoria's state visit. He ordered a spur to be built from the Nord tracks to the more glorious Gare de l'Est as a suitable gateway for the arrival of the British Queen.

If British royal travels and royal trains were splendid, they were as nothing compared to those of Napoleon III. He travelled extensively throughout France to review army parades and manoeuvres and he had special trains to take the court and his guests from Paris to Compiègne to spend the weekend in his romantic fortress-palace at Pierrefonds. The imperial train comprised nine or ten carriages, each with a heavily embossed gilded bronze N surrounded by the cipher of the empire and the crown of the emperor. The sumptuous carriages included salons and bedrooms lined in silk and the dining room carriage had four small tables with ten plush armchairs, two of which, thrones, were heavily embossed with the imperial cipher. The tables glittered with gold or silver gilt cutlery,

Sèvres porcelain and Baccarat crystal.

The imperial age in France came to an end in 1870 and carriages from the imperial train were sold to the Tsar of Russia. The ostentation, pomp and glory of the second Empire were succeeded by the stolidity of the Republic and its presidents. One President, Sadi Carnot, was murdered by an Italian anarchist when he stepped out of his Wagons-Lits salon carriage in Lyon station in 1894. One evening in 1920, President Descharvel set out in the presidential train for an overnight journey to Montbrison. The chef-de-train held a head count of everyone on board early the following morning because he had received a telegraph message telling him that someone had been seen to fall out of the train. The President was found to be missing; the 64-year-old, bruised and bleeding in dirty pyjamas, was found by a crossing keeper and then collected by the local prefect. An official bulletin stated that the President had felt unwell, got up, tried to open a window but opened the door and fell. There was widespread speculation that the President had either been drunk or was mentally deranged; there was even a popular song *Le Pyjama Présidentiel*. Descharvel suffered the speculation and insults about the incident for four months and then resigned.

The reclusive King Ludwig II of Bavaria, Richard Wagner's patron, lived a life of romantic dreams and built a number of fairytale castle palaces on the top of mountains and beside remote lakes. His railway carriage[2] on an eight-wheel frame, is painted a shiny Garter blue with a low gilded balustrade on the edge of the carriage roof with gilded putti supporting great swags of gilded foliage. The moulded shape of an enormous cushion resting on the centre of the carriage roof supports a very large moulding of the Bavarian crown complete with ermine and jewels. The interior has a large central compartment with a rather cramped smaller compartment at each end; one is a washroom and the other has a bench for equerries or attendants. The central salon is splendiferous, almost beyond description. The style is high, overwhelming baroque. Painted allegorical panels in the ceiling are surrounded by gilded mouldings. The gilded entablatures of the windows are supported by caryatids and there are gold

---

2. Preserved in the Nuremberg railway museum.

swags, tassels and royal emblems everywhere. The walls are a dark-blue silk brocade beneath all the gilded decoration. There is a marble table in the centre surrounded by heavily decorated and gilded chairs and to one side is the blue silk upholstered throne with elaborately gilded arms and with the back decorated with nymphs and putti supporting the royal cipher. The King also had a fine-weather carriage: a glass conservatory of a carriage with balconies at each end with a surprisingly plain and handsome wrought-iron frame holding it all together.

By contrast Prussian Chancellor Otto von Bismark's *salonwagen* of the same period has a green fabric interior and the only glints of gold come from the brass coat hooks and light fittings. Almost as modest was the carriage of Elisabeth, known as Sissi, the beautiful wife of Franz-Joseph, the Emperor of Austria. She found that rail travel gave her the opportunity of escaping the elaborate and laborious protocol of the Court in Vienna. She converted the interior of a standard Wagons-Lits carriage into a bedroom and a sitting room. The carriage was added to the Orient-Express or other trains to enable the Empress to travel incognito across Europe and to her *Mon Repos* villa in Corfu. In 1873 she rented a castle in Normandy for the summer; French President MacMahon went to greet the distinguished visitor at nearby Evreux station but Sissi remained behind the drawn curtains of her state carriage until after the President left; she became known as the '*l'Imperatrice errante*'.

Napoleon III presented a specially built carriage to Pius IX, the first pope to travel by train; it was half sitting-room and half oratory. The papal train also included a coach that was a long open balcony with an awning roof so that the Pope could be seen by the crowds. Three astonishing carriages were probably the last of the sumptuous royal trains; they were commissioned in 1929 by Mussolini as a present to Victor-Emmanuel III, King of Italy. Mussolini had just made his peace with the Vatican by guaranteeing its independence and he was anxious to gain favour with the king. The interior of the carriages had gilded coffered ceilings, wall coverings embossed with a violent repetitive pattern of the King's coat of arms and quite alarmingly patterned carpets: the result was bewildering rather than dazzling.

Mussolini's famous 1922 *Marcia su Roma*, March on Rome, to assume power was in fact made by train from Milan in a luxurious sleeping carriage. It's uncertain if he made the trains run on time[3], but he certainly improved a dispirited and run-down rail system.

The most famous railway carriage of all was Wagons-Lits #2419 which was modified in 1918 as a conference room and taken to a siding in Compiègne, north east of Paris. The German high command arrived by train and at 11a.m. on the 11th of November 1918 World War I ended with the German surrender. Some years later the carriage was renovated and installed in a specially built exhibition hall. Following the invasion of France, Hitler ordered the carriage to be placed exactly where it had stood at Compiègne 22 years previously and gave a French delegation ten minutes to sign up to his terms for the capitulation of France. He then ordered the carriage to be put on exhibition in Berlin. Later it was removed to a remote rail siding to avoid damage from Allied bombs and was finally destroyed by an SS unit just before the invading American forces reached it.

A meeting was arranged between Hitler and Pétain in 1940, four months after the capitulation of France. Hitler and his staff came by train from Berlin, through Belgium and then south to Montoire-sur-le-Loir, a small, disused station on a line that had been closed for passenger traffic. There was an initial meeting between Hitler and Pierre Laval, the French Vice-President. The following day Hitler continued his train journey to Hendaye to meet General Franco of Spain. He returned to Montoire; Pétain, President of Vichy France, arrived and the two leaders spent two hours together. Following the meeting Pétain issued the following statement, 'Last Thursday I met the Chancellor of the Reich ... we envisaged a collaboration between our two nations and I have accepted this principle ... Follow me.' Philippe Pétain: hero of Verdun in 1916, collaborator in 1940.

In America, candidates for the presidency traditionally campaigned from the platform of the last car of a special train. However, whistlestop campaigning became obsolete after President Truman's 1948 campaign,

---

3. The biographer of the famous antifascist writer Gaetano Salvemini wrote that 'he would rise to his feet in a rage whenever he heard the words *on time*.'

but almost every presidential candidate since, including both George Bush and Al Gore in the 2000 presidential election campaign, has made occasional use of a train for campaigning. One American train journey to have far-reaching consequences was made by President Truman and Sir Winston Churchill travelling to Fulton, Missouri in 1946. It was there that Churchill made his famous 'Iron curtain' speech.

The best-known presidential train journey was made by the body of the murdered Abraham Lincoln from Washington to be buried in Springfield, his southern Illinois hometown. A short time earlier George Pullman had designed and built the luxurious and well-appointed sleeping and saloon car that he named *Pioneer*. It cost $20,000, five times more than any other sleeping car and was known as 'Pullman's Folly'. As one of Pullman's biographers wrote: 'Never before had such a car been seen; never had the wildest flights of fancy imagined such magnificence.' None of the railway companies were interested in using it because of its expense and the fact that the body was out of gauge: although the wheels were suitable for standard 4ft 8½in gauge rails, the body was too wide. Mrs Lincoln insisted that her hero husband should ride in the greatest possible state in *Pioneer* on the journey from Chicago to Springfield. Station platforms were torn up and other obstructions were removed and *Pioneer* and the Pullman Company became famous across the land and launched luxury rail travel in America. However, the funeral train that attracted most mourners along the tracks was the train that carried Rudolph Valentino's body back from New York, where he died, to Los Angeles.

Kings and queens have been taken to their final resting places in trains drawn by locomotives with the royal or imperial coat of arms swathed in black crepe. And it was not only kings and queens that had special funeral arrangements. The London & South Western Railway added two platforms to its Waterloo station for special trains to take the dead and their mourners to the London Necropolis & Mortuary Company's enormous Brookwood cemetery in Surrey. The spur from the main line ran for three-quarters of a mile with two stops, the north 'for Protestant Non-conformists, Roman Catholics, Jews and Parsees' and the south 'for Anglicans'.

❖

By three-quarters of the way through the 19th century each European country had its own railway system; some were national systems as in Belgium, others were operated by a series of companies; in every case the railways terminated in frontier towns where passengers had to leave the train, show their passports or credentials and board another train, sometimes in a different station, to continue their journey into the neighbouring nation.

The demand for international European passenger travel was growing. The big tunnels, the Fréjus and the St Gotthard had been opened, linking southern Europe through the Alps to the nations of the north. Rail across Europe was the quickest route to the Middle East where oil was beginning to be exploited, and it provided the means for bankers and merchants to visit customers and negotiate business. The time had come to run international trains from one end of Europe to the other.

George Nagelmackers, a Belgian entrepreneur, was the man to organise international trains. He had travelled in America on Pullman cars and even went to Chicago to examine *Pioneer*. On his return to Europe he put forward a project for a luxury through carriage between Paris and Vienna. The Franco-Prussian war put the scheme on ice, but, with the support of the King of the Belgians he ran through carriages from Ostend to Brindisi, an important route[4], because it reduced the number of days needed to travel from Britain to the Suez Canal and on to India. In 1879 Nagelmackers added two sleeping carriages to a postal train that ran from Calais to Brindisi and advertised it as the *Indian Mail Train*. In 1902 Nagelmackers ran the *Bombay Express* to connect in Marseille with P&O steamships on their way to India.

Almost inevitably Nagelmackers ran into trouble with his banks and he amalgamated his Compagnie Internationale des Wagons-Lits into The Mann Boudoir Sleeping Company of Lancashire. Colonel William Mann

---

4. This route, but via Paris rather than Ostend, to Brindisi remained important for a small number of travellers until the mid-1930s. Imperial Airways provided links to the great cities of the British Empire: Karachi, Calcutta, Rangoon and, with Qantas, to Australia. With their limited range, the aircraft made the long journeys in a series of hops. The crucial Paris–Brindisi hop was missing from the schedules because of endless political negotiations about the air-space rights over Italy. Imperial Airways' passengers travelled 950 miles by rail, from Paris to Brindisi, until 1936.

was an American adventurer with a background in Pennsylvania oil and in manufacturing. One of his firms had supplied Lillie Langtry's luxury rail car with silver bath fittings, a bedroom in padded Lyons silk and the rest to match; a modern replica of Cleopatra's barge, said Colonel Mann. Following a series of disagreements, Nagelmackers, supported by a syndicate, bought out Colonel Mann's interest and the Compagnie des Wagons-Lits et des Grands Express Européens became headquartered in Belgium. Nagelmackers made it possible to travel in comfort and without changing trains from Calais to Naples, from St Petersburg to Nice, from Berlin to Athens and from Paris to Istanbul. In Istanbul, the ferry took passengers across the Bosphorus to Haydarpasa where passengers could board the *Taurus Express* to Aleppo and Baghdad or to travel on to the Lebanon and Cairo. Nagelmackers' most ambitious scheme was the *Nord-Sud-Express* between St Petersburg and Lisbon. Serving seven capital cities, the 3,000-mile journey was scheduled to take 83 hours. The 1884 cholera epidemic closed frontiers and the train never entered service.

The last years of the 19th century, the Belle Époque, was the age of social seasons: Queen Victoria spent some of the winter in the South of France and grandees from all over Europe spent the winter months in the monumental hotels in Nice and Monte Carlo or having a season of balls and parties in St Petersburg or travelling to the sun and the Winter Palace Hotel in Luxor. In the spring there were grand formal parties and festivities in London, Paris and Vienna; in summer the gilded world went to the spas and resorts – Baden Baden, Marienbad, Vichy, Bad Ischl and many others – to shake off the effects of gluttony and good living and in autumn they went to grand estates in Scotland, France or Hungary. They all travelled in the same Wagons-Lits trains; royals and millionaires felt reassured by travelling with other snoring royals and millionaires. Years later, Cyril Connolly wrote of the pleasure of going to sleep in a Wagon-Lit: 'One bids good night to the man in brown, reads in bed by the blue *veilleuse*, hangs an imaginary watch in the velvet watch pocket and goes to sleep lulled by the wheels.' Larbaud, the French poet, wrote '*J'ai senti pour la première fois toute la douceur de vivre dans une cabine du Nord Express ...*'[5].

The Orient-Express was the most famous of the great European luxury trains. In fact it was a series of trains, some going through the Simplon tunnel to Venice and Athens or Istanbul and others going through Vienna to the Balkans. In his *Journal d'un attaché d'ambassade* Paul Morand, a French diplomat, wrote about Turkish nobles and other travellers on the train:

> ... kept their veiled wives, guarded by eunuchs firmly locked in their compartments ... Prince Ferdinand locked for hours in the W.C. anxious to avoid assassins ... English milords, clad in tweeds returning after shooting wild fowl or bears in the Marnuresh and clutching their Holland & Holland sporting guns like mistresses ... Hungarian counts and Romanian boyars making for Vienna or Paris to spend the rich profits of a good harvest ... two or three pale, hungry looking French tutors on their way to teach the sons of Moldavian hospodars at their Transylvanian castles ... demimondaines who had been a pleasant distraction ... diplomatic couriers travelling in pairs like turtle doves ... secret agents and spies no longer very secret ...

The route through the Balkans gave the Compagnie management some unwanted problems in addition to the usual difficulties of operating an international train. King Ferdinand I of Bulgaria was a train buff and sometimes insisted on driving the train across his country; after stopping a number of trains at road crossings he agreed to take over only at scheduled stops. His son Boris was also a keen rail buff and tried to board the footplate of the locomotive of the Orient-Express in Paris. After a row with the Compagnie, Boris agreed that he would only drive the train while it travelled over State Railway metals in Bulgaria. One night when the Orient-Express was running late, King Boris boarded the footplate and ordered the fireman to build up the fire to a dangerously high level. There was a blowback and the fireman, covered in flames jumped from the cab to his death; Boris brought the train into Sofia ahead of schedule and waited for congratulations. In neighbouring Romania Mme Magda Lupescu, the mistress of King Carol, was forbidden entry to the country when Carol succeeded to the throne. Secret police guarded every road and byway into the country but Mme Lupescu travelled to Bucharest on the

---

5. 'For the first time, in a sleeping compartment of the Nord Express, I experienced the sweetness of living'.

Orient-Express; as usual the *contrôleur* made sure none of his passengers were disturbed when they crossed the frontier. King Carol's wife, Queen Helen, was seen as a threat to the King and was exiled from Romania. One night in 1933 the chief of police drove the Queen into a deserted and unlit section of Bucharest station and helped her into the Orient-Express for Paris. In September 1940, three Compagnie coaches were shunted into a Bucharest siding to take King Carol and Mme Lupescu to exile. They boarded the coaches with an El Greco from the palace walls and a truckload of other treasures. The coaches were attached to a train following the route of the Orient-Express into neutral Switzerland; just before passing into Yugoslavia there was a hail of bullets and Carol and Lupescu jumped to safety in the iron bathtub of the luxury Wagons-Lits carriage.

Everyone travelling east to west or vice versa across Europe travelled on the Orient-Express; some travellers were more colourful than others. The Maharajah of Cooch Behar arrived in Constantinople in his steam yacht en route for London from Bombay. The Compagnie converted two carriages into rooms of an oriental palace, with the floor covered in rugs and cushions and with divans upholstered in swansdown for his wives and silkily clad concubines; he not only travelled with his women and retainers but also with his cricket bag. Calouste Gulbenkian, the legendary oil concession negotiator, was a frequent traveller; his son Nubar was supposedly smuggled onto the train rolled up in a carpet to avoid the Turkish authorities. Lord Baden Powell, founder of the Boy Scouts, but at that time a secret agent, travelled as a butterfly collector, and Basil Zaharoff, the international armaments king, had the most extraordinary adventure of all on the Orient-Express.

One evening in January 1886 he boarded the train in Paris and noticed a great ceremony and fuss being made of a beautiful young girl and a young man climbing into the Wagon-Lits carriage. The young man was Don Francisco Prince of Bourbon y Bourbon, an important member of the Spanish royal family. The young girl was his bride Maria, daughter of a Spanish grandee, and they were on their honeymoon to stay with the Emperor Franz Josef in Vienna. Later, when Zaharoff was studying some papers, he heard a scream and someone trying to turn the door handle of his compartment. He opened the door and saw the beautiful Maria with her nightdress ripped and with a deep wound on her throat. In the corridor one of Zaharoff's bodyguards was restraining the prince who was holding a knife. Naturally, the festivities in Vienna and the court ball at Schönbrunn were cancelled: in fact, the Prince was insane and was escorted back to an asylum in Spain. News of the Prince's insanity became known and Maria was blamed as the cause of his illness and was exiled. Zaharoff got in touch with her and she became his mistress and adored friend. As a devout Catholic she didn't apply for a divorce but finally her husband, the Prince, died and she and Zaharoff married; the Monte Carlo Casino was his wedding present to the bride.

The Duke of York, later King George VI, made a number of journeys on the Orient-Express, mainly to go to his many relations' weddings, christenings and funerals. The Prince of Wales with his equerry, Major Fruity Metcalfe famously travelled to Vienna, supposedly to visit an ear specialist. In December 1936, only a few days after his abdication as King Edward VIII, the Duke of Windsor travelled on the Orient-Express to Vienna to stay with a Rothschild at Enzesfeld; a few months later, on the day Mrs Simpson's divorce became absolute, the Duke boarded the Orient-Express and travelled to France to marry her.

The heyday of the Orient-Express came to an end with the outbreak of war in 1939. A truncated version of the service was reinstated after the war, but Europe was divided and travellers boarded aircraft rather than Wagons-Lits. The Sea Containers Company purchased some of the pre-war Wagons-Lits carriages and since 1979 has used them to run a tourist, honeymoon and vacation train from the Channel coast or from Paris to Venice where the company owns a hotel. The train has flourished and Orient-Express has almost become a name for a luxury touring train; the *American Orient-Express* starts in Salt Lake City and takes its travellers to the great national parks of the west: Yellowstone, Grand Teton Arches and Canyonlands.

Other luxury sightseeing trains have followed the example of the revived Orient-Express and run through the scenery of Africa, India and Australia as well as the Highlands of Scotland or the Rhine Valley. The traveller in the Glacier Express, between St Moritz in southeast Switzerland and Zermatt 180 miles away in the southwest, is promised 'scenes of wild beauty and pastoral serenity'. There is a special railway that circles the foot of Mt Etna, the largest active volcano in Europe. The Circumetnea train takes 3½ hours and passes through villages and small towns built of lava. In America the Northern Pacific pushed for legislation for Yellowstone to be designated a National Park and even promoted itself as the Yellowstone Park Line as far back as the 1890s. The Grand Canyon Railway, revived twenty years after closure, runs a service from the Santa Fe mainline, to the south rim of the Grand Canyon. In America, trains on preserved railroads are carrying an increasing number of passengers and there are rail connections to most of the better-known National Parks including some of the civil war sites such as Kennesaw in northern Georgia where the Great Locomotive Chase took place.

'Recreational Railroading' has become an important leisure industry in the US. More than five hundred rail museums, tourist lines, steam excursion lines and special events were listed in a recent issue of *Trains* magazine. It's not only the US; there are rail events of one sort or another in practically every country. There is so much interest in railways that there even are regular sales and auctions of 'Railwayana', which includes locomotive number plates and name plates, posters and even old timetables and tickets.

❖

In America with its greater distances and longer journeys, some lasting several days, a private railway carriage or car was commonplace among the very rich. By contrast few European grandees had private rail carriages. The end of the 19th century was the age of opulence and ostentation for the wealthy and the arrangements for private rail cars were no exception. The cars were mini extensions of the sumptuous Nob Hill or Fifth Avenue mansions and were decorated in every imaginable style, high Gothic revival, Second Empire, or even mock oriental. Jay Gould, who had painful stomach ulcers, travelled in his car *Atalanta* with his doctor and chef and was reputed to have a cow, whose butterfat content suited the financier's delicate stomach, tethered in a special boxcar. Mrs Cissy Patterson's butler travelled with her and with seven sets of slip-covers for each piece of furniture in her car, *Ranger*; they were changed each day and florists at each stopping place were alerted to have a supply of fresh flowers. The soprano Adelina Patti had her own private car *Adelina Patti* that supposedly had a sunken marble bath tub. Adelina Patti was also famous for building a sumptuous private waiting room at Craig-y-Nos railway station on the Neath & Brecon Railway in Wales for the convenience of her guests who came for musical weekends at her Craig-y-Nos castle. There are many photographs of Mrs Langtry and also of Sarah Bernhardt standing on the platform of their private cars blowing kisses at the jostling crowds of admirers on the tracks. Mrs E.T. Stotesbury explained the gold-plated taps and fittings in her car, 'saves so much polishing, you know'. Paderewski had the *General Stanley* car equipped with a grand piano. Mrs August Belmont wrote to a friend: 'A private railroad car is not an acquired taste, one takes to it immediately'. Henry Ford didn't have confidence in the construction of a standard railway car and had his *Fair Lane* reinforced with a series of steel trusses that made it so heavy that its use was limited to lines with no weight restrictions. The great railroad tycoons, the Goulds, the Vanderbilts and the Stanfords, travelled in a suite of private cars hauled by special locomotives. One tycoon even had his private car tagged to the back of a commuter train to make the daily journey between Long Island Sound and New York City. The present Waldorf Astoria hotel in New York, which opened in 1931, had an underground track from Grand Central Terminal and sidings for 'garaging' its guests' private railroad cars. Only a very few of the prestige trains would not take private rail cars and in those trains passengers had to travel in reserved luxury compartments. *The New Yorker* wrote that only the *Twentieth Century Limited* and the *Broadway* seemed 'to possess that peculiar swank which compels that patronage of genuinely fastidious travellers – ladies who entertain at bridge while travelling, gentlemen who conduct big business while Pullmanized'.

However, a large number of American passengers received very different treatment from the railroads, and indeed from the law. Two years after the end of the Civil War, Congress passed the Civil Rights Act to help and give rights to the four million freed slaves. It was common practice, however, for railroad companies to continue to segregate black passengers from white passengers despite there being no law requiring it. Then state legislation, starting with Florida in 1887, and followed by most of the southern states, required railroads to sell tickets to 'respectable persons of color' and to provide 'separate, but equal in comfort, accommodation in the train'. A similar law, passed in Louisiana 'to promote the comfort of passengers' was challenged by some African-Americans and one of them, Homer Adolph Plessy, sat in a 'white' seat in a train leaving New Orleans. The conductor asked him to move to the black Jim Crow section. Plessy refused and was arrested. The resulting lawsuit went through the judiciary to the US Supreme Court who voted 7–1 to reject Plessy's case. Writing for the majority, Justice Henry Billings Brown: '… it was reasonable to assume that a state legislature is at liberty to act with reference to the established usages, customs and traditions of the people, and with a view to the promotion of their comfort …'.

Black passengers, paying the same fare as whites, were obliged to travel in Jim Crow carriages or in composite carriages with two entrances; sometimes white men came into the Jim Crow sections to smoke and Jim Crow passengers were neglected or ignored by train crews, for instance by their not putting a step-box on the platform to help them board trains. A recent *Trains* magazine article outlined the complications caused by the legal requirements in each state: black people boarding a Chesapeake & Ohio train in Washington to go to Cincinnati in southern Ohio were obliged to travel in Jim Crow accommodation through Virginia, but permitted to sit anywhere as the train crossed West Virginia moving back to the Jim Crow section as the train continued through Kentucky until it crossed the Ohio river to Cincinnati. In 1937 African-American Congressman Arthur Mitchell boarded a Pullman coach on a Rock Island train at Memphis. When the train crossed the Mississippi into Arkansas he was ordered into the Jim Crow section. He moved after he was threatened with arrest but then went to law. The case finally reached the Supreme Court in 1941 and as a result of its ruling and subsequent legislation together with the difficulty and cost of doubling up separate accommodation, many railroads abandoned segregated accommodation for their passengers. By the end of the 1950s segregation on the railroads ended, apart from a few local lines such as the Central of Georgia.

The meeting of the tracks of the Union Pacific from Omaha, Nebraska with those of the Central Pacific from California in 1869 was the trigger for transcontinental passenger traffic. In 1870, the first full year of passenger operation, 150,000 passengers travelled the new line between Omaha and Sacramento. Emigrants from the east or from Europe travelled cheapest in great discomfort and their journey often took as long as ten days. First class passengers travelled across the continent in luxury Pullman cars in four and a half days. The Boston Board of Trade organised a trip to California for 129 Boston swells in eight Pullman cars. They took an editorial office, a printing press, a library and an organ and had a church service on board the train each evening. When they arrived in San Francisco they walked ceremoniously to the Pacific and dipped a bottle half-filled with water from the Atlantic in the ocean and declaimed in their best Boston brahmin tones: 'The union of these two waters seems typical of the commingling of a great people whose future should be one'. The same year 53 members of the Cincinnati Chamber of Commerce made the journey; one of their cars 'was an elegant saloon fitted up with sofas on either side leaving a space for dancing'. They were keen on amateur dramatics and had a Pullman fitted with a stage and curtain for a series of tableaux vivants.

One passenger who made the transcontinental journey just after the completion of the line was in a car that was derailed because the frozen ground on which the track was built had thawed; all the passengers had to walk across a wooden bridge that had been weakened by the spring floods; at one stop, they were surrounded by vigilantes brandishing guns, who had strung up a local citizen who had 'committed a fiendish outrage upon the only respectable woman in the place' and were waiting for the man's friends to avenge his death. Travellers not only encountered dangers on the line, but there were also dangers in the cars. The Mississippi riverboat tradition of good-time girls and cardsharps was often a part of the long and tedious rail journeys.

The western lands and railroads needed population. There was land for sale at nominal prices and people were needed to grow crops to fill freight cars, to settle and build houses and townships. The railroads set up promotional booths in the Chicago, St Louis and Philadelphia Expositions to attract immigrants from the east. Then they advertised for immigrants from Europe in no fewer than ten languages, even including Welsh. Northern Pacific advertised the availability of free land but made no mention of the freezing winters. 'Quit the Strenuous Life and come to Washington Fruitland' was one of their advertisements. The Atchison, Topeka and Santa Fe featured a banana tree growing out of the Missouri river in its ads and the Union Pacific offered 'Farms and Homes in Kansas; Emigrants, Look to your Interests. Farms at $2 per acre and not a foot of wasteland ... ten years credit ... not taxable for six years....' And people in their thousands responded to these calls.

Europe lost a large part of its most industrious citizens. Pacifist European Mennonites, famous for their efficient farming, bargained: they wanted a guarantee of immunity from military service for 50 years and freedom from taxes levied to support any military operation, and in 1873 Secretary of State Hamilton Fish offered his assurance that the United States 'for the next fifty years will not be entangled in another war'. In order to attract German settlers and investment, the Northern Pacific (NP) changed the name of Crossing Township in the Dakota Territory to Bismarck. The temporary capital of the Territory was Yankton and a Commission, largely organised by the NP, was set up to confirm if it was, in fact, to be the established capital. Under local laws the commission was obliged to meet in Yankton, whose citizens, anxious for their town to become the permanent capital, were preparing to put an injunction on the commission. So the NP ran a train with the commissioners, complete with suitable eats and drinks, into Yankton in the middle of the night. The commission opted for Bismarck to be the capital during the two-minute Yankton stop and Bismarck eventually became the state capital of North Dakota. Congressman Charles E. Hooker said the railroads with their intense promotional campaigns had rewarded the nation with 'an empire of hardy and industrious citizens'. Then came a time when a number of European nations saw the American West as a suitable destination for convicts after they had served their time; organisations were founded to help or coerce these people to emigrate.

Passengers come all shapes and sizes. Recently there was an advertisement in an American railroad trade magazine for an Assistant Trainmaster '... the successful candidate will support all areas, directing and co-ordinating activities to ensure safe and efficient train operations'. The advert was inserted by Ringling Bros and Barnum & Bailey, who own and run two circus trains that circle the country to give performances in the main towns and cities. Trains take all the equipment the circus needs; the big top, animals[6], a big forklift to unload containers, accommodation for the performers and back-stage hands and even autos for staff to conduct business at each stop. Each train is more than 5,000ft long, nearly a mile, and weighs more than 4,000 tons. The company has its own workshops at its Florida headquarters for maintaining and adapting rail cars to their requirements. A long way on from the friendly days when the circus rolled into town with the inhabitants lining the rail yard to watch the animals unload and the circus wagons roll off the flat cars to form the parade along Main Street to the fairground.

A lot less like fun is a story from J.H. Patterson's *Man-Eaters of Tsavo*. Three officials set out to kill a man-eating lion that had killed the stationmaster and a pointsman in Kimaa, a village on the line to Mombasa in Kenya. After a fruitless hunt the three men boarded an inspection carriage to spend the night. The carriage had a sliding door, which they failed to lock shut; the lion had followed the men, then pushed the door open and entered the carriage. His weight tilted the carriage and the sliding door snapped shut. In the noise and awful chaos the lion jumped through one of the windows carrying the Police Superintendent in his jaws.

❖

Railways played an important role in the events leading up to the Russian revolution. The years before 1914 were a time of political turbulence; however, the war with Germany fired patriotic enthusiasm uniting the politicians, the army and the workers under the Tsar. The Kaiser's high command recognised that German resources were over-extended with war on both an eastern and a western front. They hoped for the collapse of Russia when Rasputin was murdered at the end of 1916 and the situation

6. Including elephants travelling just behind the locomotive for the smoothest ride.

7. Originally St Petersburg, then Petrograd, then Leningrad and finally St Petersburg.

in Petrograd[7] grew out of control with 300,000 striking workers on the rampage. Tsar Nicholas II attempted to return to Petrograd but his train was blocked by railwaymen; he went back to the front at Pskov and on March 15 he signed his abdication in the drawing room carriage of the imperial train. Again the Germans hoped for a peace settlement but were disappointed by the resolve of Russia to continue the war under the Provisional Government. A few months later U.S. Senator Elihu Root crossed the Pacific and travelled the Trans-Siberian railway in the Tsar's former imperial train from Vladivostock to Petrograd to arrange friendship and co-operation with the Provisional Government in the belief that Russia would become an American-style democracy.

Throughout 1916, and possibly before, German agents had been keeping touch with Lenin in Zurich. Lenin had founded the *League for the Liberation of the Working Class* and edited a series of revolutionary newspapers. The Germans realised both his powers of oratory and leadership and recognised that he would not let war with Germany deflect him from his objective of revolution with the overthrow of the army command, the aristocracy and the bourgeoisie. Following some months of negotiation it was agreed that the Germans would transport Lenin and his party from Switzerland to Russia. The majority of his party were hesitant to accept; being transported by the enemy might prejudice their welcome in Russia and possibly they had twinges of patriotism. Lenin was implacable and in April 1917 the fateful journey began; a sealed train, considered to be 'extraterritorial', set out from Zurich with Lenin, his wife, and 30 other Bolsheviks on board. They travelled through Mannheim and Berlin to the port of Sassnitze, a three-day journey. They went by sea to Malmø and train to Stockholm and another train to the Finnish border. They sledged across the border and travelled by train south to Russia. The train stopped to pick up Lenin's sister and then steamed into Petrograd's Finland Station in the afternoon of April 16. There was a tumultuous welcome with a band playing a thunderous *Marseillaise* opposite where Lenin's second-class compartment stopped. After the roars of welcome from the crowd, Lenin and his colleagues hurried to what had been the station's imperial waiting room for an exchange of greetings and speeches; Lenin: '... I greet you as the vanguard of the worldwide proletarian army

... any day now the whole of European capitalism may crash ...'. In May the Germans organised a second sealed train from Switzerland carrying a large number of socialist exiles to Russia.

The Bolsheviks tried to trigger revolution against the Provisional Government to coincide with a new German offensive. It was a failure, and Lenin, disguised as the fireman, escaped into Finland on the footplate of a locomotive. He returned to Petrograd by train in late October wearing a wig and with his beard shaved and led the Bolsheviks to take over the city and replace the government. The German efforts at fomenting revolution were rewarded; a peace treaty was signed at Brest-Litovsk that lost Russia a third of her population and more than half her industry. The resulting turmoil in Russia was the beginning of the revolution.

❖

Perhaps the most chilling and most awful image from World War II is the photograph of the gateway to Auschwitz, the death and labour camp. In the foreground a series of converging tracks join together to a single track that leads under the gatehouse and into the camp; the day is dark grey, deadly icy cold with snow on the ballast between the rails. It is estimated that six million Jews and a large number of the dispossessed died in the Nazi death camps or were starved and tortured as slave labourers in concentration camps. Under the Nazi scheme, Poles, Czechs, Serbs and Russians were to become subject people or slaves; the Jews were to disappear altogether. The railways of Europe provided the transportation for these people to their frightful destinations.

The biggest Jewish population in Europe was in Poland and there were large numbers of Jews in Germany, Austria, the Balkans and Western Europe. The first step in dispossessing European Jews was to take them, largely by rail, to city ghettos of which the best known were in Warsaw, Kielce, Lublin, Minsk and Lodz. The next step was to build the death camps; Chelmno, close to the original German-Polish border, and another three camps were built just to the west of the River Bug; Belzec was on the railway from Cracow to Lvov; Treblinka had a rail link to Warsaw and the last, Sobibor, was a woodland halt on the direct rail connection to the towns of Wlodwa and Chelm, all with large Jewish communities.

Most notorious of all was Auschwitz and its satellites Auschwitz-Birkenau and Monowitz death and labour camps. Auschwitz was the railway junction for lines to Riga and the Baltic States, for Vienna and the Balkans and for Berlin with its rail network covering Germany with connections to western Europe. Usually the trains stopped some distance from the death camps; Chaim Hirszman, one of the eyewitnesses to have survived: 'the entire crew was changed. SS men from the death camp replaced the railroad employees.' Very few of the dispossessed travelled in passenger carriages, most were herded into cattle trucks. One train was made up of 45 cattle wagons containing 6,000 men, women and children. There were two trains a day from Warsaw to Treblinka, or from Radom to Treblinka, daily trains from Cracow and Leinberg to Belzec; one regular schedule was for a 22-wagon train with 1,100 Jews from Vienna to Treblinka. There were 20 special trains from Macedonia and Thrace in one year, 67 trains from Drancy, a Paris suburb, to Auschwitz in 18 months, and many, many more from European towns with large Jewish populations. Journeys could last three days or even longer, one from Romania lasted eight days; if there was a shortage of locomotives, priority was given to ordnance or troops going to the eastern front. The conditions inside the wagons were awful, a misery quite beyond description. Men, women and children were jammed together with no food, no water and no sanitary facilities. In winter they froze and in summer they suffered agonies from heat and lack of air. On some trains more than half the passengers were dead on arrival, some frozen solid and some so emaciated through lack of water that they didn't survive the journey. The wagons were bolted and sealed and barbed wire covered ventilation spaces. SS men travelled with each train, shooting anyone attempting escape. Then, when the Red Army advanced into Poland, trains transported the survivors from Auschwitz to labour camps in Germany – Belsen, Dachau, Buchenwald and others – to work in factories or mines.

The organisation of the trains, their scheduling and arranging for the availability of locomotives and crews was done from the General Management, Railway Directorate in Berlin; a document survives from the Railway Directorate headed 'Special trains for resettlers'. Copies of this instruction were sent to local railway traffic offices across Europe. It was a most terrible role for the railways.

❖

Other railway systems also carried the dispossessed. The Trans-Siberian carried five million exiles to be settled in the wastes of Siberia in the 20 years following 1898 and transported the many political exiles of the Stalin era to the camps of the Gulag.

But the largest migration in American history was a happier event; the Illinois Central carried more than a million black people and freed slaves from the southern states to the big manufacturing cities of the north in the years after the civil war.

Charles Sheeler's 1939 oil on canvas *Rolling Power*

10 Pictures of Rails and Trains

In the second half of the 19th century artists and writers became excited and enthralled by the new age of railways and trains. These were new subjects to paint or to write about; a new landscape and machinescape of fire, smoke, noise and speed. It was not only the trains and rails that excited their interest, it was also the drama of the great railway stations that inspired them. They saw crowd scenes of meetings and farewells taking place in architectural surroundings as different, as modern and as new as the trains themselves. The world of the railway and the train became popular subjects for paint, prose, poetry and song.

❖

Rain, Steam and Speed, J.M. Turner's 1844 painting of a Great Western express train belting over Maidenhead bridge, is one of the most significant 19th century pictures. It was the first really dramatic painting of the power of man and machine, an unprecedented portrayal of the modern world of steam and train overcoming the elements. The science historian Michael Serres was so impressed by Turner's rendering of the locomotive's heat and power that he called him an 'intuitive genius of thermodynamics'. As well as being a landmark in British painting, *Rain,*

Steam and Speed was an inspiration to French Impressionist painters. In 1872, Claude Monet, one of the greatest, took his easel to the railway yard in the north-west Paris suburb of Argenteuil and painted a scene of locomotives pouring smoke and steam into a dark thundery sky; the point of the painting was the atmosphere. Then, to quote from a catalogue, 'he began to think about the representation of trains themselves. Within a short five years he had them hurtling across bridges, arriving in wintry suburban stations, chugging through snow filled landscapes, rushing by private gardens ...'. His most famous railway work is a series of twelve paintings of Paris's St Lazare railway station, the terminus for the lines to Normandy.

As early as the 1830s, some 14 years before Turner's masterpiece, railways had already become popular subjects for illustrators and artists and a large number of pictures of trains, civil works and opening ceremonies were printed by Rudolf Ackermann and other publishers. The most magnificent early images of the railway are John Bourne's *The London and Birmingham Railway,* published in 1839. The lithographs detail the construction of the railway from the entrance of the Euston terminus to the station buildings in Birmingham. Excavation of cuttings, the removal of false-work from arches and building viaducts, are shown so accurately and with such clarity that no series of photographs could equal their impact. The often-reproduced scene of the working shaft of Kilsby tunnel shows horses and workmen caught in the vertical light from the shaft shining into the deep gloom of the tunnel. Bourne also published *Bourne's Great Western Railway;* this book includes one of the best-known early railway pictures of a broad-gauge train leaving a tunnel with a traditional rope design decorating the portal.

Victorian painters were enthusiastic about narrative pictures and excelled at painting them; anything with a story was fair game. There are hundreds of Victorian scenes of railway activity, mainly departures and arrivals in stations. William Frith's 1863 *The Railway Station* depicts the agitated bustle surrounding a train that has just arrived at Paddington station. There are about 60 beautifully painted individuals on the station platform, porters with barrows, mamas embracing children, passengers desperate for their luggage in the chaos, ladies in white crinolines and even two policemen arresting a fugitive. George Earl's *Going North, King's*

Cross Station and *Perth Station, Coming South* are particularly popular paintings of railway station activity; possibly because there are almost as many dogs as there are fashionable people on their way to or from a sporting holiday in the Highlands.

There were, of course, paintings of encounters inside the railway carriage. Abraham Solomon painted *First class: The Meeting ... and at First Meeting Loved*; it shows the interior of a first-class carriage with a beautiful young woman facing a young man leaning forward with admiration while her father sleeps in the corner. The painting was considered shocking and a year later Solomon painted a second version with a benevolent and encouraging father sitting between the admirer and the young woman. In the first version the young woman looks down modestly at her needlework. In the second she gives the eye to the young man from behind her father's shoulder. Abraham Solomon also painted a touching picture of a mother embracing her sailor son goodbye in a second-class compartment.

Charles Rossiter's 1859 *To Brighton and Back for Three and Sixpence* is a picture of a bedraggled crowd in a third-class carriage after spending an unsatisfactory day at the seaside.

Travelling Companions by Augustus Leopold Egg shows the interior of a luxurious first-class carriage with two stylishly dressed young women facing each other; one is reading and the other sleeping. The atmosphere of the painting has been described as 'richly sensual, slightly erotic, the dress of the sleeping girl undone at the breast'. Léonor Fini, a fringe Surrealist painted a sequel in the early 1930s with one of the girls making a lesbian assault on the other.

Giorgio de Chirico, a precursor of the Surrealist movement, was the son of a railway engineer working in Greece. He painted a series of evocative, haunted pictures of the small towns in which he had lived. A classical arcade, a tower, outsize shadows and statues all appear in painterly conjunction, and there is almost always a train that chugs along in the background.

The Surrealists felt that civilisation was gaining too tight a grip over nature. They visited sites such as Angkor in Cambodia and were delighted by the sight of the jungle overwhelming and reclaiming the temple buildings. This enthusiasm for rampant nature was the subject of an article by the faithful Surrealist Benjamin Péret, *La nature dévore le progrés et le dépasse*[1], illustrated by a photograph of a locomotive abandoned after de Lesseps had given up his attempt to build the Panama Canal. The form of the engine is obliterated under a forest of tropic rain-jungle greenery. Blaise Cendrar's[2] poem about the construction of the canal implores 'send me the photograph of the forest ... which now smothers the 400 steam engines abandoned by the French contractor'.

Many of the Surrealists including Max Ernst made a series of paintings of vegetation that threaten to explode out of the pictures. Romance and reality of the railway was a potent ingredient in the imagination and work of other Surrealists including René Magritte and Paul Delvaux. Max Ernst made a collage of a Victorian engraving, *Rape of the Sabine Women in a Railway Station* with the decapitated heads of roosters collaged onto the people in the picture. Another Ernst collage, *Le Lion de Belfort* shows lion headed and maned travellers in ordinary clothes in a passenger carriage.

In 1962 Magritte painted *The Nightingale* in which an express passenger train pounds along in the foreground under a vague god-like figure looming above in the clouds. In his *Time Suspended* a locomotive steams out of a domestic fireplace into an empty room. In Paul Delvaux's moody and sometimes erotic paintings, naked female figures stand abstractedly as trains and tramcars rumble on their eternal journeys along the deserted street of industrial towns.

Perhaps most astonishing in the Surrealist canon was Salvador Dali's view of and his relationship with Perpignan railway station. He would forward his luggage from the station even if he travelled to Paris in his Cadillac. The railway station was the boundary marker between a summer of hard work in his studio in nearby Spain and life in Paris with his friends.

---

1. Nature consumes progress and overtakes it.

2. Blaise Cendrars was a leading figure in the literary avant-garde in the first thirty years of the 20th century. Aged 15 he ran away from school and travelled in Russia, Asia and the Orient with a jewel dealer. He wrote his melancholy story of travel, both real and fantasy, in the astonishing *La prose du Transsibérian et de la petite Jehanne de France*. It was published in an enormous format with the text interwoven with Sonia Delaunay's abstract paintings. *Le Panama ou les aventures de mes sept oncles* followed five years later in 1919 and was in the format of a railway timetable.

In his memoir, *The Unspeakable Confessions of Salvador Dali*, he wrote:

> The setting sun was ablaze and the flood of its light created flames on the
> facades and especially the central skylight of the station that seemed to
> become the centre of an atomic explosion. About the station I could see a
> radiating aura in a perfect circle: the metal trolley cables of the streetcars that
> ringed the edifice and gave it a crown of glinting light … I had seized truth, I
> was living it. Everything became overpoweringly evident. The centre of the
> universe was there before me.

This revelatory vision of Perpignan station was so powerful that he painted
a famous and telling canvas of the station peopled with bizarre images of
his wife Gala and himself. Dali died in 1989. In the late 1990s three young
women were murdered in Perpignan, their bodies horribly mutilated in a
manner reminiscent of Dali's most extreme paintings. The murders have
not been solved.

One of the most dramatic and astonishing paintings is John Martin's
1853 apocalyptic sublime work, *Last Judgement* with its demon train,
filled with soldiers falling off Satan's bridge into the chasm of chaos.
Later Martin made a popular print, *The Broad and the Narrow* that
included showing Sunday trains as a social and religious evil. L.S. Lowry,
the British artist famous for his paintings of figures against an industrial
background, included steam trains in many of his pictures. His 1946 *Level
Crossing* has a crossing keeper waving a flag to stop passers-by, children
and dogs from being run down by an LNER tank engine. Eric Ravilious,
Paul Nash and Stanley Aarhus are among the other well known artists who
painted railways and their activities. Edward Burra's large watercolour,
The Cutting with its vivid red-brown railway cutting running through
feminine folds of hills and landscape can be viewed as a sexual metaphor.

A number of artists have painted locomotives and railway life with
astonishing realism. A locomotive painted by Terence Cuneo conveys the
immediacy of the 150-tons weight, the smell of ash, steam and smoke. The
beat of the exhaust seems almost audible as his engine heads a heavy train
up Camden Bank.

❖

The earliest American paintings to include a train were in great contrast to Turner's *Rain, Steam and Speed* in which the train is both the centre and the point of the picture. *River in the Catskills* painted in 1843 by Thomas Cole, the founder of American landscape painting, is a dreamy romantic landscape of river, trees, fields and a distant view of mountains with a train, only just discernible, puffing its way across a bridge in the middle ground. In much the same genre, George Innes painted three different views of the *Delaware Water Gap* between 1857 and 1861 but the railway, although present, has little significance in the composition of the pictures. In 1865 Jasper Cropsey used the same Hudson River School formula of an idealised setting with a placid river and with mountains in the distance in his *Starucca Viaduct, Pennsylvania*. The railway curves along the valley on a magnificent viaduct and the train has a more important role.

Probably the best-known early American portrayal of a train is George Innes's *Lackawanna Valley*, commissioned by the President of the Delaware, Lackawanna & Western in 1857. It shows a rustic valley with the beginnings of industrial buildings, a roundhouse and all three Delaware, Lackawanna & Western engines pouring out smoke. Innes was instructed to add a little salt to the subject of the painting; an interview published as part of one of his obituaries quoted him as saying, ' You see I had to show the double tracks and the round house whether they were in perspective or nor.' However salt or no salt, the President did not like the painting and, by chance, Innes came upon his picture in a Mexican curiosity shop shortly before he died.

One of the most dramatic images of the early railway is the American primitive painter A.Tapy's painting of an enraged stallion in the foreground with a train winding its way in the background. Currier and Ives, the great New York firm of lithographers, helped popularise the image of the railroad with its dramatic and folksy prints of railroads. *The Lightning Express Trains* of 1864, painted by Fanny Palmer, shows two express trains, probably on the Hudson River Railroad, getting under way, belching clouds of dark smoke and sparks from their chimneys. Currier and Ives prints showed trains in every kind of landscape or situation, even one with the engine pouring out inky black smoke while being dug out of a snowdrift. Different movements and different artists emphasised different aspects of the railway; in 1916 Georgia O'Keefe painted a somnambulistic winding train in her *Train at Night in the Desert*.

The school of painting known as Ashcan because of its focus on industrial subjects took over the portrayal of railroads in all their grime and dirt in the early years of the 20th century. Some painters, particularly George Luks and George Bellows gave their scenes a gloomy significance.

New York City at night became a particularly important subject for American painters. John Sloane's 1922 *The City from Greenwich Village* shows an el train snaking its way past the Flatiron building in lower Manhattan on a wet winter evening and he made a number of other paintings with the city's street life framed by the shapes of the overhead els. Other painters, especially John Marin, Max Weber and Joseph Stella absorbed influence from Italian Futurism[3], the style of motion and dynamic sensation and they portrayed New York in a hysterical confusion of images that included els, subways and tracks. Charles Sheeler was recognised both as a painter and a photographer and his work was in complete contrast to the Futurists. His 1920 *Church Street El* is a disciplined geometric view down the walls of high buildings to the tracks of the el and his 1930 *American Landscape* and *Classic Landscape* are classical academic style paintings of the industrial landscape of the Ford River Rouge plant. Sheeler is best known for his painting *Rolling Power* commissioned by *Fortune Magazine* in 1938. It is a hyper-realist painting of the cylinder, piston rod, side rods and front two wheels of a Hudson-type locomotive used for hauling the *Twentieth Century Limited*. It presents more definition than any photograph and emphasises the function of every bearing and split pin. When critics claimed that *Rolling Power* was little more than a photograph, Sheeler responded, 'Photography is nature seen from the eyes outward, painting from the eyes inward'. Later after a retrospective exhibition at the Museum of Modern Art, Sheeler said, 'Since I could not camp beside the locomotive for the three months required to paint it, I made a photo.'

---

3. The Futurists' 1909 manifesto included 'We declare that the world's splendour has been enriched by a new beauty; the beauty of speed ... of broad chested locomotives prancing on the rails, like huge steel horses bridled with long tubes ...'

Edward Hopper, who died in 1967, was the last classic American artist to paint a major series of pictures of railroad scenes. According to Professor Gail Levin's 1995 Catalogue Raisonné, Hopper 'depicted trains still and moving, interior and exterior views, American and European trains, commuter and long-distance trains, freight and passenger cars, railroad crossings, views from trains, and views of trains and trains passing through the landscape'. Each painting, whether a girl sitting alone in a passenger car, a signal-box beside the tracks in a deserted landscape or a bleak hotel room with a man smoking a cigarette looking out over the tracks, is a portrayal of stillness, loneliness and chill.

Saul Steinberg's marvellously mad series of railway images drawn mainly for *The New Yorker* show tracks criss-crossing and jostling into magnificent train sheds and there are mazes of lines with improbable signals and the occasional train; seemingly crazed drawings but which are, in fact, carefully constructed playful fantasies.

Rail buffs may prefer more handsome and straightforward images of trains such as the painting by Walter E. Greene, *Eastward, Westward*, of the two *Twentieth Century Limited* trains standing side by side in Buffalo station, one about to head for Chicago and the other for New York and each halfway on its 950-mile journey, and they may prefer Leslie Ragan's dramatic night scene of the *Pittsburgher* express running at speed alongside the Monongahela River, seemingly underneath the blast furnace of a giant steelworks.

❖

The Lackawanna line from New Jersey to Buffalo NY, which competed for passenger business against giants like the New York Central System, devised one of the more delightful advertising campaigns. Their engines burned anthracite rather than the dirty bituminous coal of the competition and they conjured up a heroine called Phoebe Snow, 'Phoebe Snow all dressed in white Rides and the Road of Anthracite' and 'Says Phoebe Snow / About to go / Upon a trip to Buffalo / "My gown stays white / From noon till night / Upon the Road of Anthracite." They even called their premier express *The Phoebe Snow*. It ran for over 60 years.

Between the two world wars, the most brilliant and striking railway posters were by Adolfe Mouron who worked in Paris under the name Cassandre. He is one of the few artists to be given a retrospective poster exhibition at the New York Museum of Modern Art. His most famous posters were in a cubist style and advertised a series of French Pullman expresses, *Etoile du Nord*, *Nord Express* and *L'Oiseau Bleu*. They dramatised the locomotive, the rails and the whole glamorous dream of travelling on an express train.

British railway advertising in the 1920s and 30s focussed largely on holiday destinations. The most interesting ads were collages of the sights in historic British cities and there were posters promoting York and Chester and a dozen other cities. Many posters reflected the prevalent British class distinctions of their day. The resorts that wished to project an image of catering to the serious-minded commissioned posters featuring sensibly dressed, rather prissy visitors looking out to sea from on top of a cliff or walking over the hills. Resorts catering to a less select clientele usually showed scenes of happy fun. A classic ad featured a jolly pink-faced seafisherman bouncing along the beach, 'Skegness is so Bracing'. Another memorable image promoted both Bridlington seaside resort and the journey on the LNER. It featured a beach complete with children, sandcastles and happy heads of bathers bobbing all around. An ecstatic, triumphant bathing beauty stands in the foreground on the bow of a rowboat, her arms above her head holding a large fluttering towel; she looks as if inspired by the second century BC sculpture *Winged Victory of Samothrace* in the Paris Louvre.

The map of the London Underground system has become almost as much a symbol of London as Big Ben. It was designed by Harry Beck who began his professional life as a draughtsman in the signal engineers' office. He had lost his job when he designed the system map which was first printed in 1933. Beck refined and improved the map until 1960 when updating was taken over by London Underground's publicity department. The Underground system lines are shown as a series of horizontal, vertical and diagonal lines. Each line is a different colour and the River Thames, the only landmark on the map, threads its way across the diagram from left to right. The map is recognised as a masterpiece of clarity and design and has been adapted for metro lines around the world. In 1992, the artist Simon Patterson made a fantasy facsimile version of the map with each line dedicated either to celebrated engineers or authors or saints and so on. The stations on each line were rechristened and named after artists, authors, saints or celebrities; for instance, Morden station, the southern terminus on the movie star line, was named *Anjelica Huston*. A wittier version of the Underground map was made by Beck himself in the form of an electrical circuit-wiring diagram. In it, Morden is now *Circuit Earth*, Cockfosters *Aerial*, the Bakerloo becomes the *Bakerlite Tube*, Hampstead becomes *Amp* and so on.

From the very beginning cartoonists and caricaturists satirized the railways, their staff and the promoters. In particular, *Punch* printed cartoons over a period of more than a hundred years that were critical of the railways; one contributor found some railway schemes so impractical as to cast doubt on the sanity of the proposers and drew a handsome *Railway Lunatic Asylum*. Another cartoon shows Macbeth's three witches, called Great Western, North Western and South Western, cooking a brew of railway company amalgamations. The variations of satire and scorn of management, late trains, railway sandwiches and railway grime are endless. Peter Arno, the American cartoonist of the chromium-plated 1930s did some memorable railway cartoons. In one, two eminent men walking along the carriage corridor glance through a crack in the doorway of a sleeping compartment and see the conductor waking a sleeping woman passenger with a chaste kiss: 'By George, the other railroads certainly have a lot to learn from the Chesapeake and Ohio.'

A number of artists created fantasy railway worlds that were published as books. W. Heath Robinson who drew and compiled *Railway Ribaldry* to celebrate the Great Western's centenary is the most widely known. Rowland Emmett created a bucolic dream world of an infinitely small branch line with locomotives festooned with birds' nests, the side rods half tied on with bits of string and with high chimneys puffing away as the engine slips and slides along an overgrown track. Albert Dubout, known as the *Rabelais of Marseilles*, also created a fantasy world of trains, all cobbled together and chuffing along the curvy lines of southern France with crowds of shouting, screaming and frantic passengers. In each case it's the fantasy and fascination of the drawings and detail that is the pleasure rather than any narrative.

In the 1970s when graffiti first appeared it was considered a disfiguring nuisance, as indeed it still is, except by a handful of New York dealers. It was first perceived as an art form on the New York subway and its beginning was recorded in a 1971 New York Times article: 'Taki is a Manhattan teenager who writes his name and number everywhere he goes. He says it is something he just has to do … He has spawned hundreds of imitators …'. Subway cars became the canvas for the artists, many of whom developed their own distinctive style of spray-painting their names and sometimes a message or icon of the moment. Kids whose names appeared most frequently or in inaccessible places became folk heroes and graffiti artists aspired to be a 'king' and often tagged their graffiti with a crown. Recognised kings and their supporters tried to monopolise all the cars on a particular line or section. Their writing and painting developed into planned and garish artwork covering subway cars from top-to-toe along the whole car length, even including windows and doors. For instance, on one car the names *Blade and Dolores* were painted in thick, thick comic mag letters, black and edged in bright lemon yellow, and with wild colours and hearts making a dazzling background that covered every square inch. Not surprisingly, the Subway Authority was less than enthusiastic and the police department organised squads of detectives to raid yards and tunnels to catch the artists; a cops and robbers game developed, and in 1978 a graffiti artist called Lee did a top-to-bottom, end-to-end whole car painting of a huge caricature Sherlock Holmes looking through a magnifying glass at the message 'Stop Real Crime' and a balloon; 'f…ed up again'.

One curious effect of working beside a railway occurred in Bulgaria. After WWII Bulgaria severed diplomatic relations with the West. However, the authorities supposed that everyone travelling to Istanbul or the Near East would have little choice other than to travel on the Orient-Express or one of the other international trains routed through Bulgaria (they hadn't reckoned with air travel and passengers crossing Bulgaria at 30,000 ft). They wanted influential and powerful international travellers to form a favourable opinion of their country. It became mandatory for Art

Academy students to spend their weekends at the collective farms in the vicinity of the railway in order to instruct farmers to park their machines and tractors well in view from the track and to place their hay stacks on top of hills, so that the train passengers could see a dynamic and prosperous landscape. Among the art students was young Christo Javacheff who years later, as the artist Christo, working with his wife Jeanne-Claude, created monumental works of art such as *The Pont Neuf Wrapped, Paris*; *Surrounded Islands, Miami*; *Wrapped Reichstag, Berlin* and *The Gates* in New York's Central Park. These projects have changed how millions of people look at landmarks and landscapes – with a wholly different view and finding a different meaning. Possibly his role in helping to change the appearance of the landscape beside the Bulgarian railway line provided one of the influences for their great projects.

❖

In January 1839 Louis Daguerre and William Fox Talbot announced their respective photographic processes and launched the age of the photograph just fourteen years after the opening of the world's first public steam railway.

Images of locomotives, railway civil works and tourist destinations started to become popular in the 1860s. In America the stereograph[4] supplemented the printed photograph: in the late 1860s Alfred Hart, Central Pacific's official photographer produced 30,000 stereographs from 300 negatives showing construction progress of the railroad for stockholders and public officials as well as the general public.

By the late 1850s locomotive manufacturers included clear and handsome photographs of their products[5] as part of their sales information and by the 1860s railway companies were using photographs to advertise resorts and towns on their networks.

4. The stereograph comprises two photographs in a stereoscopic device to produce a seeming three dimensional image.

5. One of the earliest extant photographs is of the London North Western *Eugenie* photographed in 1855 for the Paris Universal Exhibition.

Not only professional but also amateur enthusiasts have taken thousands or even millions of photographs of locomotives and railway scenes and many have been published in a never-ending flow of railway picture books. Railway photography became a genre in its own right.

There are some glorious exceptions to the general monotony of train photographs: Bill Brandt's railway photographs have the same spirit and drama as Doré's drawings of railway viaducts high over rows of tenement buildings a century earlier. Man Ray shot a witty photograph of a seedy hotel next to a railway embankment in a shabby Paris suburb. The top floor is level with the tracks and seems almost immediately next to the rails; painted very large above the top windows is the hotel's name, *Au Château Tremblant*. Alfred Stieglitz's 1902 photograph *The Hand of Man* shows a locomotive and train pulling away from a rail yard surrounded by industrial buildings and chimneys on a grimy smoky, wet and overcast morning. A contemporary critic who had been travelling overnight by train wrote 'In the morning, I could hardly trust my eyes when I beheld one *Hand of Man* after another coming toward me down the track. The audacity of the Pennsylvania Railroad to plagiarise this idea.'

The photographer Andrew J. Russell was employed by the Union Pacific to record the construction of the last stages of the railroad from Wyoming to Utah. He not only recorded railroad construction but also introduced the world to the geological and natural wonders of the American West. In 1869 he took what is possibly the best-known of all rail photographs, *East and West Shaking Hands at the Laying of the Last Rail*, the historic scene of the completion of the first transcontinental railroad.

O. Winston Link made a deserved world reputation with his series of photographs of the last days of steam. He was a well-known New York City advertising photographer who was on location in Virginia close to the Shenandoah Valley line of the Norfolk & Western Railroad, one of the last American lines to run steam locomotives. His work is memorable because of the attention he gives in it to the people working on the railway or living their lives beside it; his pictures portray the relationship of the men and their families with the railroads. Most of his photographs are night shots and although amazing in their clarity and interest, appear to be natural rather than set up with batteries of floodlights. One of the most remarkable pictures shows a Y6 350-ton locomotive at the head of a heavy coal train palpably rumbling along the track laid down the middle of Main Street, North Fork, West Virginia; the huge articulated locomotive is almost adjacent to and only about ten feet from the columns and entrance of the town bank.

At a time when glamour girls were a selling accessory they were more often seen draped over the bonnet of a new car model rather than spread-eagled over a locomotive. However, there are exceptions: the most glorious glamour girl of all, Marilyn Monroe, was photographed at Jasper, Alberta standing on the sill of a Canadian National boxcar when she was filming *River of No Return*. Ava Gardner on the footplate in *Bhowani Junction* is a spectacular combination of beautiful woman and locomotive. Less glamorous but more interesting is a 1930 photograph of *Four Aces,* a 350-ton demonstration locomotive fitted with roller bearings, being hauled at the end of a rope in a Chicago station by three girls wearing high heels.

One of the most affecting pictures of a pretty woman and a locomotive was taken in the early 1950s by railwayman Chard Walker, on the Santa Fe's rails at Summit at the head of the 4,000-ft Cajon Pass that separates Los Angeles from the Mojave Desert. A slim girl, Mickey Andersen, was a train-order operator in this desolate place. Standing in a short-sleeved blue shirt and blue gingham skirt with wind blowing through her thick chestnut hair, she holds up a long cleft stick with the train orders for the engine crews of two enormous black 2-10-2 locomotives growling slowly past and dwarfing her. Beauty and the Beast.

A new genre of railway publishing has developed recently: books of photographs that have high artistic aspirations. Graeme Outerbridge's *Trains* is a lush publication of random train photographs; the introductory chapter is entitled *The Photographs are the Journey* and includes '… The resulting project was to span five years and forty journeys on every continent save Antarctica … I circled the globe three times catching trains.'

❖

One of the earliest-ever moving pictures was Louis Lumière's 50-second film, shown in Lyon in January 1895, of a train arriving at La Ciotat station. In his *Chez les Lumières*, Georges Reyes wrote 'Suddenly a train appeared. Women cried out with terror. Men threw themselves to one side to avoid being run over. It was panic. And triumph.' This account may have been exaggerated but certainly early audiences were astonished. According to one viewer 'It was a thrilling experience, something entirely unprecedented and the few who saw it found it miraculous'. Lumière made a second version the following year, which featured members of his family, and altogether he made 55 films that included trains. Some of these were shown in London with a man off-stage simulating the noise of the steam with a compressed air bottle.

Trains featured in Wild West stage shows long before the first movie was made. *Under the Gaslight* was a hit in 1867 with an engine thundering out of the wings, just missing the gallant hero, bound and gagged on the line. *The Fast Mail* had two trains chasing each other on stage and Buffalo Bill Cody's tent show featured a train hold-up. The plots were usually versions of much the same set of clichés: hero rescues heroine in the nick of time or salvages a trainload of gold.

A train also occupied centre stage in a quite different sort of theatre performance. Howard Hawk's comedy *Twentieth Century,* first performed in New York in 1934, stages the action in a luxury car of the NY Central System's *Twentieth Century Limited*. The play was recently revived and in his review the critic John Lahr said the train 'epitomized the American delirium of momentum'[6].

When Thomas Edison saw a staging of *The Great Train Robbery*, the usual plot but more dynamite and gunshot than usual, he was so impressed that in 1903 he helped to produce the first Western movie, *The Great Train Robbery*. It is now regarded as a milestone in motion picture development. Its runaway success was followed by an enormous number of railway films featuring almost every genre of drama or story. Every Western seemed to feature a train; the best known has to be Fred Zinneman's 1952 *High Noon* where Gary Cooper as the beleaguered town marshal waits for

---

6. Railways are not often the setting for serious-minded plays. All the action in Brian Phelan's 1969 *The Signalman's Apprentice* takes place in the signalbox of a London railway yard. Through a clerical error the jobs of the signalmen were not included in the closure and they continue their lives in fantasy, self delusion and ultimately murder.

the fatal shoot-out as the train arrives at Hadleyville depot. Trains featured in war movies as well as Westerns; the 1927 *The General*, with lovelorn Buster Keaton riding on the side rod of a moving locomotive, is the most loved and best known. *The Bridge on the River Kwai* and *The Train* are among other war movies that had great success.

Love and passion are at the centre of a number of well-known movies featuring trains. There is a wry and marked contrast in the portrayal of national characteristics between the English movie *Brief Encounter* and its theme of the hopelessness of love, the power of seduction set in the *Twentieth Century Limited* in the American movie *North by North West* and the conflict between duty and passion on the Paris-Le Havre line in the French film *La Bête Humaine*. However, the enginemen at Le Havre presented Jean Gabin, one of the French film's stars, with an 'oil can of honour' in recognition of his aptitude on the footplate. Another masterpiece was André Delvaux's 1968 movie, *Un soir, un train* with Yves Montand and Anouk Aimée, a beautiful but melancholy story of dream and reality merging. More terminus than train, set almost entirely in Rome's Stazione Termini, Vittorio de Sica's *Indiscretion of an American Wife* is a story about the ending of a romance between an American matron and a handsome young Italian.

At least two big movies took rail history as their theme: John Ford's 1924 *The Iron Horse* and Cecil B. DeMille's *Union Pacific* are about the building of the first American transcontinental line. Humour and even farce lies at the centre of some films; *Some Like it Hot*, with its sleeping-car scenes and The Marx Brothers *Go West* are classics and so is Gene Wilder's 1976 *Silver Streak*. *Union Station* made by Rudolf Maté in 1950 and set in Los Angeles Union Station, starring William Holden ('I'm a cop twenty-four hours a day. All I care about is my railroad station.') is one of a large number of rail detective or crime movies which range from the charmingly fantastic such as *Murder on the Orient Express* to the suspenseful – *Thirty-Nine Steps*, *Stranger on a Train*, and *The Lady Vanishes* by Alfred Hitchcock. Another movie, *Deathline*, featured scenes shot on the London underground with a cannibal living in the tunnels who picks off stray passengers. *The Titfield Thunderbolt*, *The Ladykillers* and *The Ghost Train*, starring Will Hay, are classic examples of a certain genre of British-made movies' whimsical and gentle fun. The scope of rail movies is far-reaching, from the charm of *The Railway Children* to the avant garde of Jean Mitry's 1949 *Pacific 231*, a study of the movement and synchronization of the driving wheels, side rods and piston rods, reciprocating motion transformed into rotary motion, with rails, steam and smoke, set to a score by Arthur Honegger.

A number of surprisingly interesting rail documentary films were made in the UK. Most memorable is the 1936 *Night Mail* directed by Harry Watt, with W H Auden's poetic commentary about the Anglo-Scottish mail train. After WWII, British Transport Films produced documentaries about every aspect of travel. In addition to showing the pleasures of travelling by train and the contribution the railways were making to the national economy, they portrayed, according to one commentator, 'railway workers in an idealised light that makes even Soviet documentaries about heroic workers seem understated.'

These days the general public sees few heroic or impressive pictures of trains. Most views in the media are of crowded platforms with delayed and discontented crowds. Sadly, sadly the interest and romance of the railway has almost disappeared from view.

Paris-Mantes; Emile Zola on the footplate

11 Words and Song

The railways made a great impact on life in Britain but disappointingly little impact on the British literary scene. Charles Dickens spent almost all his adult life with a background of railway construction and rail travel and the first episode of *The Pickwick Papers* appeared in 1836, just as the railway age was beginning. The Pickwickians set off on their adventures by stagecoach; no doubt their adventures would have been very different had they been written ten years later and they had travelled by train. One of the chapters is described as '*Strongly illustrative of the Position that the Course of True Love is not a Railway.*'

Dickens's 1848 *Dombey and Son* includes a dramatic account of the chaos caused by building the great cuttings of the London & Birmingham Railway in North London and a number of scenes take place on railways including the violent death of the principal villain. *Mugby Junction*, a short story that appeared in the 1866 Christmas number of *All the Year Round,* has Barbox of Barbox Bros, a Scrooge-like character who takes a train to anywhere in a fit of loneliness and despair. He winds up at Mugby Junction where he meets a railway lampman and his family and then becomes jolly and generous. *Mugby Junction* is followed by a humorous piece:

> I am the boy at what is called the Refreshment Room, at Mugby Junction, and what's proudest boast is, that it never yet refreshed a mortal being … a metallic object that's at times the tea urn and at times the soup tureen ….

The same issue of *All The Year Round* also includes *The Signalman,* a supernatural story about a lonely signalman manning a box at the bottom of a deep and dark cutting just by the portal of a tunnel; it is a story of loneliness, gloom and horror. Without the railways, Dickens's extensive travelling in Britain and America to give public readings would not have been possible. In *American Notes* he wrote about some of his travels:

> There are no first or second-class carriages as with us; but there is a gentlemen's car and a ladies' car. The main distinction between which is that in the first, everybody smokes and in the second, nobody does ….

Dickens always thought trains were dangerous; he nearly had a bad accident on a train from Belfast to Dublin and in 1865 he was involved in a serious accident at Staplehurst on the South Eastern in which ten people were killed; the shock affected his health and he never wholly recovered.

William Wordsworth moved to Grasmere in the English Lake District in 1802 and although a stockholder in a railway company, he vigorously opposed the building of the railway to nearby Windermere on the grounds that bringing crowds from the cities to the heart of the Lake District would overwhelm it with people. He wanted to reserve Sublime and Divine Nature for '… any man who has an eye to perceive and a heart to enjoy'. In October 1844, aged 74 and Poet Laureate, he sent a sonnet *On the Projected Kendal and Windermere Railway* to the *Morning Post,*

> Is then no nook of English ground secure
> From rash assault?....

Almost two months later he wrote a 3,000 word letter[1] of protest and only nine days later followed up with a second 3000-word letter that included a poem and two sonnets, one entitled *Steamboats and Railways*. The letters were printed in the *Morning Post* and brought a 'torrent of abuse'. Finally the Board of Trade's report recommending the construction of the Kendal & Windermere line countered the grounds of Wordsworth's protest with

> We must therefore state that an argument which goes to deprive the artisan of the offered means of occasionally changing his narrow abode, his crowded streets, his wearisome task and unwholesome toil, for the fresh air, and the healthful holiday which sends him back to his work[2] refreshed and invigorated … appears to us to be an argument wholly untenable.

The railway from Kendal to Windermere opened in 1847.

John Ruskin hated the very idea of railways but could not help being entranced by the drama of the steam locomotive. He saw the countryside with its defined social order becoming desecrated by the spread of railways. When a railway was built through Derbyshire's beautiful and remote Peak District he wrote 'and now every fool in Buxton can be in Bakewell in half an hour, and every fool in Bakewell at Buxton…'.

Anthony Trollope, author of the Barchester Chronicles, was an official in the Post Office, where he introduced the pillar-box. A prolific writer, he did a lot of his work while travelling by train. He describes Willesden Junction, on the line from Euston in his book *The Prime Minister* (1876),

> … some six or seven miles distant from London, lines diverge east, west, and north, north-east, and north-west, round the metropolis in every direction, and with direct communication with every other line in and out of London. It is a marvellous place, quite unintelligible to the uninitiated, and yet daily used by thousands who only know that when they get there, they are to do what someone tells them.

1. The letter included the word *tourists*. Wordsworth was one of the first to use the word 'tourist' in the sense of a circuitous journey; returning to where the journey began.

2. Notice that the report makes no reference to happiness or pleasure, only 'back to his work'.

In the US Nathaniel Hawthorne wrote the *Celestial Railroad*, a parody of Bunyan's *The Pilgrim's Progress*: 'The passengers being all comfortably seated we now rattled away merrily, accomplishing a greater distance in ten minutes than Christian probably trudged over in a day.'

'Too many trains and too many crimes' wrote one critic of Emile Zola's 1890 *La Bête Humaine*[3]. The Compagnie de l'Ouest's line from Paris through Rouen to Le Havre is the centre of the novel and all the characters are railwaymen or their women; it is not only the greatest 'railway novel'; it is the only one. Nothing comparable has been written in English or any other language. It is a compelling story of duty, sexual passion and violence. All the main characters meet violent deaths; there is a collision staged by a jealous lover and the novel ends with a fight and death on the footplate of an express troop-train of cattle wagons filled with drunken shouting and singing boy soldiers on their way to carnage, fighting the Prussians on the Eastern Front.

When Zola was planning *La Bête Humaine,* a visitor reported that he envisaged a railway network as its setting:

> There will be a large station in which ten separate lines converge, with each line having its own plot and all of them linked to the main station; and the whole novel will be imbued with the colour of the locale, and you will be able to hear like background music, the rattle and roll of this hectic life, and witness love on a train, a tunnel accident, the toil of the locomotive, collisions both head on and from behind, disasters, fleeing passengers, the whole dark, smoke-filled, noisy world.

Zola, complete with pince-nez, and stiff collar, travelled on the footplate from Paris to Mantes as part of his research and the novel describes the happy comradeship between Jacques Lantier the engine driver, Pecqueux the fireman and La Lison, their engine, as a *ménage à trois*.

In Russia the coming of the railways had a massive impact on such an immense country – and on its epic writers, in particular Tolstoy, writer, mystic and philosopher. The railway played a significant part in his second great novel, *Anna Karenina*, a tragic love story. Anna has come from

3. May be translated as *The Demon in Man*.

St Petersburg to Moscow where she is being met at the station by her brother. Count Alexei Vronsky is also at the station to meet his mother. By chance the two ladies share a compartment for the journey and Vronsky, glimpsing Anna for the first time as he goes into the compartment to greet his mother becomes aware, in an instant, of her great attraction for him. As they climb down there is a commotion on the platform. A train conductor has slipped under the wheels of a nearby moving train. As Anna and her brother leave the station he notices that she is having difficulty holding back tears and asks her what is the matter. 'It's an omen of evil', she says. Anna loses everything to be with Vronsky – her child, her husband, her friends and her position in society – but he feels increasingly bored and trapped. In a fit of deep despair she orders her coachman to take her to the railway station. She recalls the man crushed by the train the day she first met Vronsky, and 'she knew what she had to do'. She throws herself under the wheels of a wagon of a passing train.

At the end of his life Tolstoy handed over his estate to his wife, Sonya and lived according to his principles, as a peasant in poverty. Then family quarrels made him flee his home and he died in a siding at the remote Astapovo railway station.

A starry-eyed Théophile Gautier wrote,

> The Railway Station will soon be the cathedral of humanity, the meeting place for nations, the centre where everyone gathers and the centre of gigantic stars with steel rails stretching to the ends of the earth … in antiquity, architecture provided the temple, in the Middle Ages the church and in our day it will build the railway station.

Franz Kafka visited Paris in 1923 and was less starry-eyed when he wrote that, whenever possible, Métro passengers preferred to travel 'facing the door'.

In his monumental narrative *À la recherche du temps perdu*[4], Marcel Proust uses the railway as much more than just a convenient means of travel. Travelling in the train allows the narrator streams of introspection that parallel the view through the carriage window. And the narrator even

---

4. *Remembrance of Things Past*

has a reverie and dreams up a small country line; he relishes the names of imaginary stations: Égleville, Pont-à-Couleuvre, Grattevast and Saint-Frichoux. The railway also provides a theatrical setting for critical moments in the story: the narrator's inebriation in the train after leaving his mother or his devastating upset when, his train delayed by a breakdown at a country station, the bored narrator goes to the little casino near the station and finds his love, Albertine, dancing lasciviously with another woman. On one journey the narrator and Albertine find themselves sharing a compartment with an old and ugly lady '... and I amused myself wondering to what social category she could belong; I at once concluded that she must be the manageress of some large brothel, a procuress on holiday. Her face and her manner proclaimed the fact aloud.' Later he discovers she is the high-born Princess Sherbatoff and then, on another journey, finds himself sitting next to her. The hideously sociable narrator tries to cultivate her friendship by bombarding her with questions. She 'could scarcely bring herself to reply to my questions and finally told me that I was giving her a headache'.

Basset Digby, an American journalist who lived in Siberia in the first part of the 20th century was much more down to earth as well as romantic. He writes of looking at the destination board in Leningrad railway station,

> Trains are leaving for Archangel, up on the White Sea, and the Crimean seashore resorts down on the Black Sea, for Romania, for Vienna, for Central Asian destinations within a morning's horse-ride of the frontiers of mysterious Afghanistan, and for Manchuria and China.

Many writers of the age had their heroes and characters travel on trains, including Mark Twain, Stephen Crane and Robert Louis Stephenson but only a few seem to have been fascinated by the actuality of the locomotive, the line and the train. Kipling's[5] 1896 *Captains Courageous* is a cracking narrative that includes an epic high-speed journey by a multi-millionaire railway tycoon whose son is swept overboard from a transatlantic liner and picked up in the nets of a Grand Banks fishing vessel. His family in San

---

5. Many of Kipling's early short stories such as *The Phantom Rickshaw* and *Under the Deodars* first appeared in A.H.Wheelers Indian Railway Library Series.

Diego have given him up for lost when suddenly they get news that he is alive in Boston. The tycoon father orders the *Constance*, his private rail car, to be coupled to an express engine and telegraphs railroads across the nation to have their roads clear and to have locomotives and crews available to make the journey from California to Boston in record time: 'division superintendents will accompany this special over their respective divisions'. The description of the epic journey across America may have inspired the eccentric California gold miner, Death Valley Scotty, who paid the Santa Fe to take him on a record dash from Los Angeles to Chicago in forty five hours; the 1905 journey required relays of 19 locomotives and it caught the nation's interest.

Kipling's *007* is a good railroad story about a new engine fresh from the outfitting shop spending its first night in the roundhouse. The Pittsburgh Consolidation, the Massachusetts Compound and the Flying Freight Mogul are all rude and insulting to the newcomer. 'But manners was left out when Moguls were made', said Pony the Switcher, 007's only friend. The outcome is predictable: the Flying Freight is derailed and on his first night 007 goes to the Mogul's rescue with a wrecking crew. The story is a great read, told in convincing American roundhouse-speak.

Jules Verne's *Around the World in Eighty Days* is one of the best travel stories of any time anywhere. Mr Phileas Fogg and his servant Passepartout travel overland by rail wherever possible, with one of the more memorable descriptions of travelling across India on the Great Indian Peninsula Railway: '... the locomotive guided by an English engineer and fed with English coal threw out its smoke upon cotton, coffee, nutmeg, clove and pepper plantations, while the steam curled in spirals around groups of palm trees'. An equally colourful description of smoke from a speeding engine is in Flaubert's *Sentimental Education* 'A gigantic ostrich feather whose tip kept blowing away'.

Jules Verne uses railway journeys to revel in the poetry of place names; in his *Kéraban le têtu* he writes:

> After leaving Constantinople the railway leads to Andrinople with a branch to Iamboli ... and the itinerary for crossing southern Russia is through Iassi, Kisschenneff, Kharkov, Taganrod, Nachintschewan, to the foothills of the Caucasian mountains.

In *Claudius Bombarnac* Verne uses the railway to poke fun at the constant hurry of the 'Anglo-Saxons'; an American man and an English girl board at Tiflis, get married in the train and divorce when they arrive in Peking. Apollinaire wrote of a less fanciful world when, in 1915, he travelled in a troop train to Chaumont and wrote a poem about his journey and of his love for Lou. He sent Lou the poem with a letter describing how the train was being shadowed by an overhead Zeppelin.

Toward the end of the 19th century, Robert Louis Stephenson wrote the story of his transcontinental rail crossing of America in *Across the Plains*. He travels the first part of the journey with a Dutch widow and her children whom he amuses and for whom he buys candies and fruit. He even sleeps on the floor to give them more room. Despite all this 'she had conceived a great aversion to me', and when they leave the train in Ohio, ' "I am sure" said she "we all *ought* to be very obliged to you".' In Chicago he crosses town to another station and travels to Council Bluffs. There he boards a Union Pacific emigrant train that rolls west over the Missouri and across the Plains to Ogden, Utah where he changes onto a Central Pacific emigrant train to Oakland and the Pacific Ocean. Stephenson describes the stench from the emigrant cars as 'pure menagerie, only a little sourer'. He not only writes about his fellow passengers, who include a jokester who shouts 'All aboard' when they are half-way through a lunch stop, but he writes feelingly about the endless horizons of the Great Plains, the very few lonely inhabitants that the train passes, the fate of the Plains Indians and about the extreme prejudice against the Chinese.

It is not surprising that the Orient-Express provided the setting for a number of best-selling novels. There was nothing improbable about the gathering together of a wide variety of characters from different nationalities and backgrounds on an international train; there was no need to explain why such a mixture of people was together. Graham Greene's *Stamboul Train* was followed by Eric Ambler's *The Mask of Dimitrios* and Agatha Christie's *Murder on the Orient Express*, which, of course, has Hercule Poirot on board the train from Istanbul. The plot has the train snowed-in to enable the great detective to do his work with no possibility of escape for any of the suspects. In fact, five years earlier the Orient-Express was snowed in for six days on the Romanian border with Turkey.

Den Doolard's *Orient Express* and Ethel White's *The Wheel Spins,* which became the basis of Hitchcock's movie *The Lady Vanishes*, were written in the late 1920s or early '30s. One of the notable incidents in D.H. Lawrence's *Lady Chatterley's Lover* happens on the Orient-Express as it nears Paris, when Connie tells her father she is expecting a child; she doesn't add that her husband's gamekeeper is the father. The most notable post-World War II novel featuring the Orient-Express was Ian Fleming's James Bond thriller *From Russia with Love*, with Bond travelling from Istanbul with a Russian beauty who is, of course, a SMERSH operative.

La Madone des Sleepings or *The Madonna of the Sleeping Cars,* written by Maurice Dekobra in 1925 has the best title of any novel about train travel. The cover of the 1972 Livre de Poche edition includes a photograph of the 1935 LMS steam turbomotive at speed, presumably to encourage train buffs to purchase it. In fact it is a kitsch story about the adventures of Lady Diana Wynham and her secretary Prince Selim and there is no mention of trains until the last chapter. The beautiful and perverse Lady Diana shocks London society by dancing nude at a charity gala and by becoming engaged to marry a Bolshevik commissar. She loses her fortune and loses heart in quick succession but soon makes a new start in search of adventure. The last scene has her secretary and devoted friend, Prince Selim, saying goodbye on the platform of Paris's Gare de l'Est and asking where she is going. Lady Diana replies 'I have a ticket for Constantinople. But I might only go as far at Vienna or Budapest. It depends on chance and the colour of the eyes of the man sharing my compartment. I have reserved suites at the Imperial on the Ring and at the Hungaria on the Promenade at Pesth but perhaps I will wind up in a flophouse on the Josephtadt or in a palace high on the hill above Buda ... .'

Paul Theroux's *The Great Railway Bazaar* is another seductive title that should make rail enthusiasts running to buy. It is a story of travelling to Japan and back by rail and includes endless tedious conversations with fellow travellers and petty officials. But there is no interest in the trains, apart from the comfort and food, nor any indication of interest in the construction and story of the railways that transported the author.

In his 1884 *À Rebours,* the symbolist writer J.K. Huysmans has his hero Des Esseintes compare '*la Crampton à une adorable blonde et*

243

l'Engerth à une monumentale et sombre brune'. Lucky blonde; the Crampton engine was a lean, racy, elegant locomotive used on various lines in France for express passenger work in the 1840s and '50s. Unfortunate brunette; the Engerth was originally designed for toiling over Semmering, and it was a lumpy, heavy, stretched out tank engine. His *Les Soeurs Vatard* has the sisters living in an apartment overlooking the tracks into Paris's Montparnasse station. They get to know the rosters of each locomotive and take great pleasure in observing and commenting on the trains and their movements.

It is generally supposed that humour is in short supply in railway literature but there are many exceptions and, surprisingly, there is a book of railway jokes, published in New Delhi in the 1960s. *A Train Load of Jokes and Anecdotes* is a collection of incidents culled from the Indian railway system but also from around the world. Proof of its fun? It was reprinted five times in its first four years. Even A.E. Housman, classical scholar and the lyric poet of *A Shropshire Lad*, had moments of playfulness:

> "Hallelujah! was the only observation
> That escaped Lieutenant-Colonel Mary Jane,
> When she tumbled off the platform in the station
> And was cut in little pieces by the train.
> Mary Jane, the train is through yer;
> Hallelujah, Hallelujah!
> We will gather up the fragments that remain.

Lawrence Durrell's hilarious *The Ghost Train* is about a party of diplomats travelling from Belgrade to Zagreb to attend a Liberation Day exhibition of Yugoslav heavy industry in the 1950s: the passenger carriages were specially decorated to give the 'effect of a Sicilian market-cart with painted and carved side-boards or the poop of some seventeenth-century galleon'. The carriage for the Heads of Mission 'was about thirty degrees out of centre and was only, it seemed held upright by the one immediately before and behind it'. The occupants sat on the higher elevation of the carriage 'like people on a sinking ship'. A.G. Macdonell's *England Their England*, published in 1933, is a humorous account of the researches of Donald Cameron, a young Scotsman shell-shocked in Flanders in 1917,

into the habits and characteristics of the English. He sets off on a series of
adventures and encounters, one of which starts from Marylebone station,

> quietest and most dignified of stations, where the porters go on tiptoe and the
> barrows are rubber-tyred and the trains sidle mysteriously in and out with
> only the faintest toots on their whistles so as not to disturb the signalmen.

Donald bought a ticket and was told that the train would leave 'as soon as
the engine driver had come back from the pictures, and the guard had been
to see his old mother'. When he was in the train 'Donald fancied, but he
was not quite sure, that he heard the guard whisper to the engine-driver, "I
think we might make a start now, Gerald," and he rather thinks the engine-
driver replied in the same undertone, "Just as you wish, Horace."'

P.G. Wodehouse has Lord Ickenham at Paddington Station comparing
its calm with the bustle at Waterloo,

> At Waterloo all is hustle and bustle, and the society tends to be mixed. Here
> a leisured peace prevails, and you get only the best people – cultured men
> accustomed to mingling with basset hounds and women in tailored suits who
> look like horses.

John Betjeman describes county people arriving at Liverpool Street
Station: 'The ladies often travel second class, most of the men go first,
except of course, the vicars.' Harold Nicolson's *Lord Curzon's Valet* is an
amusing account of his accompanying the olympian Lord Curzon and his
drunken valet from London to Switzerland on a diplomatic mission to
meet Mussolini in 1922. It's a most enjoyable read and evokes rail travel
of the period: '... from time to time a station would leap up at us from the
gathering dusk, flick past the train in a sudden rectangle of illuminated but
unfocussed shapes, be lost again in the brooding darkness.'

All Aboard with EM Frimbo, World's Greatest Railway Buff is a
collection of charming and witty articles for the *New Yorker* in the 1940s
and '50s. Written by Rogers E.M. Whitaker and his collaborator Tony
Hiss, it relates the adventures of Whitaker's alter ego, curmudgeonly rail
buff, EM Frimbo who travels nearly three million miles by rail, but mainly
in North America on ordinary trains and also as a guest of millionaire train
buffs, who put together special trains to travel along remote lines. 'Frimbo

professes to prefer bad weather, because, he says, then he can think of all the hundreds of grounded planes, and all the thousands of people sitting in airports listening to bad music and not getting to where they want to go....'

Perhaps the most delightful and at the same time dramatic story centred around a railway is Bohumil Hrabal's 1965 *Closely Observed Trains*. It is told in the first person by the apprentice train dispatcher in a station in Bohemia during the German retreat from the Eastern Front. The story ranges from the stationmaster's prized pigeons and the scandal of the horny train dispatcher using the station's official rubber stamps to make a pattern over the bottom of the beautiful young telegraphist to a very dramatic ending.

❖

Over the decades the railways have inspired poets as diverse as Mary Coleridge and her romantic *The Train,* Emily Dickinson with her verse *I like to see it Lap the Miles,* Rupert Brooke, Hart Crane, Robert Graves, Lawrence Durrell, Stephen Spender and John Betjeman. In 1968 the London Underground introduced *Poems on the Underground*; a poem replaced an advertising panel in some passenger carriages. 'We hoped two million commuters would be charmed to discover poems by Shelley and Burns, Seamus Heaney and Grace Nichols enlivening their tube journeys'[6]. City transit systems as far apart as New York, Paris, Shanghai and Moscow have followed London's lead and poems are translated and exchanged between the metro systems and the subsequent books are often best sellers.

W.H. Auden recognises the silent heroics and romance of the railway in his poem *Night Mail* about the Anglo-Scottish mail train hounding north in the night past sleeping towns and houses; *Night Mail* includes the lines,

> In the farm she passes no-one wakes
> But a jug in a bedroom gently shakes

Edward Thomas's *Adlestrop* is one of the best-known and best-loved of all English poems:

---

6. Part of an introduction from a recently published collection of *Poems on the Underground.*

Yes. I remember Adlestrop –
The name, because one afternoon
Of heat the express-train drew up there
Unwontedly. It was late June.
The steam hissed. Someone cleared his throat
No one left and no one came.

Even T.S. Eliot included Skimbleshanks, the Railway Cat, in his 1923 *Old Possum's Book of Practical Cats*.

Thomas Hardy wrote a number of poems about travelling on trains. At the beginning of his career he was an architectural assistant and helped supervise the reburying of bones in St Pancras cemetery during the construction of the Midland line into London. His two poems, *The Levelled Churchyard* and *In the Cemetery* spring from this experience.

The writer and poet Philip Larkin was 42 years old when he passed his driving test and bought his first car. Until then he often used railway journeys as the basis for his observations about fellow passengers, the passing countryside and townscapes. Perhaps his best known poem *Whitsun Weddings* is an extraordinary evocation of a train journey from Hull to London and that same journey being the starting point into married life for a host of newly-weds. As the young couples board the train at each of a series of stops on the way to their honeymoons and their futures he observes them with puzzlement and love.

William McGonagall, an inhabitant of Dundee, is famous for his poem about the Tay Bridge. He was a disaster poet whose poems like *The Clepington Catastrophe* and *The Horrors of Majuba* are described in a biographical dictionary as '… uniformly bad, but possess a disarming naivety and a calypso-like disregard for metre which still never fail to entertain'. In fact he wrote three poems about the Tay Bridge, which are best heard recited in a rich, Scots accent. The first, *The Railway Bridge of the Silvery Tay*, celebrated the opening of the bridge and includes the lines:

I hope that God will protect all passengers
By night and by day,
And that no accident will befall them while crossing
The Bridge of the Silvery Tay.

The second poem *The Tay Bridge Disaster* begins:

> Beautiful Railway Bridge of the Silv'ry Tay
> Alas! I am very sorry to say
> That ninety lives have been taken away
> On the last Sabbath day of 1879
> Which will be remember'd for a very long time

and finishes after another 45 lines:

> I must now conclude my lay
> By telling the world fearlessly without the least dismay,
> That your central girders would not have given way
> At least many sensible men do say,
> Had they been supported on each side with buttresses,
> As many sensible men confesses

The opening lines of his third lay to the Tay Bridge are:

> Beautiful New Railway Bridge of the Silvery Tay,
> With your strong brick piers and buttresses in so grand array
> And your thirteen central girders, which seem to my eye
> Strong enough all windy storms to defy.

A few workers on the railway had a real gift for words, such as Alfred Williams, born in 1877, who was employed in the stamping shop of the Great Western Swindon railway works. He wrote a number of poems, corresponded with the Poet Laureate and his best-known book, *Life in a Railway Factory,* includes descriptions of the trains passing through Swindon:

> These wagons, if they could speak, would tell you they have visited every station and town on the system ... They have gone through dark tunnels, over dizzy viaducts, past cathedral cities and quaint old market towns, villages and hamlets, sleeping and waking at all hours of the day and night...

These evocative images compare with a verse written by a Cardiff engineman:

The wind was high
The steam was low
The coal was small and plenty of slate
That's the reason we were late

To a Locomotive in Winter, written by Walt Whitman in 1876, envisages the train almost as a sexual being – he certainly catches the energy and rhapsody of a locomotive tearing along through the winter night:

Thee in thy panoply, thy measur'd dual throbbing and thy beat
    convulsive,
Thy black cylindric body, golden brass and silvery steel,
Thy ponderous side bars parallel and connecting rods, gyrating, shuttling
    at thy sides
Thy metrical, now swelling pant and roar now tapering in the distance.

Carl Sandburg in his 1916 *Chicago Poems* focuses on a different view:

I am riding on a limited express, one of the crack trains of the nation.
Hurtling across the prairie into blue haze and dark air go
    fifteen all-steel coaches holding a thousand people
(All the coaches shall be scrap and rust and all the men and women
    laughing in the diners and sleepers shall pass to ashes.)
I ask a man in the smoker where he is going and he answers:
    "Omaha."

❖

There is an endless stream of railway literature for the enthusiast; every locomotive type is studied and every branch line is catalogued in minute and meticulous detail. A selection at random might include *The Nailsworth and Stroud Branch*, 176 pages long with 170 photographs and 11 maps; *Zanzibar and the Bububu Railway; Watauga and Yadkin River Railroad*, 120 pages, 100 photos; *The Schull and Skibbereen Railway; Angus & Kincardineshire's Lost Railways,* and it may not be long before there is a book on *Les Rails de la Canne à Sucre* that takes passengers most of the way from the Rum Distillery to the Banana Museum in Martinique. A recent issue of *Trains* magazine included an advertisement for the *Steam Whistle Patents Book, 216 US patents for whistles, valves, sirens, horns and more*. There are even sugar-sweet titles such as *Twilight of Steam, Masterpieces in Steam* and *Symphony in Steam*. These are only a small sample of the specialist publications available for the enthusiast.

There have been railway picture books, puzzles and alphabets for children ever since the first wheel turned on a rail. Possibly the most successful children's railway books are the Rev. W. Awdry's *Thomas the Tank Engine* series. The spin-offs are equally successful: there is a Thomas Land in Japan and hundreds of thousands of visitors flock to special Thomas the Tank Engine events in America and Britain. One American museum director said his staff referred to 'Thomas the bank engine' because of the revenue it attracted. The stories of *Thomas the Tank Engine*, have superseded *Sammy the Shunter* by Eileen Gibb: '...."What's the matter Sammy?" asked Mr Buffin his driver. "You're making a queer kind of noise this morning." "There's a nasty pain in my boiler," whispered Sammy in a trembly voice. "Oh dear, I do feel ill! My wheels are shaking." '

In *Through the Looking Glass*, Lewis Carroll's Alice is in a train without a ticket. '"Don't make excuses," said the guard: "you should have bought one from the engine driver." And once more the chorus of voices went, "The man that drives the engine. Why, the smoke alone is worth a thousand pounds a puff!"' The Tenniel drawing shows a prim Alice in the railway carriage opposite a gentleman in white and a goat, while she is being scrutinised by the guard with opera glasses.

Readers of *The Wind in the Willows* will remember Toad's scrape with the authorities and his escape from custody '...They piled on more coals and the train shot into the tunnel, and the engine rushed and roared and rattled ... as the train slowed down to almost a walking pace he heard the driver call out "Now, jump!"... Then out of the tunnel burst the pursuing engine, roaring and whistling...'. In Germany almost every adolescent was brought up on Gerhart Hauptmann's tragic *Bahnwarter Thiel*, the story of a philosophic crossing-keeper. Fred Fearnot and Railroad Jack were young heroes in American teen magazines in the first years of the last century, 'Just then the express dashed into view, coming out of the canyon and Fred sped forward ...'. Another hero, Frank Merriwell, finds a seat for a lady in a crowded train '..."You are a cheap cad," Fred told the overdressed Harvard bully...'. Railway fantasy had a tremendous boost when the Hogwarts Express became the preferred mode of transport for the characters in J.K. Rowling's Harry Potter books. The steam locomotive *Taw Valley,* painted red, left from Kings Cross platform 9¾ (naturally). Chris Van Allsburg's 1985 book *The Polar Express* has been made into a Christmas movie featuring every small boy's dream of a locomotive[7].

Of all the many books about trains for the young, there is one that enchants. *Boy on a hill top* by Peggy Blakeley, and illustrated by Kota Taniuchi, is a sublimely happy story of a little boy watching trains that turn into captivating and delightful fantasies.

Toy or model trains as well as railway books were an intrinsic part of every small boy's life. Possibly the oldest surviving toy train, probably dating from the late 1820s, is in the Bowes Museum, County Durham. The boiler has painted wood cladding, a stovepipe chimney and an inclined track with sleepers under and parallel to the rails. A label says 'This train belonged to John Pease'. He was the son of Joseph Pease, one of the principal backers of the Stockton & Darlington Railway.

❖

Popular songs and classical music have featured railways from their beginning. The moving train has inspired dances, two-steps, gallops, marches and a number of Strauss waltzes that echo the rhythms of a moving train. Rossini and Berlioz included references to the sounds of trains in some of their music. Jules Massenet composed the *PLM March*[8] to celebrate the 50th anniversary of the *Paris Lyon Méditerranée*. Dvorak was a keen train watcher when he was an organist and a young composer in Prague. Steve Reich's 1998 *Different Trains* is an interesting composition based on train travel. His parents separated and he spent

---

7. The engine in the movie was a Lima 2-8-4 Berkshire supplied to the Pere Marquette Railway which gave it the 1225 number. After restoration 1225 has become a centre piece of Owosso, Michigan, Steam Railroading Institute.

8. World War II Rhodesian railway employees adopted a rather different song, '*I'll Walk Beside You ...*'.

1939–1942 travelling by train with his governess between his New York father and Los Angeles mother. In his composition he sadly speculates that he might well have ridden very different trains in Europe. In his autobiography, Rudolf Nureyev, the great dancer, describes how, when he was a boy, he climbed a hill to look down on the railway at Ufa, 'watching the trains slowly starting and getting up speed ...' He claimed that his birth in a compartment of the Trans-Siberian Express gave him a lifelong love of railways and trains. 'In later years in Leningrad before creating a role in a new ballet I would often go to the station and just look, until I could feel the movement become part of me, and I part of the train.' Nureyev defected to the West in 1961, leaving behind all his possessions. The one he most regretted was 'my very first purchase in Paris – a beautiful electric train, symbol of the fascination I have felt ever since I was a baby for railways, trains and smoky stations.'

Perhaps the best-known popular songs that feature trains are *On the Atchison Topeka and Santa Fe* and of course Glenn Miller's 1943 recording *Chatanooga Choo Choo*, the first-ever gold record. Steve Goodmans's *The City of New Orleans* with its heroic flavour should be better known:

> Goodnight America! How are you?
> Say, don't you know me? I'm your native son,
> I'm the train they call *The City of Orleans*,
> I'll be gone 500 miles when day is done.

Sentimental Journey, *Train of Love*, *Wabash Cannonball* and many other songs were popularised by singing stars such as Johnny Cash, Hank Snow and Boxcar Willie. The Grand Funk Railroad was something else. The band founded in 1968 was called 'the world's worst rock band' by *Rolling Stone*, the rock establishment's flagship publication but their recordings sold in millions and at the Atlanta Pop Festival they played to an audience of 125,000.

The USA is the only country with an extensive tradition of railway folklore and folk music. One of the earliest railway minstrel songs is reputed to date from the 1840s:

> Oh, de steamboat makes a mighty splutter
> And when de biler bursts it lands you in de watter
> Do hoss boat can trabel, if de wedder wet or dry
> An noffin can stop you if de ole hoss don't die
> Railroad trabel's gettin all de go
> 'Kass de hoss boat an' steamboat goes so might slow

John Henry is an American folk hero in the same pantheon as Davy Crockett or Daniel Boone. His story is based on the introduction of the steam-powered drill for drilling holes for placing explosive in hard rock when building tunnels. To safeguard jobs, John Henry was determined to show that manual drilling was faster than the steam drill. In the man versus steam competition, the steam drill bored nine feet and John Henry fourteen feet but the gigantic effort cost him his life. John Henry told his captain,

> I am a Tennessee man
> Before I would see that steam drill beat me down
> Die with a hammer in my hand
> Die with a hammer in my hand.

There were many ballads and songs about the hardships and dangers of working on railroads:

> Twas only a poor dying brakeman
> Simply a hard lab'ring man
> And the smoke and the soot of the engine
> Had covered his face of tan

The most famous of all railroad ballads is Wallace Saunders's *Ballad of Casey Jones*. Jones was recognised as a brilliant but arrogant engineman on the Illinois Central and on one fateful night in 1900 he was scheduled to take over the southbound *New Orleans Special* crack train known as the *Cannonball*. It was wet, conditions were bad and the train was late into Memphis; Casey Jones was determined to make up the lost time. Ahead, at Vaugn two freight trains were signalled into a passing siding but the siding was not long enough and two cars remained on the main line. The freight train conductor laid explosive warning signals on the line but Casey

Jones, intent on speed, didn't hear them. When he saw the taillights of the freight train's caboose he screamed to his fireman to jump while he heroically remained at his post to shut off the steam and wind down the brake. Casey Jones was the only fatality of the accident:

> Come all you rounders if you want to hear
> The story told of a brave engineer;
> Casey Jones was the rounder's name,
> A high right wheeler of mighty fame.

For a time his image featured on a US postage stamp and bore a striking resemblance to Elvis Presley.

The Wobblies, officially known as the Industrial Workers of the World, was founded in Chicago by union men who were dissatisfied with the lack of progress made by their craft unions. They handed out a songbook entitled *To Fan the Flames of Discontent* with each union card; the songs included *We're bound for San Diego,* Joe Hill's famous *Pie in the Sky* and his *Casey Jones, the Union Scab* which Hill wrote during an Illinois Central shopman's strike.

❖

For some, the railway became the metaphor for man's pilgrimage through life, not only in song and ballad but also in stone. A memorial tablet in the south porch of Ely Cathedral, England, commemorating the death of two young men in a railway accident is titled *The Spiritual Railway* and begins,

> The line, to heaven by Christ was made
> With heavenly truth the Rails are laid,
> From Earth to Heaven the line extends
> To Life Eternal where it ends.

There are American verses in the same style,

> So the old train of life rolls away in the distance
> Laden with souls that are heavenward bound.
> But many alight at the little side 'stations'.

She moves slowly on, as the curve passes round
So when at length the journey is ended
May you be on board with the passengers be
Who turned not aside, but attended the signals
And alighted at last in Eternity.

An 1877 number of *The Engine* compares man to a locomotive travelling along the 'Narrow Track of Fearless Truth',

Oh! What am I but an Engine, shod
With muscle and flesh by the hand of God

There have been a variety of images for the transition from death to the hereafter: crossing the River Styx in antiquity, Christians crossing the Jordan or riding in Elijah's Chariot, and in its time the railway became a new form of travel for crossing to the next world. Trains can travel in opposite directions, as was clearly understood in a broadsheet entitled *The Spiritual Journey*; the sheet is divided in half, one half with verses for the Upward Line and the other for the Down Line. The fate of passengers on the Down Line stimulated a number of ballads. The 'Noted National Evangelist and Power in Jehovah's Quiver', Rev. A.W. Nix wrote the *Black Diamond Express to Hell*; 'Sin the Engineer holding the throttle wide open. Pleasure is the headlight and the Devil is the Conductor ... the moanin' of the Drunkards, Liars, Gamblers and other folks who have got aboard. They are hell-bound and don't want to go.'

Smiling Ed McConnell's the *Hell Bound Train* is in the same league. One verse;

The boiler was filled full of lager beer,
And the devil himself was engineer
The passengers were a mixed-up crew–
Church member, atheist, gentile and Jew.

❖

There were other more serious aspects to rail travel (or the lack of it) in America. Slaves were prevented from travelling and hearing the sound of an approaching train, watching it pass and listening to its sound recede symbolized freedom and escape, the metaphorical 'Underground Railroad that the Fugitive Slaves took from the House of Bondage to the Promised Land of Freedom'[9]. Whether picking cotton, working with mule teams to build the levees to contain the great river, constructing railroads, or even serving time in the Angola State Penitentiary, for the slave the sound of a passing train was the only hope of a different life and freedom in the big northern cities with their industries and jobs. An early folk song included

> Let the midnight special
> Shine its ever-loving light on me.

Emancipation came at the end of the Civil War and Reconstruction became the hope of a democratic future. However, Reconstruction came to an end after the 1875 Shooting War and by the beginning of the 20th century the 200-mile section of the Mississippi delta south from Memphis was in the hands of a few large-scale plantation owners; there was autocratic white domination and black subjugation. It was here that the blues were born.

The birth of the blues is supposed to have hppened in Moorhead where the Southern Railway and the Yazoo Delta line cross at right angles. The YD painted on the freight cars gave the name *Yellow Dog* to the line. In 1903, W.C. Handy, the father of the blues, in nearby Tutwiler train station heard the song 'Where the Southern crosses the Dog' scored it and later published it as *Yellow Dog Blues*

> Easy rider hit this burg today
> On a southbound rattler beside the Pullman car
> I've seen him there and he was on the hog
> Easy rider had to go away
> And he's had to vamp it but the hike ain't far
> He's gone where the Southern crosses the Yellow Dog.

---

9. On the other side of the world the train was a symbol in a quite different context. Georgii Plekhanov, the founder of Russian Marxism, 'We have boarded the train of history which is taking us at full speed to our goal.' Not long after, in a letter to the newspaper *Pravda* a worker protested 'Lice have eaten us to death and soap is *only* given to railroad workers.'

The Railroad Blues is another early song,

> Every time you hear me sing this song
> You may know I've caught a train and gone
> I get a letter and this is how it read:
> Stamped on the inside "Yo' lover's sick in bed."

In the 1920s many of the best known blues singers recorded railroad songs: Blind Lemon Jefferson's *Lemon's Cannonball Moan*, Bessie Smith's *Ticket Agent, Ease your Window Down* and many others. Clara Smith[10], promoted as *The World's Champion Moaner*, sang

> When a woman gits de blues she lays down and c—r—i—e—s
> A man gits de blues he takes a freight train an' r—i—d—e—s

The blues developed with many references to the train and there were even specially devised instruments, including Leadbelly's twelve-string train-whistle guitar and Washboard Sam's locomotive washboard; some bands such as the Cannon's Jug Stompers even orchestrated locomotive onomatopoeia.

The blues travelled up the great river system to Kansas City, then to Chicago and the world. Few would have thought that Huddie Leadbetter, Leadbelly, making a recording of the blues in the Angola penitentiary in 1934 would go on to play at New York's Carnegie Hall. The programme included a performance of *The Rock Island Line*, a song that was later a mass hit for Lonnie Donegan in Britain and America.

Over and over again the sound of the locomotive or the train features in the blues and jazz. Count Basie's bell-like piano chorus playing against the steady four/four of the bass fiddle, guitar and cymbals in *One O'Clock Jump* suggests a train pulling out of a station and the Oscar Peterson Trio's *Night Train* is a very compelling impression of a heavy train gathering speed. Louis Armstrong's *Wolverine Blues* includes a solo call of a train whistle and the ensemble response of pistons and rumbling boxcars.

10. The legend on one of her record sleeves reads 'Every blues thinks it's full of misery until Clara Smith goes to work'… and it becomes 'a melodious melody of moans and groans when Clara gets warmed up to her work.'

Armstrong also recorded *Hobo, You Can't Ride This Train* and Duke Ellington recorded *Happy Go Lucky Local*, *Across the Track Blues* and *Daybreak Express*. The train continued to be an influence on jazz: Billy Strayhorn's *Take the A Train*, the IND express subway train connecting Harlem to the rest of Manhattan, became the Ellington Band's theme tune.

For railway buffs, and for everyone with spark, the last word comes from Aunt Hagar, famous in W.C. Handy's *Aunt Hagar's Blues*:

> When my feet say dance, I just can't refuse
> When I hear that melody they call the blues.

The world's fastest trains. Japan Railways-Central X01-1 Maglev trains passing on the Yamanashi test line

12 Change

Good communications make a critical contribution to national prosperity. Roads, city streets, railways, airports and airlines, telecommunications and an efficient postal service all have an essential role in providing an infrastructure in which large concentrations of population, industry and commerce can flourish. The contribution made by these communication networks is measured in terms of cost, reliability and efficiency and, in the case of transportation, by speed, convenience and safety.

Modern technology, together with commercial or national ambition, has speeded up every form of transportation – trains, autos and aircraft. Road and air travel have now reached their practicable maximum speeds. Speeds are limited on roads for reasons of safety and to make optimum use of the road network's capacity; nearly every country imposes a limit between about 60–80mph even on its superhighways. Cars are unlikely to exceed these road speeds in the foreseeable future; automotive technology is mainly devoted to improving safety and reliability, reducing pollution and providing increased comfort. In any case, maximum speed on roads is becoming largely academic because of increasing traffic and congestion. It is reported that between 1970 and 2002 the population of the United States grew by 40%, registered road vehicles increased by nearly 100% and road

259

capacity increased by 6%. Similar rates of growth are forecast for the future. A recent report[1] in Britain estimated the annual cost of congestion at £15 billion which will double in ten years. Statistics for other nations may not be as dramatic but they follow a similar pattern. Aircraft already fly at close to their maximum practicable speeds, and even when the aircraft are available, speeds faster than the speed of sound are uneconomic and in any case only permitted on flights over the ocean. Congestion and delays at airports seem likely to increase as the demand for air travel grows. Rail is the only transport system that has not reached its maximum in terms of either speed or volume of traffic.

Like any industry or organisation, the railways have evolved to serve their market place. From the late 1830s and over the next 80 years the demands and opportunities of the market encouraged growth of the railways and the variety of services they offered. The following 80 years saw a contraction in the extent of the many rail systems and a reduction in the range of services they offered. Cars or buses became the standard transport for most people apart from those working in the centres of the largest cities. Aircraft took the place of the passenger train for most journeys over 300 miles and for many shorter journeys. Road transport has taken an overwhelming share of freight transportation, leaving railways with a market share that would be considered derisory in any other industry. By the 1950s, decline in the role of railways seemed irreversible; there appeared to be no way to pull them out of decline especially in the realm of long-distance passenger traffic. Then the climate changed.

On 1 October 1964 the dedicated Tokaido Shinkansen line for express passenger trains was inaugurated between the two great centres of Tokyo and Osaka. The line and the trains incorporated notable technical advances: 25kVac power, lineside signals replaced by information displayed in the driver's cab, traction on the train axles in the place of a single or double driving unit and an Automatic Train Protection System to enhance the margins of operational safety. A year after it opened, express trains covered the 322 miles at just over 100mph. The speed of the Nozomi trains has been increased to about 130mph to link Tokyo and Osaka in 2½

1. Royal Academy of Engineering

hours. The Tokaido line also provides a high-frequency service of 285 trains a day: 51 Nozomi trains, 147 Hikari trains making only two or three stops and 87 Kodama trains stopping at all stations. It has been calculated that three jumbo jets leaving every five minutes or a 40-seat bus leaving every ten seconds would be needed to replace the capacity of the Tokaido Shinkansen. The train became the standard method of travel between the two cities and was admired and envied by rail operators and travellers around the world. By the third year revenue exceeded costs including interest and the depreciation on the initial investment. The Japanese rail companies built other Shinkansen lines and had a steep rise in traffic; the East Japan Railway Company responded to this increased demand by introducing a double-deck train running at 150mph and transporting 1,634 seated passengers in comfort. The Shinkansen system has been extended from Osaka through a tunnel under the Kammon Strait to the south island of Kyushu and north through the Seikan tunnel to Hokkaido and plans are being made for a new Tokaido line to parallel the existing line to accommodate increasing demand between Tokyo and Osaka.

France was the first nation to benefit from the lessons of the Shinkansen and recognise the advantages of a line for use only by high-speed express trains, and a dedicated express line, the LGV, *Ligne à Grand Vitesse*, was opened between Paris and Lyon in 1983. The line was designed for TGV (*Trains à Grand Vitesse*) express passenger trains cruising at 168mph, later increased to 186mph, and the line was extended to Marseille, to provide a start to stop speed of about 160mph over the 485 miles from Paris to the Mediterranean. Plans are being made to increase capacity on the line by introducing a second generation of double-deck trains seating 1,124 passengers. Recently, signalling and TGV braking have been upgraded to enable peak time departures at intervals of only four minutes. LGVs have been built to link Paris to the North and West and construction of the line linking Paris and Lorraine in the East is nearly complete. In May 2001 the SNCF ran a demonstration TGV train directly from Calais to Marseille[2]; it covered the 663 miles in a little less than 3½ hours.

Italian railways are completing a dedicated Milan-Rome-Naples high-

2. From the English Channel to the Mediterranean.

speed passenger line. Spain's AVE high speed train has almost replaced air travel on the dedicated high speed line between Madrid and Seville; the railway company is so confident about the reliability of their AVE service that passengers have their fare reimbursed if their train is more than six minutes late. The Madrid–Barcelona line will open shortly. German Railways introduced their ICE super express train in 1991; their ICE Series 3 train is designed to run along dedicated lines at over 200mph. Taiwan is constructing its dedicated high speed line from Taipei 250 miles south to Kaohsiung and South Korea has inaugurated most of its high speed line for the 256 miles between Seoul and Pusan with locally built TGV train sets. The economic viability of building and operating dedicated high speed lines with a very high density of passenger traffic has been demonstrated as have other benefits such as substantially reduced numbers of domestic flights and car use. The operating feasibility of the recent advances in train, in track and in signalling technology have been and continue to be proved on the high-speed rail systems of an increasing number of nations.

These high-speed lines and projects are all based on yesterday's technology; the 320mph world speed record for a train on rails was made in France as long ago as May 1990. Since then French, German and other railway researchers have done extensive work on the behaviour of the wheel on the rail, the ride of bogies at very high speeds, vibration effects on the rail bed and structures and the problems of high-speed trains passing in tunnels. The evidence indicates that today's technology can be developed to build trains to run safely at more than 300mph along dedicated rail tracks.

Trains running at speeds greater than 300mph would change the travel pattern between cities as far as 1,000 miles apart. Trains would replace aircraft as the preferred way to travel along densely travelled passenger corridors such as Los Angeles to San Diego or to Las Vegas, or between Boston, New York, Philadelphia and Washington. Downtown Chicago would be 3½ hours from Manhattan, including two or three intermediate stops. Travel time between downtown San Francisco and Los Angeles, or between London and Glasgow, with intermediate stops, would be less than 1½ hours. But the cost of constructing and maintaining new, dedicated high speed rail lines can only be justified on routes with very high year-round demand for travel.

Not only does the traditional steel wheel on a steel rail have scope for travelling at higher speeds than the current 125 or 200mph, but engineers around the world, especially in Japan and Germany, are investigating the possibilities of Maglev or Magnetic Levitated Guided Transport Systems. So far applications have been for short distances at low speed. The 1984 Birmingham Airport Shuttle was among the first, if not the first, and other lines include the Vancouver Skytrain and the line to Pudong Airport from downtown Shanghai. It is likely that the next will be for a metro line with a maximum speed of 60 mph in Nagoya, Japan. The increased construction cost of this metro line is justified by the silent operation of the trains, no noise of the steel wheel on the rail, making the system suitable for elevated and surface operation in densely populated areas.

Many believe that future long-distance high speed surface transportation will be Maglev and Japan Railways-Central have constructed a test track to develop and test high speed trains. The theory is simple: two superconducting magnets with their very high force characteristics are mounted on each bogie to interact with a continuous series of energised coils in the sidewalls of the guideway to lift the vehicle, push it and maintain its central position in the guideway through curves and cross winds. There are practical difficulties for high speed Maglevs despite the system's apparent simplicity. Superconducting magnets need to be maintained at close to absolute zero temperature to levitate and propel the train; this requires liquid helium coolant, which boils at minus 459°F, and the refrigeration plant to re-liquify the gas. Other difficulties include constructing and maintaining the guidepath to very exacting standards of accuracy and precision and reducing the excessive aerodynamic sound of a very high speed train. Despite the difficulties, Maglev trains have reached a speed exceeding 360mph, have passed each other at a relative speed in excess of 1,000 km/hr or about 620mph and recently a test train covered nearly 1,800 miles in a single day. Maglev is now being seriously considered for a new Tokaido line to increase passenger capacity between Tokyo and Osaka.

❖

Passengers are interested in high speed in order to reduce their travel times; they want to reach their destinations as quickly as possible. Many of the Eurostar Channel tunnel trains, on their way to London's St Pancras station from Continental Europe, will stop at Stratford in East London where passengers will be able to interchange to Central or Jubilee line Underground trains or the Docklands Light Railway, taking them directly to London's commercial, shopping and entertainment centres. Parkway-type stations on the edge of big towns with their large car parks, regional rail connections and connecting tram or bus services have started to play an important part in reducing passenger travel times. It is planned that the new TGV line from Paris east to Strasbourg will have three intermediate stations, Champagne-Ardenne, Meuse and Lorraine, designed to serve their hinterlands rather than just a major town in the region. Each will have extensive car parking and each will radiate connecting regional express trains or trams to the suburbs and centres of the towns of the region. Manchester, Paris, Lyon, Frankfurt, Amsterdam, Newark and some other major airports now have their own mainline rail station to reduce travel time and increase convenience for travellers.

A number of interesting trials are being conducted, both to help reduce transfer times in stations and to help passengers continue their journeys as effortlessly as possible. Time lost buying tickets or passing through crowded inspection barriers is substantially reduced by the use of magnetic travel tokens covering different transport modes and which don't need to be produced from a pocket or handbag. Continental European rail timetables include a bicycle symbol on an increasing number of express and regional trains; large bike decals on the outside of carriages indicate storage sections and the SNCF is well into a *velo+train* advertising campaign. The city of Turin has gone a stage further by providing 500 well-equipped bikes latched to parking posts in the main railway station and the city. Swiss National Railways recently purchased 75 Smart cars and plan to increase the number to 400 for use by passengers who need to travel a further ten or fifteen miles from the railway station to their destinations; the passenger receives a token card with the rail ticket that replaces the ignition key and enables the traveller to jump into the Smart without completing the normal rental formalities.

CHANGE

❖

Everyone recognises the need for a safe and reliable railway system to serve industry, business and travellers. Who should own and operate the railway system is still open to debate in a number of countries; so too are the decisions concerning the amount of resources that need to be committed to upgrading a system in addition to maintaining it.

A large number of variations or formulas for railway ownership already exist. These include tracks and trains owned and operated by a single company; tracks maintained by one company and trains operated by a series of different companies; the state, either directly or indirectly, owning the tracks and independent companies operating the trains or the state operating the main intercity lines and independent companies owning and operating the feeder lines. In Europe the liberalisation policies of the Brussels eurocrats through their CSSPF quango (*Le Conseil Supérieur du Service Public Ferroviaire*) will doubtless encourage even more permutations of railway ownership and operation. It is to be hoped that the emphasis of their rulings will encourage co-operation rather than competition between companies. No one system is the correct or best system, other than, perhaps, the ideal of a single body owning both tracks and trains and taking responsibility for operating them efficiently as part of a planned transportation system serving the nation.

Almost all passenger rail travel is subsidised in one way or another by local or national government. The principle of subsidy is not in question; without it the very nature of big cities and the pattern of commerce and industry would change. The question that needs to be asked is how much subsidy provides value for money for the nation. Is it good value to reduce travel time between two centres, say, 250 miles apart, by an hour through investment in new track and trains to increase train speed from 90mph to 140mph? Clearly it is good news for travellers on the line but is it value for money for the nation or the regions served by the line?

The need for new highways, road improvements or new airports is decided on economic rather than financial criteria. Parallel economic criteria should apply for investment in the railway system. And there are other factors also to be taken into consideration such as reduced noxious pollution, reduced congestion on highways and in cities and the safety of travellers.

The choice of either maintaining and improving an existing railway network or investing in a modern rail system lies with the legislators and ultimately with the people who elect them. Whichever choice is made, investment has to be combined with direction and leadership to build and operate railways to serve the nation in the present century.

❖

Britain is a nation of railway enthusiasts. There are more preserved locomotives, more steam lines, more books for the specialist about closed, remote and uninteresting railway branch lines or the steaming characteristics of forgotten locomotives and more railway periodicals than in any other country.

We can therefore be sure of one aspect of the future: as long as there are trains speeding, running or stumbling on tracks, and as long as there are steel wheels on steel rails, there will be railway buffs and enthusiasts cheering them on.